The
**Survival
Guide** for
Teachers of
Gifted Kids

The
Survival
Guide for
Teachers of
Gifted Kids

How to Plan, Manage, and Evaluate Programs for Gifted Youth K–12

Jim Delisle, Ph.D., & Barbara A. Lewis

Edited by Marjorie Lisovskis

free spirit
PUBLISHING®

Library of Congress Cataloging-in-Publication Data
Delisle, James R., 1953-
    Survival guide for teachers of gifted kids : how to plan, manage, and
    evaluate programs for gifted youth / by Jim Delisle and Barbara A. Lewis.
        p. cm.
    Includes bibliographical references and index.
    ISBN 1-57542-116-X
        1. Gifted children—Education—United States—Handbooks,
    manuals, etc. I. Lewis, Barbara A., 1943- II. Title.

LC3993.9 .D45 2003
371.95—dc21   2002013573

Cover design: Marieka Heinlen
Interior book design: Percolator
Assistant editor: Douglas Fehlen

10   9   8   7   6
Printed in the United States of America

Free Spirit Publishing Inc.
217 Fifth Avenue North, Suite 200
Minneapolis, MN 55401-1299
(612) 338-2068
help4kids@freespirit.com
www.freespirit.com

For more than twenty years, Ann Wink, my cherished friend and colleague from Texas, has been an inspiration to my work and my thinking. This book is dedicated to her because so much of who she is, and what she believes, is within its pages. Ann, thank you!
J.D.

My husband, Lawrence, who is one of the most gifted people I have known, has devoted much of his life to developing the intellectual abilities of others. I dedicate this book to him, my dear friend, who has also led my mind across bridges to the unknown.
B.L.

ACKNOWLEDGMENTS

If I listed the name of every person whose thinking and other work contributed to the content of this book, there would be no room for anything *other* than the acknowledgments! What this tells me is that the learning I now possess in relation to designing programs for gifted kids is due, in great part, to the parents, professional educators, and gifted students I have met in my twenty-five-year career quest. I acknowledge and thank each of these individuals for the unique insights that have helped to shape the beliefs and principles I now espouse. Thanks to my colleagues, friends, and students, this book has become a reality.

Of course, the crack editorial team at Free Spirit Publishing was invaluable in making all the pieces and parts of the book come together. Thank you to all, but especially to Margie Lisovskis and Douglas Fehlen, whose patience rivals Job's and whose detective skills would give Sherlock Holmes a run for his money.

—Jim Delisle

Just as it takes the work of many to build a bridge over which others may travel, the work of many people has served to inspire and shape this book. First, I would like to thank the Park City School District and those administrators who allowed me to design the PATHS gifted program for Park City, Utah: Dr. Nancy DeFord (a superintendent with both vision and tenacity) and Merry Haugen (who allowed freedom of thought).

I will always be indebted to my mentor, Sally Lafferty, Salt Lake City School District, for her generosity in sharing all she knew about the field of gifted education. Other people have also influenced my thinking and shared materials with me: Becky Odoardi, Davis School District; Phyllis Embly, Jordan School District; Sue Sakashita, Granite School District; Scott Hunsaker, Utah State University; Connie Amos, Salt Lake City School District; and Kay Erwin, Murray School District. All of them have in some way left their footprints on the bridge of this book.

My thanks to Sally Walker for generously sharing the Illinois plan with me. Thanks, too, to numerous national consultants who have inspired, mentored, and befriended me: Dr. Linda Silverman (who has time for anyone), Barbara Clark (who enlightened my brain), and Sally and Joe Renzulli (who provided some theory upon which I could ground my practice).

My thanks also go to the organizations that have left their imprint upon me, and thus upon this book: NAGC, UAGC, and NRC/GT. I've been truly lucky to have had such a broad network of caring individuals to help design my education, both directly and indirectly.

I am delighted to have shared the writing of this book with Jim Delisle, who has such a broad historical scope on gifted education and who is also talented and easy to work with.

Finally, my gratitude goes to my publisher, Judy Galbraith, who always exemplifies integrity (and who is a gifted child herself), for her continued support, enthusiasm, and friendship; and to my editor, Margie Lisovskis, and assistant editor, Douglas Fehlen.

—Barbara Lewis

Contents

List of Figures

List of Reproducible Pages

Introduction

Teacher of the Gifted: Fainthearted Need Not Apply

What's your job title? Resource teacher? Gifted specialist? Gifted coordinator? Half-time classroom/half-time gifted teacher? G/T paraprofessional? Parent member of the gifted education committee? Whatever your official designation, the fact that you're reading this book means that you probably work with, or on behalf of, gifted kids. Depending on your particular role, the job you do may call for some or all of a laundry list of written and unwritten qualifications like these:

- completion of graduate coursework in gifted education
- experience teaching gifted children in a school setting
- ability to work well with parents and professionals
- knowledge of curriculum models and differentiation strategies for varying grade levels
- capability to conduct staff development sessions within the school district
- skills in persuasiveness and finding common ground among disparate voices
- capacity to tirelessly and creatively advocate, troubleshoot, solve problems, and apply for funding

And, as though the list weren't long enough already, there is one more unwritten qualification for teaching gifted children and coordinating their education, one that is probably the most valuable credential of all:

- possession of a *very* thick skin

To be sure, no job in education is easy, but the job of a gifted teacher or coordinator* is often among the most difficult of all. Why? Because gifted education is

---

* Just like in the real world of gifted education, in this book we use the terms "coordinator" and "teacher" pretty much interchangeably. A myriad of titles can apply to the same job description, and two people with similar job titles may have different responsibilities.

one of the few fields for which some people, professionals included, question the need for the position at all—indeed, they may question the need for *any* programming for gifted kids. Not only must you do your job, but also you're likely to find yourself called upon to smile in the face of criticism as you defend its very existence. Thus, the most vital qualification for someone in the role of gifted teacher/coordinator/specialist/volunteer is a personal sense of conviction about the field itself. Without you, many gifted students (and their parents) may have no professional advocate at all. And, as you already know or will soon realize, advocacy is an element of nearly every aspect of the work you do.

Indeed, this is not a field for the timid!

Why We Wrote This Book

The beginnings of this book can be found in our own personal experiences in gifted education:

Jim: *When I took my first job as a teacher of gifted children in Stafford Springs, Connecticut, it was a part-time position for a resource (pull-out) program in grades 4–6. The district had never had a gifted program before, and there was no budget (other than my salary) and no classroom space (I worked out of a school library). There were also no materials and no guidelines for identification, curriculum planning, program evaluation, working with other teachers, staff development, or parent involvement. Nada. Zippo. Zero.*

Equally frustrating, there was not a text or resource book I could find that pointed out, usefully and succinctly, the steps to establishing a gifted program. Nuts-and-bolts questions were many, but answers were few: Should the gifted program curriculum coordinate with the regular curriculum or be separate from it? Could homework be assigned? Would the kids receive report-card grades for their involvement in the gifted class? Should students be required to make up the work from their regular classroom? Added to these implementation concerns were the more overarching issues about program philosophy, identification, and the politics of running a program that was seen by various groups as either necessary or frivolous, equitable or elitist.

This was in 1978, which coincided with my first year as a doctoral student in gifted-child education. The two years I spent in this program were instructive in every way. I learned who gifted kids were and what I should (and shouldn't) expect of them. I learned what strides could be made when a group of people pulled together to work on building a program for gifted kids. At the same time, I learned to count to ten when confronted with "gifted disbelievers" who questioned why we were providing specialized services for kids who already succeeded in school.

Barbara: *I served as a classroom teacher before entering the field of gifted-child education in 1985. Thanks to many innovative "gifted pioneers," I landed in an established program in Salt Lake City, Utah, where I taught ethnically diverse and economically disadvantaged gifted children. Within a few years, my students' problem-solving activities garnered national and international kudos and helped reinforce the concept that gifted children can be found in all populations.*

Fueled with enthusiasm for working with gifted kids, I then initiated, designed, coordinated, and taught in a program for gifted students in the Park City, Utah, school district. With a supportive administration and the dedication of teachers and parents, the program received recognition and converted many skeptical souls into recognizing the needs of accelerated learners. People who had previously considered gifted education to be unnecessary, unfair, or elitist changed their minds.

Today, a generation after we started on our own "gifted journeys," levels of programming and support for gifted education vary widely from district to district and school to school. One thing remains the same, though: resource books to answer teachers' questions remain few. And that's why we decided to bring together our expertise and experience and write this book. We wanted to create a comprehensive, hands-on resource that addresses the diverse needs and challenges inherent in developing and implementing a gifted program and the vital skills required to teach and direct it.

. . . and Who We Wrote It For

It's possible that there are as many different job descriptions for those who work in gifted education as there are positions to fill. As we wrote *The Survival Guide for Teachers of Gifted Kids,* the readers we had in mind fell mainly into four broad categories:

Full-time coordinator of gifted programming for a large school district. If you are in this role, you are often more an administrator than a teacher. Generally, you work in a large city, suburban, or consolidated school district (5,000 students or more, K–12) and are responsible for multiple buildings and grade levels. You are probably part of the district's central office staff rather than an employee assigned to a specific classroom or building. You have responsibilities for hiring (and firing) staff; planning an array of identification options that respect the diversity within your district; answering calls that are "delicate" in nature from parents, principals, and journalists; and preparing a budget. This is by no means a complete list of your responsibilities, so your days (and nights) are usually quite full. If you're lucky, you have the part-time support of a secretary or an administrative assistant who shields you from too many interruptions and apprises you of paperwork that's due.

Full-time teacher of gifted children who is also assigned various administrative responsibilities. In our experience, this is the most common description of a gifted coordinator. If it fits your position, you probably work in either a rural or suburban setting. Your gifted program services are concentrated in some, but not all, grade levels (often, grades 3–8). You teach kids all day, every day, except for occasional release time to complete administrative assignments. You are not usually required to do any supervision or hiring of other gifted personnel (although you may be asked to sit in on interviews). It's likely that you're responsible, at least in part, for completing various forms required by your State Department of Education, and that you're involved to some degree in student identification (although this may be someone else's main job—the director of special education, perhaps). You may be asked to lead inservice workshops within your building and, if you coax a bit, might be allowed to attend the state-level gifted conference. (With luck, some of your expenses might even be reimbursed.) You're probably expected to write and distribute a newsletter to parents and staff about the gifted program's happenings. Last, if there are small jobs to be done (sending in payment for the Destination ImagiNation teams, scheduling a school bus for a field trip), they are no doubt yours to do. Your budget may be quite small, or nonexistent. Relying on the goodwill of your building principal may garner you the funds you need to purchase resources or curriculum materials. Clerical assistance? Most likely, that would be *you* typing your letters.

Classroom teacher with supplemental responsibilities in the gifted program. Usually, this position category is found in school districts where the majority of services received by gifted children are delivered in the regular classroom (through cluster grouping or various means of differentiation) or in homogeneous classrooms of high-ability students. Beyond the hands-on teaching that you do, your tasks may include providing materials and curriculum ideas to the other classroom teachers who serve gifted children; reporting to the State Department of Education on the numbers of gifted children identified in your district; and keeping your principal informed of matters that you hear about from assorted kids, parents, and teachers in your building. Generally, someone else handles the broader administrative responsibilities, either at the central office or through a county liaison responsible for multiple school districts. It's possible that you have a supplemental contract for your services, but more likely that you get release time of a very limited nature. Though in essence your main job is as a classroom teacher, people are likely to look to you for leadership regarding the gifted program or services offered in your school.

Off-site gifted coordinator serving multiple districts. This is a particularly difficult assignment, as your role may encompass several school districts that have different levels of interest in and services for gifted children. Your office might be miles removed from the actual schools you serve, and individual districts purchase your services by the day—25 days per year in Hoboken, 35 in East Orange, and so forth. Your tasks involve student identification, staff development, communicating with various school personnel who work with gifted students, and procuring curriculum materials for teachers who request them. You generally don't work directly with students, and much of your time is spent putting out fires lit by others. Since you're not based in any single district, you probably have little clout with the schools you serve and may be viewed by some as an outsider. Your lack of consistent presence in any one building requires you to wear a name badge so people will recognize you, and at the end of the month, your mileage reimbursement comes close to equaling your paycheck. Your car resembles a used bookstore and is often littered with leftover wrappers from the fast-food outlets you frequent between here and there.

If you don't find your situation among these four positions, read on. A second audience we felt our book would be important for were gifted educators whose focus was more pinpointed. You may be such an educator. For example, you might be a full-time classroom teacher who has volunteered (or been asked) to conduct a pull-out program in a specific area—say, math or science. You may be a paraprofessional or parent volunteer charged with introducing and running a particular program such as a Great Books group. Or, perhaps you're a director of special education with a small percentage of your time slated for gifted education.

Whatever your role in the design and operation of your district's or county's gifted programs, we've written this book to provide you with practical, effective advice for surviving and thriving as a gifted educator. It is our hope that the book's structure, strategies, recommendations, examples, and forms—gathered through our own combined 40+ years' experience in working with and for gifted children and the parents and professionals who come with them—will help you become the finest advocate you can be for the young people we all care so much about: gifted kids.

The Challenges You Face

Working in our home districts and traveling the United States and Canada speaking with other gifted educators, we have found that teachers face some universal concerns. In fact, it may well be one or more of the following challenges, echoed by teachers across North America, that led you to open this book to begin with:

1. "There isn't much funding, if any. How can we have a sound program without money to pay for it?" Plenty of funds are earmarked for students with special needs ranging from learning disabilities to speech and language impediments to behavioral challenges. Often, though, when it comes to funding for the unique learning needs of gifted children, dollars seem scarce. Educational money is competitive; this means that specialized educational opportunities for students with exceptional ability are rarely given financial priority. To overcome this challenge, people working in the trenches of gifted education routinely find it necessary to both advocate and search for additional funding to pay for special programs, trips, or resource materials. Tracking down and harnessing money for your program is only part of this challenge, though. Equally important is finding ways to help those people in charge of the purse strings recognize the critical need to establish and support a solid budget for gifted education.

2. "Many education professionals don't recognize or understand the learning needs of gifted students." Often in a school system there are administrators, teachers, and parents who argue that fast learners can fend for themselves and therefore do not need special programming or advanced learning opportunities. For these people, the fact that many gifted students already know much of the curriculum stands as proof that those kids are "doing fine on their own" and that additional services aren't necessary. A common related perspective many gifted teachers face is the view that all students, not just those who are gifted, deserve the same advanced and enriched learning opportunities. Demonstrating exactly how and why gifted learners need unique educational experiences calls for a host of knowledge and skills: You need to know where to find resources and information. You must learn to listen so you fully understand people's objections and concerns. You need to find ways to respond with respect and evenhandedness and to be compelling when you present your case.

3. "Providing specialized instruction for gifted students is considered elitist." Many people feel that any special accommodation for gifted students is a form of snobbery. They say (or think), "Why should those who already have so much get more?" The charge of elitism is an especially frustrating one to anybody who cares deeply about students whose appetite for knowledge and growth seems insatiable. You know that the term "gifted" is no more of a value judgment than the term "dyslexic" or "musical" or "at grade level" or "brown-haired." You know that giftedness is a trait; it isn't *better than* or *worse than, superior to* or *inferior to*—it just is. The challenge is to help others come to know this, too.

For some teachers and coordinators, an added burden tied to the question of treating giftedness as if it were a value is that other teachers are either judgmental about the gifted program or seem jealous of the gifted teacher's involvement in it. In other words, people sometimes assume that it's an "easy job to work with kids who always want to learn." But it's not.

You may have also heard the charge that placing gifted children in special programs reinforces "intellectual segregation." If you want a hot-button word in our egalitarian society, it is the term *segregation*. The very sound of it sends chills up the spine of any caring and thinking individual. However, when it comes to designing unique programs for gifted learners, the term is misapplied (sometimes for dramatic effect by critics of gifted education). Gifted coordinators are challenged to demonstrate that separating gifted learners from the rest of the class for a portion of their school time doesn't divide students but rather opens up broader opportunities for all.

"A child miseducated is a child lost."
—JOHN F. KENNEDY

4. "Administrators don't support gifted programs." This is not universally the case, and you can count yourself fortunate indeed if you work with a curriculum coordinator, principal, or superintendent who is a strong backer of gifted education. Unfortunately, however, there are still many administrators who don't recognize the unique educational needs of gifted children, or who give those needs a low priority. (Conversely, what principal has ever said, "You know, I always wondered if we *really* needed fourth grade. Can someone justify this to me?" Or, "I don't really believe there is such a thing as a learning disability, so let's cut the special education program and just let these kids learn on their own.") This challenge is a critical one, because the administrator is essentially the captain of that ship called *The Gifted Program*. If the captain isn't on board, how can the program even stay afloat, let alone cruise full-steam ahead?

5. "It's difficult to get parents organized and supportive of the gifted program." From the so-called pushy parent to the one who is reluctant to have his or her child singled out for gifted education, moms, dads, and other family adults can help or hinder your cause. Yet you need them on your team. In fact, parents can be tremendous allies in advocating for gifted students and gifted education in a school or district. Forming those alliances is essential.

6. "I can't get everything done, and I constantly have to advocate for gifted students. It never ends. How do I keep from burning out?" Though we often joke about this issue, there's really nothing funny about burnout—and finding ways not only to prevent it but also to keep a positive perspective on your job is critical for you and for the students who depend on you. Yes, this is a high-stress field, but others who share your concerns and questions are many. Finding people with like concerns, seeking out mentors and other people who can help you, and figuring out when and where to draw the line on the time you can put in are some of the strategies that can help you stay balanced.

7. "How can I train teachers so they can be the ones differentiating instruction in their classrooms?" Classroom teachers, typically overwhelmed already with their many obligations, are not always eager to take on additional training and classroom duties. Gifted coordinators face two hurdles here: helping teachers see that learning to differentiate can make their job more manageable while they reach more students, and finding a way—on their own or by hiring a qualified presenter—to provide the training teachers need in order to do this. Easy tasks? No. Worthwhile in the long run? You bet.

8. "I'm not a psychologist, and I don't know how to help my gifted students cope with their own differences and get along with other kids and teachers." Some gifted kids have problems with behavior in school. At times they turn to the gifted teacher to discuss some of their deepest emotional concerns. This can be unnerving for the adult involved, who cares about the students, wishes to help, but wants to be sure to do and say the right things. The fact that it is among the concerns teachers routinely bring up is probably actually a positive thing—it means that educators have come to see gifted students as more than simply great brains, but as real people with real feelings and problems.

Your Greatest Challenge (and Opportunity): Turning Skeptics and Critics into Stakeholders

Obviously, the challenges are many and diverse. Yet they all move along a common undercurrent: a need for understanding and collaboration among gifted students, their teachers, administrators, parents, and all the other people who play a role in gifted education.

What we're talking about here can be summed up in a one word: buy-in. The need for buy-in is something all of these challenges have in common. With buy-in, school boards and administrators see the importance of funding and staffing for gifted educa-

tion. With buy-in, parents, others teachers, and students are interested in getting involved with the gifted program. Why? Because they've come to see and understand the value of gifted education, to care about the educational needs of gifted students, to consider themselves stakeholders who want to have a voice and a part in these kids' lives.

How do you achieve buy-in? There are a host of ways, large and small, to make this happen. The ways include sharing information and resources, bringing everyone to the table to imagine a vision for gifted students in the school or district, exploring the academic needs of gifted kids in the school or district, working together to chart a course for the program and to determine how to identify students for it, continually evaluating what and how the program is doing, and inviting ideas and participation wherever possible. And, perhaps most important of all, listening. There is probably no surer path to buy-in than through listening to what the stakeholders have to say. Few educators or parents really "have it in" for gifted kids or gifted ed, but sometimes their frustrations with general education spill over into your arena. Listening—and patience—go a long, long way toward calming these waters.

The strategies in this book can help you join with others in your school or district to develop a thriving community for gifted education. Doing so won't be quick or easy, and there's no guarantee of cooperation and smooth sailing. As an advocate for gifted kids and gifted programming, your role is to be assertive, passionate, inclusive . . . and persistent. It will be worth your while. Working to help all of the parties involved in gifted kids' education be engaged in the process may be the most important effort you make. Though you may feel alone right now, you won't be on your own for long. Within your school community there is at least one administrator, one teacher, or one parent who really cares about providing challenging opportunities for gifted kids. That person may be waiting for someone to take the first step. With the help of this book, you can be that someone.

"Education is all a matter of building bridges." —RALPH ELLISON

How to Use This Book

The Survival Guide for Teachers of Gifted Kids addresses the interests of people working with gifted children in all grades. The book presents a set of survival strategies that comprise both map and guidebook for designing, building, implementing, sustaining, and growing a gifted program from the ground up.

SURVIVAL STRATEGY 1: SET A SOLID FOUNDATION FOR YOUR PROGRAM

This strategy gives an overview of the elements involved in planning how to develop a new gifted education program or enhance and enlarge an existing one. It includes information on crafting a philosophy and mission for gifted education in your school or district and recommendations for gathering the information you need in order to focus programming and services.

SURVIVAL STRATEGY 2: CAST A WIDE NET TO IDENTIFY GIFTED STUDENTS

Covered in this strategy are the factors to consider in developing a definition of giftedness that fits your mission and focus and in determining ways you will screen and select students for gifted programming. Addressed in detail are pitfalls to avoid, advantages and disadvantages of different methods of assessment, fair and inclusive means of identification, and effective ways to use information from varied sources in selecting students for gifted services. We also discuss ways to communicate the results of your search, steps to take when a decision is challenged, and factors to weigh in planning an exit policy.

SURVIVAL STRATEGY 3: LAY THE GROUNDWORK FOR A WELL-STRUCTURED PROGRAM

Here you'll find steps for examining learning opportunities your school already has in place that can benefit gifted students, noting gaps to be filled, and setting program goals that take into account both those factors and the mission and philosophy you have already established for your gifted services. The strategy also presents a research-based model for planning a balanced, comprehensive gifted education program that includes services in the regular classroom, special classes, and special schools.

SURVIVAL STRATEGY 4: PLAN PROGRAMMING YOU CAN BUILD ON

In this strategy we present detailed descriptions of programming options for each of the three dimensions of the planning model set forth in Survival Strategy 3. Described under the first option—gifted services in the regular classroom—are early entrance and acceleration, in-class grouping, and differentiated instruction and curriculum. For the second option—special classes—we explore pull-out programs, ability grouping, self-contained gifted classes, high school honors

and Advanced Placement options, weighted grades, and seminar series. The chapter examines the benefits and drawbacks of both regular-classroom service delivery and pull-out programs, presents examples of specialized institutions such as magnet schools, and discusses additional programming options including mentorships and various support and enrichment programs.

SURVIVAL STRATEGY 5: PLAN AND CONDUCT ONGOING EVALUATION

Survival Strategy 5 presents a best-practice approach to systematic evaluation focused on measuring and improving the depth, breadth, and quality of a gifted education program. You'll find both step-by-step guidelines for an exemplary evaluation process and a set of "just the basics" recommendations for getting started with evaluation when time and financial resources are in short supply. The goal is to help you establish an ongoing evaluation process that is realistic for your school or district and free of bias in addressing the interests of all those involved in gifted education, recognizing what's working well, pointing out areas where change or improvement are called for, and providing direction for follow-through.

SURVIVAL STRATEGY 6: STRENGTHEN YOUR PROGRAM BY COMMUNICATING AND BUILDING RELATIONSHIPS

This survival strategy highlights some of the challenges involved in forming alliances with administrators, parents, and other teachers in order to sustain and strengthen the gifted education program. You'll find ideas on where to look for data and information that can help you and your administrators state the case for program funding; suggestions for establishing parent groups and developing a newsletter; tips for supporting classroom and G/T teachers; recommendations on planning inservice training for teachers; and strategies for resolving problems with parents and students. The chapter also discusses the unique social and emotional needs of gifted kids and the actions you and other adults can take to help children cope with perfectionism, peer ridicule, high intensity, stress, and other personal challenges they face. This final strategy concludes with first-person narratives from teachers and coordinators on sustaining *yourself* and reaping the personal rewards of working in gifted education.

Along with step-by-step guidelines, each strategy includes a wealth of real-life examples; recommended books, organizations, Web sites, and other resources specifically related to the strategies; and reproducible forms to help you implement procedures we recommend. At the end of the book, you'll find a glossary of terms related to gifted education, a short biographical history of the people whose research and efforts have shaped the field, and an expanded list of resources.

Our goal has been to make *The Survival Guide for Teachers of Gifted Kids* as thorough as possible in order to meet the needs of many different readers. Please don't let the broad scope of the book intimidate you! You may be in the position of spearheading a comprehensive gifted education program in your school or district. Or, you may need information pinpointed to implementing a teaching strategy, exploring enrichment options, or arranging for teacher training. If you are inaugurating your district's first-ever gifted program, we suggest you read this book from cover to cover to get a good feel for the various elements of program operation. If you want information or strategies regarding a specific topic, such as identification, evaluation, or gaining administrative support, use the contents and index to point you to the sections of the book that are of interest to you.

Whatever your goal, don't be afraid to start small. Small efforts, carefully planned and implemented, hold the best promise of success for you, your program, and the gifted students you serve.

Before You Begin

In writing this survival guide, we realize that nearly all states (and Canadian provinces, too) have specific regulations regarding identification, gifted teacher certification, and almost every other aspect of programming addressed between these covers. These rules are constantly changing, as are the people responsible for monitoring their compliance. Thus, we recommend that before reading this book, you first acquaint yourself with the national organization that supports gifted education in the United States:

National Association for Gifted Children (NAGC)
1707 L Street NW, Suite 550
Washington, DC 20036
(202) 785-4268
www.nagc.org

Visit the NAGC Web site, find your way around it, and then use its links to visit the association of your own state. (If you teach in Canada, visit the Gifted Canada Web site at *www3.telus.net/giftedcanada* and click the link to provincial organizations.) Here you will find specific information governing gifted education programming where you work, general information about gifted kids and the programs that serve them, and links to other organizations and Web sites. Then, when you return to *The Survival Guide for Teachers of Gifted Kids*—which is filled with advice and suggestions that deal little with law and more with logistics—you can weave the "have to's" of your locale with the "how to's" revealed in this book.

We're interested in learning how our book has helped you survive and thrive as a teacher of gifted kids. Which recommendations have worked best for you? Which haven't? What other strategies have you found helpful? Please share your experiences by writing to us in care of our publisher:

Free Spirit Publishing Inc.
217 Fifth Avenue North, Suite 200
Minneapolis, MN 55401-1299
help4kids@freespirit.com

We wish you all the best on your adventure!

Jim Delisle, Ph.D.
Barbara A. Lewis

1

Set a Solid Foundation for Your Program

Eight-year-old Ada is obsessed with bugs. She collects them in jars, dissects them, and draws them with skillful, meticulous detail on the corners of her assignments. For Ada, the best part of her school week comes on Wednesday afternoon when she meets with her mentor, a biology teacher from the middle school, to pursue her study and experiments in entomology.

Contrary to Ada, Mario detests bugs and bug parts, but he is passionate about Einstein's theory of time dilation. He maroons himself at the back of the classroom and works on writing his own science fiction book about time travel. In a meeting with Mario, the gifted resource teacher, and Mario's sixth-grade math and English teachers, the group devised a project Mario could do to replace the science unit on plant species, which he already knew, with research into time travel. He could then work on his novel as part of the creative writing unit in English class. The resource teacher found sources and Web sites Mario could use to learn more about the genre of science fiction.

Carson, a gregarious fourth grader with a huge vocabulary, worries constantly about the homeless families in his community. Recognizing Carson's intellectual and leadership abilities and his strong social conscience, his teacher recommended that he participate in the district's Future Problem Solving Program (FPSP). Carson quickly became intensely involved, and has now recruited a group of kids from the program to work on the issue of homelessness in *their city through the Community Problem Solving Component of FPSP.*

At sixteen, Xiang struggles with her world history class and works with an English as a Second Language teacher every day. At the same time, she has already completed or tested out of all of her high school math choices and is currently working on her second college-level calculus course through an online independent study with a local university.

All of the preceding examples point out how important it is for a gifted program to provide a broad base of services focused on the specific needs of the students. A successful gifted program requires funding and commitment from the district. In a perfect world, a full-fledged gifted education program would include a consistent continuum of services, with a scope and sequence all the way from kindergarten (or prekindergarten) through twelfth grade, and into all curricular areas. It would allow for flexible groupings of students and would be incorporated into the regular school educational plan, as opposed to being an after-school enrichment club. Instruction would be differentiated and fast paced to meet the academic needs of individual students.

Sound a little too good to be true? While many districts do offer such a thoughtfully structured array of accommodations for gifted kids, many more provide a narrower range of programming or are continually working to add services one step at a time. And, as you probably know, some districts offer a bare minimum of opportunities to stimulate and challenge their gifted learners.

No matter how much or how little formal gifted education your district currently offers, you can start from that point to develop broader and improved programming. Maybe you're part of a committee charged with imagining and designing a comprehensive set of services. If so, lucky you! Maybe your district has a mix of services, but they have gaps or don't seem well thought out. Or, maybe you're starting out with little more than $1,285.32 from the PTA bake sale. Don't despair! Begin with what you have. Do something well on a small scale, maybe a pilot program in one building or training on differentiation for a couple of enthusiastic classroom teachers. Then, as you gain appreciation and approval for the services, you can work with others to expand the programming. Use the skills and talents that you have in place. Complete gifted programs are not "built in a day."

Keys to Developing a Successful Gifted Education Program

Services for gifted students might be organized in many ways. Whether you're starting with a lot or a little, a successful gifted program is built on a similar set of elements. Here is a brief summary of these fundamental components, which are covered in detail in the remainder of this book.

The Gifted Education Committee

If you are the district's gifted coordinator, the job of spearheading the formation of this committee may fall to you. It might also be the responsibility of another administrator, who may assign leadership for different tasks to one or more individuals. Regardless of who's in charge or what your specific role may be, the committee will set or help set the direction for your program. Its members will work in various capacities, often with people outside the group, to accomplish the different tasks and processes of building and sustaining a districtwide program. Ideally, the committee will include representation from all the people with vested interests: administrators, teachers, parents, interested PTO or PTA members, community leaders, and even a few students.

Program Development and Planning

Tasks here include:

- writing the program mission or philosophy statement and goals

- writing, implementing, and reviewing policies and procedures
- setting a focus for gifted education programming
- seeking approval for the program plan from the district and State Department of Education, if necessary

Individuals charged with actually designing the program will want to poll teachers, administrators, and parents to determine what student needs are of particular interest or concern and to see what types of services people feel will be most useful. It will also be important to research different exemplary programs. NAGC (the National Association for Gifted Children—see page 7) and state gifted organizations can be excellent resources here, as can other districts in your region known for high-quality gifted services. With this information in hand, the next tasks are:

- determining who participates in programming and how it is delivered
- selecting curriculum, programs, and other services and materials

Identification, Selection, and Placement of Students

Means of identification will depend on the types of programming that will be offered. Beyond programming, selection and placement will also depend on the number of students your resources (human and monetary) will allow you to serve.

Staff Development and Involvement

Inservices for teachers in gifted education philosophy, instructional strategies, identification, and implementation can make the difference between a program that plods or limps along and one that thrives. Equally important are regular meetings for teachers involved with the program. Often these meetings can be used for training and education. They will also give teachers a forum for sharing strategies, discussing problems or concerns, and supporting each other.

"Combine two or more people in the pursuit of a common purpose and you can achieve more with less. Together we are able to accomplish what none of us could achieve alone."
—DAN ZADRA

Publicity

Local media outlets present the opportunity to spotlight your program's successes, inform the community about what's happening with gifted students in the school or district, and invite people into the process. Newspapers, TV and radio stations, and the Web sites of your district and the local gifted organization are all forums for educating people about the need and value inherent in gifted education and for cultivating buy-in. Best of all, this publicity can be free.

Parent Involvement

Parents want and need to be involved with the school's gifted education services. Your planning should consider all of the following:

- **Parent meetings several times each year.** During the meetings, you can encourage advocacy and participation in your program. You can also present information and host discussions of topics of interest to parents of gifted kids, such as social and emotional needs, ability testing, giftedness coupled with another learning difference, or planning for college.

- **A parent newsletter.** Send this out several times a year to keep parents informed about what's going on and about trends in gifted education.

- **Parent advocacy.** Encourage parents to develop a parent advocacy committee, making sure that school personnel attend the meetings to keep abreast of parents' concerns and to support their involvement in their children's education.

- **Volunteer opportunities.** Invite parents to volunteer, in and out of the classroom, and provide appropriate training if they will work directly with students or staff.

Program Evaluation

From the beginning, you will need to collect data that gives a snapshot of how the program is succeeding and what changes or improvements are called for. Plan to submit to the school board an annual report of the strengths and weaknesses of the program. Include ways for all "players"—teachers, parents, students, and administration—to evaluate gifted services. Set in place a procedure for reviewing the information gleaned from evaluations and using it to improve your program and services so they truly meet the needs of gifted kids in the district.

Networking and Trend Monitoring

Time and money need to be allotted so that gifted education personnel can attend local and national workshops to keep informed about current trends and strategies in gifted education. This should include membership in local, state, and national gifted organizations as well as plans for someone to serve on district, state, and professional committees that have the power to make decisions impacting gifted students. In addition, no matter what programs and services you decide to implement, you will want to plan for a resource center. Even if this starts out as a single shelf in the office or library, it's important to initiate this early on. Include books, pamphlets, videos, and other resources for parents, teachers, and students. The resource center is also the place to house publications from national and state gifted organizations.

Yes, the list of elements for developing a successful gifted program is a long one. Your planning will take time and patience. As with many endeavors, to build or strengthen your program, start at the foundation. The remainder of this chapter will look at three essential pieces of groundwork: determining your mission and philosophy, conducting a needs assessment, and setting the focus for your gifted program.

Getting Started: Stating Your Mission and Philosophy

"If you don't know where you're going, you'll end up somewhere else."
—ALFRED ADLER

Writing a mission and philosophy statement can be a challenge, especially when doing it as a committee, but is essential to know your parameters and follow them to design the path your program will take. The process is necessary in order to allow all parties with a vested interest to identify with the program. This is creative, buy-in time for the participants. Much enthusiasm and built-in advocacy can be generated at this step.

We recommend that you think in terms of three types of information here:

- philosophy *(what)*—the focusing, identifying, descriptive information

- mission, or purpose *(why)*—your stated reasons for the program

- goals *(how)*—outlining specific steps and some details about the way you will address the philosophy and accomplish the purpose (goals are addressed in Survival Strategy 3; see pages 64–66)

Look First at Your District's Philosophy and Mission

Your statement will need to align with the district's stated mission, so start by looking at the official language your district has put in place. Virtually every school district and many individual schools have written philosophy and mission statements—sometimes separate, sometimes combined. These statements are usually quite short, seldom longer than a few sentences, and have generally been sanctioned by the board of education in some type of formal approval process. Though some schools start with their philosophy and move to their mission, often they begin by thinking about their mission—the purpose behind what the school district wants to project for its overall image and goals.

Mission statements tend to take on a particular tone and character. Some emphasize the child's developing role as a "global citizen," while others focus on the child as a "lifelong learner." Still others address the student as a member of a "democratic society." Very rapidly, you can sense in a mission statement whether the school district sees its primary educational job in terms of benefiting the individual child or in serving as the conduit for acculturating the child into a larger world.

Close to a school's mission statement is its philosophy of education. A natural link to the mission, the philosophy is usually a bit longer and more detailed. Also, it is here that you will almost always find language and values that can support the idea of services for gifted students. Nearly all philosophy statements include elements on which a gifted education mission can be founded, as there is often mention of something akin to "allowing each child to reach his or her potential." Here are some examples of mission and philosophy statements:

The mission of the Shattuck Public Schools is to produce responsible, educated citizens who are equipped with the skills required for success in an ever-changing, highly diverse, technological world.

Figure 1.1 This combined mission/philosophy statement puts the emphasis on children's future employment and the role they will play in society. Though individual children's needs are not noted as a particular focus, diversity is acknowledged.

The Redfern School District will foster an academically excellent educational system to develop critically thinking, civic-minded learners who will contribute to our global society. To accomplish this mission, the district will encourage and support a committed partnership with staff, parents, and the community.

Figure 1.2 This mission includes a bit of philosophy as well as some direction for goals. The statement would appear to have a direct link to services for gifted students, as it emphasizes academic excellence and critical thinking as fundamentals. It's apparent, too, that the district values collaboration.

The mission of public education for Los Manos District #22 is for every student to develop the attributes necessary to become a lifelong learner, to reach personal fulfillment, and to contribute productively to a democratic society. This calls for an educational system that responds to the differing abilities, needs, interests, and aspirations of the entire student body.

The philosophy of public education for the Los Manos District #22 is to provide every student with the maximum educational experience the student can absorb, subject only to each individual's limitations. This includes providing the maximum educational experience for fast, average, and slow learners and for those children with disabilities and learning differences.

Figure 1.3 Here's a wonderful statement that emphasizes personal growth within a larger society and clearly expresses a commitment to individual student needs. It just follows that gifted students can be served well within this mission and philosophy.

Develop a Statement That Fits Your District's Focus

If you are working from a base of statements similar to any of these, it should be relatively easy for your committee to construct a gifted program philosophy and mission that complements what the board of education says it wants to provide for all students. It's particularly easy to do this when districts state their commitment to being "responsive to the differing needs, interests, abilities, and aspirations of the entire student body," to "academic excellence," or to having students "achieve personal fulfillment." It's not a stretch, either, to link the value of gifted education to district missions and philosophies that emphasize "commitment to quality," "critical thinking," or "lifelong learning." It can be a little more challenging to connect the dots from language like "basic knowledge and skills for making constructive use of the law" or "acquisition of skills, attitudes, and interests which allow an individual to be aware of the options available, not of the absence of restraints" (these latter statements are both from actual district missions), but this can legitimately be done.

Indeed, it will be in your best interest to do as in the following examples: refer back to the district's mission or philosophy as the reason behind your desire to offer specific services for gifted students.

> The Shattuck Public School District has a responsibility to foster in all students critical-thinking, leadership, and academic skills that are necessary for succeeding in a global society. Fulfilling this mission for all students requires that the district's schools capitalize on students' inherent and developed talents and abilities. Therefore, it is incumbent upon the district to provide gifted students with individual learning prescriptions, resources, and experiences that capitalize on their inherent and developed talents and which provide the potential for self-fulfillment, creativity, and responsible production in our society.

Figure 1.4 By identifying attributes required in students' future roles as workers and contributing members of society, this statement makes a clear link between the school district's mission and philosophy and the needs of gifted students.

> Meeting the individual learning needs of children is a well-established mission in Los Manos District #22. It is acknowledged that no single learning prescription fits all children. In recognition of this diversity, Los Manos District #22 will provide services to identified gifted children. We will provide a wide range of opportunities that accommodate the learning differences of these children and that incorporate the academic, psychological, and social needs of gifted children into program structure.

Figure 1.5 Some pretty big promises are made in this gifted program philosophy, which is clearly tied to a stated district mission. Note that the statement on gifted education includes specific accommodation for gifted kids' psychological needs—a critical area that is often overlooked at this early stage in the process.

Though not usually a difficult task, writing your gifted program philosophy and mission may be one of the most important steps you take in establishing your program, as it defines both what the program will offer and why it needs to exist in the first place. Think of your statement as a compass that will provide direction for the program and services you will provide. *Focus* is the operative word here.

> **GIFTED EDUCATION MISSION AND PHILOSOPHY STATEMENT CHECKLIST**
>
> ✔ The statement is consistent with district and state goals.
>
> ✔ The statement matches the identification and programming practices currently in place.
>
> ✔ The statement aligns with the gifted education committee's agreed-upon vision.
>
> ✔ The language in the statement provides an umbrella for all the elements the committee knows it wants to include in the gifted program.
>
> ✔ The statement is clear and unambiguous.

Figure 1.6

Conducting a Needs Assessment

There are lots of reasons for starting or changing a gifted program. Most commonly, there is pressure from some community group—usually, parents of gifted kids—to do more for highly able students than is currently being done. At other times, a school board member or superintendent may see a need for such a program, either because of a lack that is noted or in response to parents' or teachers' calls for more attention to the needs of the gifted. Or, the state may have a new mandate requiring services for the gifted.

Whatever the reason, one of the best things you can do to get the ball rolling at program onset or expansion is to do a formal needs assessment. A key purpose in doing this is to learn about the specific educational needs of the gifted children in your school or district—the kids who are actually being served or who will be served. The needs assessment process leads to creating a focus for your curriculum. For example, if the assessment results in a demand for a strong English program, then the focus can be centered on writing, reading, research, speaking, critical thinking, and problem solving. A needs assessment also lets you take the temperature of key players in gifted education when it comes to their views both on the school's approach to gifted programming and on gifted education in general. It can tell you where your pockets of support and struggle are likely to be as your program begins or changes. A third value of the needs assessment is in seeking buy-in: people like to be asked for their views and feel more connection and commitment to a program when their concerns and ideas are heard and they are allowed to contribute in this way.

Input from a variety of people can help the gifted education committee shape a new program or tailor an existing one. You'll want to seek information from:

- teachers who work with gifted children—both those in the regular classroom and those who specialize in gifted education

- parents of identified gifted students (if there's an existing program) or interested parents from PTA or PTO (in any case)

- administrators—particularly principals, assistant principals, and school counselors

---

WHAT ABOUT INVOLVING STUDENTS IN NEEDS ASSESSMENT?

Student input can be very helpful at this stage. One approach is to gather a group of identified gifted students or students recommended by teachers (probably high-achieving or creative kids likely to be identified for services). Have this group sit down with you and brainstorm what components they think a gifted program should have—a wish list. After brainstorming, invite discussion and ask students to select and prioritize the elements they think are most important. Keep notes about this input to use in conjunction with the information from the written needs assessments completed by adults.

Another approach is to invite some high school students—those identified as gifted or who are in National Honor Society, student council, or debate, for example—to engage in a similar discussion. Tap the memories of these students to learn what they appreciated, didn't appreciate, and wished for in terms of gifted services in elementary and middle school.

Students involved in the development of the Park City, Utah, G/T program insisted upon one thing: they wanted to go to space camp. The planning committee included this as an enrichment option in the gifted program, and space camp developed into one of the most motivating and challenging programs for the students. From then on, the crafty kids who were responsible for requesting it walked tall among their peers.

Figure 1.7

An effective way to gather information about needs is through anonymous questionnaires. Pages 16–33 provide reproducible needs assessment forms you can photocopy and distribute to teachers, parents, and administrators. (Use the "Gifted Services" forms for beginning a new program and the "Improving Gifted Services" forms for enhancing or expanding existing services.) You may also have forms available to you through your school or district, or wish to work with others to develop questionnaires that fit your school's particular circumstances.

Formal (written) assessment is important because it gives you paper in hand with data that can be compiled and interpreted. Be prepared to hear some things you don't want to hear. Since the questionnaire is anonymous (to encourage honest responses), people may reveal their biases. For example, some respondents may dismiss the whole idea of gifted programming because their child wasn't included in a program years ago. Or, a teacher may resent "losing" his or her "best kids" to another teacher. Who knows? Some adults, and even kids, may think that gifted education programs are elitist, undemocratic, or unfair, and use the questionnaire to air these views.

Of course, you may also learn that there is great support for a gifted program, or come to realize that while a self-contained gifted class will never fly, many teachers would appreciate a cluster grouping of gifted kids in particular classrooms.

Whatever the results, you will learn more by doing a formal needs assessment than by forgoing this critical early step in your program planning.

Tips for Gathering and Using Information

1. If you create your own questionnaires, avoid jargon wherever possible, or define your terms. For example, if parents or teachers aren't familiar with the terms *AP* or *curriculum compacting* and you use the words in your form without explanation, people's responses may not be helpful to you.

2. If you are going to distribute the needs assessment to different schools, use different-colored paper for each building. You'll be able to tell where your greatest (and fewest) numbers of respondents are from, and you can send reminders accordingly.

3. Think of attaching a piece of candy or some other small goody to each form you distribute. You'll be amazed how such a small courtesy can increase your response rate.

4. Most high schools do not have gifted programs. Instead, they offer *services* that benefit gifted students— AP classes, honors courses, drama club, forensics, and so forth. So, don't survey the high school staff unless you plan to alter or add to the existing options for those students There is nothing more frustrating for teachers than to take time to complete a survey, only to discover that little or nothing will come of the results. This isn't to say that high school services are unimportant—on the contrary. But concentrate your needs assessments on the grade levels where program services are to begin or where they are to be modified or expanded.

5. Give school personnel no more than ten days to return the needs assessment to you. Also avoid distributing it right before a weekend or vacation, the week before grades are due, or the day before open house. Although no time is convenient, some times are more *inconvenient* than others.

6. Invite parent participation by announcing the survey in your PTO or PTA newsletter, on a school Web site, or along with another mailing. In this announcement, tell parents how to get the survey (perhaps by stopping at the school office, calling to request one, or downloading it from the Web). If possible, provide a self-addressed stamped envelope for returning surveys. In some cases, it can also be valuable to hold a needs assessment discussion with parents rather than ask them to complete a questionnaire. This open-ended format sometimes reveals information that might not emerge on a structured form.

7. Don't be surprised by a small return rate on surveys. We consider fifty percent to be an excellent return, but the percentage of completed questionnaires you get back may be considerably lower. This is okay, because you can still get enough information to identify trends.

8. Once you determine you have gathered or received as many responses as you are going to get, compile the data in a short report that can be shared with administrators and the gifted education committee. You might want to separate out data based on which group of participants gave input (parents, teachers, administrators, students). With the committee, discuss your results in terms of ideas that emerged and directions these might give to the gifted program.

9. Write a one-page letter (no longer) and share the highlights of the findings with teachers and parents. There's no need to distribute the entire summary to every respondent, but do invite them to ask you for one if they have a particular interest in seeing it. Create a brief kid-friendly report or letter for student participants as well, thanking them for their input and letting them know what you learned from them and from others who participated in needs assessment.

10. Probably the best way to compile the data is to note any trends that develop. For example, teachers

may believe that gifted children should not be identified until third or fourth grade, while parents may want identification to occur in kindergarten or first grade. Likewise, some groups or individuals may wish services to be offered within the regular classroom, while others would prefer a more "visible" program, like a pull-out or self-contained class. Your job is *not* to say things like, "Because sixty percent of the respondents want a pull-out program in grades 4–6, that's what we should have." Instead, rely on the data as points of information that your gifted education committee can use as they discuss the pros and cons of various program designs. Remember: needs assessment results provide a snapshot, not a panorama, and they are intended as an initial source of feedback and information from people who can ultimately make or break whatever you design.

Setting a Focus for the Gifted Education Program

Another early step is to take some time with your committee to think about the general focus for the gifted education you will provide.

What programs or accommodations does your district already have in place? Is there a particular school that specializes in math, science, performing arts, or another area? Are practices like differentiation or cluster grouping already being used? If so, those particular services should be included in your focus.

Are you starting from scratch? In this case, you might want to keep your focus smaller, so that you are better able to carry out the program. The program can always expand, but it's difficult and defeating to return back home from first base.

Consider the strengths, resources, interests, and skills of your district to design the focus of the program. Who will get the services? What will the services be? Who can help provide services in the district?

The majority of gifted programs have an academic focus; however, your program may have a single focus or be a combination of choices. Programs are generally grouped into these categories, with critical thinking and leadership opportunities incorporated throughout:

- academic overall
- math
- literature, writing, publishing, and speaking
- science and technology

- social problem solving
- visual arts
- performing arts: music, dance, theater

With your philosophy and mission in place, your needs assessment conducted, and your focus set, you are ready to begin identifying students for the gifted program, setting your goals, and designing the programs and services you will provide in order to meet those goals.

Resources

The following resources apply specifically to topics addressed in this strategy's chapter. For a complete list of gifted education resources, see pages 146–154.

Gifted Programming Today: A National Sample, 2d ed., by Elizabeth Pinkney Coyne (Washington, DC: NAGC, 1998). A 430-page guide for anyone involved in program planning for elementary and secondary students. Includes state directors of gifted education and much more.

"National Association for Gifted Children Pre-K–Grade 12 Gifted Program Standards" *(www.nagc.org/webprek 12.htm).* This Web page is the online source for a document that delineates both requisite and exemplary standards for gifted education programming in seven areas: Curriculum and Instruction, Program Administration and Management, Program Design, Program Evaluation, Socio-Emotional Guidance and Counseling, Professional Development, and Student Identification.

Dear Teacher:

Our school/district is considering providing specialized services for gifted students, and we need your input. Would you please take a few minutes to complete this anonymous survey and return it to

_____ at _____ on or before

_____.

Thank you for taking the time to help us determine how best we might serve highly able students. We will get back to you with a summary of the results and keep you informed as our plans progress.

Sincerely,

_____

1. For each statement, write the letter that best expresses your view:

A=Agree   N=Not Sure   D=Disagree

A. _____ Gifted children need specialized gifted services.

B. _____ Gifted students have special learning needs.

C. _____ Gifted students have special social and emotional needs.

D. _____ All children are gifted.

E. _____ I currently tailor teaching strategies and curricula for gifted students in my classroom.

F. _____ I differentiate instruction for gifted students in my classroom.

G. _____ I incorporate critical-thinking, reasoning, and problem-solving skills into my lessons.

H. _____ I use lessons that require a student to be creative.

I. _____ I provide enrichment and acceleration in my classroom.

J. _____ Only students who demonstrate achievement in the regular classroom should receive gifted program services.

K. _____ Some type of special learning opportunity should be available to students who may be gifted but who do not excel in the regular classroom.

MORE

2. How do you think a gifted program should be focused? Please rank your top 3 choices, with 1 being the highest priority:

A. _____ academic overall

B. _____ math

C. _____ literature, writing, publishing, and speaking

D. _____ science and technology

E. _____ critical thinking

F. _____ social problem solving

G. _____ visual arts

H. _____ performing arts: music, dance, theater

I. _____ other: _____

3. Please rank order the following methods for identifying gifted students, with 1 being the highest priority:

A. _____ standardized intelligence and achievement tests

B. _____ teacher nominations, recommendations, and anecdotal information

C. _____ parent checklists and anecdotal information

D. _____ student portfolios or work samples

E. _____ instruments that measure creativity and problem-solving ability

F. _____ interviews with students

G. _____ other: _____

4. Please rank order the following arrangements for meeting the academic needs of gifted students, with 1 being your strongest preference:

A. _____ in the regular classroom by their classroom teachers

B. _____ in the regular classroom, with occasional assistance from a teacher trained in gifted education

C. _____ in cluster groups of several gifted students

D. _____ in a pull-out program once or twice a week

E. _____ in a full-time classroom where all the children are identified as gifted

F. _____ in a resource room where children work independently

G. _____ other: _____

MORE

5. Please rank order the 5 gifted education topics for which you would most like to receive inservice training, with 1 being your highest priority:

A. _____ characteristics and identification of gifted children

B. _____ teaching strategies

C. _____ differentiation (varying instruction to meet students' individual needs)

D. _____ cluster grouping

E. _____ acceleration

F. _____ curriculum compacting

G. _____ Bloom's Taxonomy

H. _____ Internet activities

I. _____ service projects

J. _____ enrichment

K. _____ underachievement/undermotivation

L. _____ multiple intelligences

M. _____ twice exceptional (gifted students with LD)

N. _____ underrepresented student groups

O. _____ social and emotional needs

P. _____ creativity

Q. _____ intensity

R. _____ perfectionism

S. _____ student stress

T. _____ discipline/behavior issues

U. _____ other: _____

6. Additional comments:

_____

_____

_____

_____

_____

_____

_____

_____

_____

_____

Dear Parent/Caregiver:

Our school/district is considering providing specialized services for gifted students, and we need your input. Would you please take a few minutes to complete this anonymous survey and return it to _____ at _____ on or before _____.

Thank you for taking the time to help us determine how best we might serve highly able students. We will get back to you with a summary of the results and keep you informed as our plans progress.

Sincerely,

_____

1. Has your child ever been identified for gifted services in a school setting? _____ Yes _____ No

2. Do you believe your child is gifted? _____ Yes _____ No

3. For each statement, write the letter that best expresses your view:

A=Agree   N=Not Sure   D=Disagree

A. _____ Gifted children need specialized gifted services.

B. _____ Gifted students have special learning needs.

C. _____ Gifted students have special social and emotional needs.

D. _____ All children are gifted.

E. _____ My child's classroom teacher(s) currently adapt teaching strategies and curricula to meet the needs of gifted students.

F. _____ There are adequate resources and materials for gifted students in our school.

G. _____ The school provides appropriate opportunities for gifted children's social and emotional growth.

MORE →

H. _____ The school provides sufficient opportunities (such as music, art, drama, sports) for nurturing students' special talents.

I. _____ Only students who demonstrate achievement in the regular classroom should receive gifted program services.

J. _____ Some type of special learning opportunity should be available to students who may be gifted but who do not excel in the regular classroom.

4. How do you think a gifted program should be focused? Please rank your top 3 choices, with 1 being the highest priority:

A. _____ academic overall

B. _____ math

C. _____ literature, writing, publishing, and speaking

D. _____ science and technology

E. _____ critical thinking

F. _____ social problem solving

G. _____ visual arts

H. _____ performing arts: music, dance, theater

I. _____ other: _____

5. How should students be identified for gifted programming? Please rank your choices, with 1 being the highest priority:

A. _____ standardized intelligence and achievement tests

B. _____ teacher nominations, recommendations, and anecdotal information

C. _____ parent checklists and anecdotal information

D. _____ student portfolios or work samples

E. _____ instruments that measure creativity and problem-solving ability

F. _____ interviews with students

G. _____ other: _____

MORE ➤

★ **Parent Survey: Gifted Services** (cont'd)

6. How should the academic needs of gifted students be met? Please rank your choices, with 1 being your strongest preference:

A. _____ in the regular classroom by their classroom teachers

B. _____ in the regular classroom, with occasional assistance from a teacher trained in gifted education

C. _____ in small groups of several gifted students

D. _____ in a pull-out program once or twice a week

E. _____ in a full-time classroom where all the children are identified as gifted

F. _____ in a resource room where children work independently

G. _____ other: _____

7. Please rank order the 5 gifted education topics you would like to see addressed at parent meetings, with 1 being your highest priority:

A. _____ characteristics and identification of gifted children

B. _____ how to support gifted children's education at home

C. _____ teaching strategies

D. _____ Internet activities

E. _____ service projects

F. _____ enrichment

G. _____ underachievement/undermotivation

H. _____ learning styles and multiple intelligences (different ways children process information)

I. _____ twice exceptional (gifted students with LD)

J. _____ underrepresented student groups

K. _____ social and emotional needs

L. _____ creativity

M. _____ intensity

N. _____ perfectionism

O. _____ student stress

P. _____ discipline/behavior issues

Q. _____ other: _____

8. Additional comments:

_____

_____

_____

★ Administrator Survey: Gifted Services ★

Dear Administrator:

Our school/district is considering providing specialized services for gifted students, and we need your input. Would you please take a few minutes to complete this anonymous survey and return it to _____ at _____ on or before

_____.

Thank you for taking the time to help us determine how best we might serve highly able students. We will get back to you with a summary of the results and keep you informed as our plans progress.

Sincerely,

_____

1. For each statement, write the letter that best expresses your view:

A=Agree   N=Not Sure   D=Disagree

A. _____ Gifted children need specialized gifted services.

B. _____ Gifted students have special learning needs.

C. _____ Gifted students have special social and emotional needs.

D. _____ All children are gifted.

E. _____ Teachers in my district/school currently tailor teaching strategies and curricula for gifted students in their classrooms.

F. _____ Teachers in my district/school differentiate instruction for gifted students in their classrooms.

G. _____ Teachers in my district/school incorporate critical-thinking, reasoning, and problem-solving skills into their lessons.

H. _____ Teachers in my district/school use lessons that require a student to be creative.

I. _____ Teachers in my district/school provide enrichment and acceleration in their classrooms.

J. _____ Only students who demonstrate achievement in the regular classroom should receive gifted program services.

K. _____ Some type of special learning opportunity should be available to students who may be gifted but who do not excel in the regular classroom.

MORE

★ Administrator Survey: Gifted Services (cont'd)

2. How do you think a gifted program should be focused? Please rank your top 3 choices, with 1 being the highest priority:

A. _____ academic overall

B. _____ math

C. _____ literature, writing, publishing, and speaking

D. _____ science and technology

E. _____ critical thinking

F. _____ social problem solving

G. _____ visual arts

H. _____ performing arts: music, dance, theater

I. _____ other: _____

3. Please rank order the following methods for identifying gifted students, with 1 being the highest priority:

A. _____ standardized intelligence and achievement tests

B. _____ teacher nominations, recommendations, and anecdotal information

C. _____ parent checklists and anecdotal information

D. _____ student portfolios or work samples

E. _____ instruments that measure creativity and problem-solving ability

F. _____ interviews with students

G. _____ other: _____

4. Please rank order the following arrangements for meeting the academic needs of gifted students, with 1 being your strongest preference:

A. _____ in the regular classroom by their classroom teachers

B. _____ in the regular classroom, with occasional assistance from a teacher trained in gifted education

C. _____ in cluster groups of several gifted students

D. _____ in a pull-out program once or twice a week

E. _____ in a full-time classroom where all the children are identified as gifted

F. _____ in a resource room where children work independently

G. _____ other: _____

MORE →

★ Administrator Survey: Gifted Services (cont'd)

5. Please rank order the 5 gifted education inservice-training topics you believe would be of most benefit to teachers, with 1 being your highest priority:

A. _____ characteristics and identification of gifted children

B. _____ teaching strategies

C. _____ differentiation

D. _____ cluster grouping

E. _____ acceleration

F. _____ curriculum compacting

G. _____ Bloom's Taxonomy

H. _____ Internet activities

I. _____ service projects

J. _____ enrichment

K. _____ underachievement/undermotivation

L. _____ multiple intelligences

M. _____ twice exceptional (gifted students with LD)

N. _____ underrepresented student groups

O. _____ social and emotional needs

P. _____ creativity

Q. _____ intensity

R. _____ perfectionism

S. _____ student stress

T. _____ discipline/behavior issues

U. _____ other: _____

6. Additional comments:

_____

_____

_____

_____

_____

_____

_____

_____

★ Teacher Survey: Improving Gifted Services ★

Dear Teacher:

Our school/district is considering some different approaches to meeting the needs of our identified gifted students, and we need your input. Would you please take a few minutes to complete this anonymous survey and return it to _____ at _____ on or before _____.

Thank you for taking the time to help us determine how best we might serve highly able students. We will get back to you with a summary of the results and keep you informed as our plans progress.

Sincerely,

_____

1. For each statement, write the letter that best expresses your view:

A=Agree   **N=Not Sure**   **D=Disagree**

A. _____   Gifted children need specialized gifted services.

B. _____   I have adequate knowledge concerning giftedness.

C. _____   I feel adequately informed about the gifted programs and services in our school.

D. _____   I have adequate time to serve gifted students in my classroom.

E. _____   There is adequate communication among parents, teachers, and administrators about the gifted program.

F. _____   There are adequate opportunities for staff development in the area of gifted services.

G. _____   There are adequate resources and materials for gifted students in our school.

H. _____   Gifted students have special learning needs.

I. _____   Gifted students have special social and emotional needs.

J. _____   I understand how to differentiate instruction for gifted students.

K. _____   I incorporate critical-thinking, reasoning, and problem-solving skills into my lessons.

MORE ▶

L. _____ I use lessons that require a student to be creative.

M. _____ I provide enrichment and acceleration in my classroom.

N. _____ Only students who demonstrate achievement in the regular classroom should receive gifted program services.

O. _____ Some type of special learning opportunity should be available to students who may be gifted but who do not excel in the regular classroom.

P. _____ All students are gifted.

2. In what area(s) (for example: general academic, a specific subject, social-skills development, community service projects, a visual or performing art) do you feel your gifted students would benefit from having more challenging activities?

_____

_____

_____

3. Please rank order the following methods for identifying gifted students, with 1 being the highest priority:

A. _____ standardized intelligence and achievement tests

B. _____ teacher nominations, recommendations, and anecdotal information

C. _____ parent checklists and anecdotal information

D. _____ student portfolios or work samples

E. _____ instruments that measure creativity and problem-solving ability

F. _____ interviews with students

G. _____ other: _____

4. Please rank order the following arrangements for meeting the academic needs of gifted students, with 1 being your strongest preference:

A. _____ in the regular classroom by their classroom teachers

B. _____ in the regular classroom, with occasional assistance from a teacher trained in gifted education

MORE

C. _____ in cluster groups of several gifted students

D. _____ in a pull-out program once or twice a week

E. _____ in a full-time classroom where all the children are identified as gifted

F. _____ in a resource room where children work independently

G. _____ other: _____

5. Please rank order the 5 gifted education topics for which you would most like to receive inservice training, with 1 being your highest priority:

A. _____ characteristics and identification of gifted children

B. _____ teaching strategies

C. _____ differentiation (varying instruction to meet students' individual needs)

D. _____ cluster grouping

E. _____ acceleration

F. _____ curriculum compacting

G. _____ Bloom's Taxonomy

H. _____ Internet activities

I. _____ service projects

J. _____ enrichment

K. _____ underachievement/undermotivation

L. _____ multiple intelligences

M. ___ twice exceptional (gifted students with LD)

N. _____ underrepresented student groups

O. _____ social and emotional needs

P. _____ creativity

Q. _____ intensity

R. _____ perfectionism

S. _____ student stress

T. _____ discipline/behavior issues

U. _____ other: _____

6. Additional comments:

_____

_____

_____

_____

_____

Dear Parent/Caregiver:

Our school/district is considering some different approaches to meeting the needs of our identified gifted students, and we need your input. Would you please take a few minutes to complete this anonymous survey and return it to _____ at _____ on or before _____.

Thank you for taking the time to help us determine how best we might serve highly able students. We will get back to you with a summary of the results and keep you informed as our plans progress.

Sincerely,

_____

1. Do you have a child in the gifted program? _____ Yes _____ No

2. Regardless of placement, do you believe your child is gifted? _____ Yes _____ No

3. For each statement, write the letter that best expresses your view:

A=Agree   N=Not Sure   D=Disagree

A. _____ Gifted children need specialized gifted services.

B. _____ I understand the school's identification process for placing students into gifted programming.

C. _____ I feel adequately informed about the gifted programs and services in our school.

D. _____ I have a positive view of the services, programming, and teaching gifted students in our school receive.

E. _____ There is adequate communication among parents, teachers, and administrators about the gifted program.

F. _____ There are adequate resources and materials for gifted students in our school.

G. _____ Gifted services in our school provide appropriate opportunities for gifted children's social and emotional growth.

MORE

H. _____ The school provides sufficient opportunities (such as music, art, drama, sports) for nurturing students' special talents.

I. _____ Only students who demonstrate achievement in the regular classroom should receive gifted program services.

J. _____ Some type of special learning opportunity should be available to students who may be gifted but who do not excel in the regular classroom.

K. _____ All students are gifted.

4. In what area(s) (for example: general academic, a specific subject, social-skills development, community service projects, a visual or performing art) would you like to see gifted students have more challenging activities?

_____

_____

_____

5. How should students be identified for gifted programming? Please rank your choices, with 1 being the highest priority:

A. _____ standardized intelligence and achievement tests

B. _____ teacher nominations, recommendations, and anecdotal information

C. _____ parent checklists and anecdotal information

D. _____ student portfolios or work samples

E. _____ instruments that measure creativity and problem-solving ability

F. _____ interviews with students

G. _____ other: _____

6. How should the academic needs of gifted students be met? Please rank your choices, with 1 being your strongest preference:

A. _____ in the regular classroom by their classroom teachers

B. _____ in the regular classroom, with occasional assistance from a teacher trained in gifted education

C. _____ in small groups of several gifted students

MORE →

D. _____ in a pull-out program once or twice a week

E. _____ in a full-time classroom where all the children are identified as gifted

F. _____ in a resource room where children work independently

G. _____ other: _____

7. Please rank order the 5 gifted education topics you would like to see addressed at parent meetings, with 1 being your highest priority:

A. _____ characteristics and identification of gifted children

B. _____ how to support gifted children's education at home

C. _____ teaching strategies

D. _____ Internet activities

E. _____ service projects

F. _____ enrichment

G. _____ underachievement/undermotivation

H. _____ learning styles and multiple intelligences (different ways children process information)

I. _____ twice exceptional (gifted students with LD)

J. _____ underrepresented student groups

K. _____ social and emotional needs

L. _____ creativity

M. _____ intensity

N. _____ perfectionism

O. _____ student stress

P. _____ discipline/behavior issues

Q. _____ other: _____

8. Additional comments:

_____

_____

_____

_____

_____

_____

_____

Dear Administrator:

Our school/district is considering some different approaches to meeting the needs of our identified gifted students, and we need your input. Would you please take a few minutes to complete this anonymous survey and return it to _____ at _____ on or before _____.

Thank you for taking the time to help us determine how best we might serve highly able students. We will get back to you with a summary of the results and keep you informed as our plans progress.

Sincerely,

_____

1. For each statement, write the letter that best expresses your view:

A=Agree   **N=Not Sure**   **D=Disagree**

A. _____ Gifted children need specialized gifted services.

B. _____ Gifted students have special learning needs.

C. _____ Gifted students have special social and emotional needs.

D. _____ All children are gifted.

E. _____ Teachers in my district/school currently tailor teaching strategies and curricula for gifted students in their classrooms.

F. _____ Teachers in my district/school differentiate instruction for gifted students in their classrooms.

G. _____ Teachers in my district/school incorporate critical-thinking, reasoning, and problem-solving skills into their lessons.

H. _____ Teachers in my district/school use lessons that require a student to be creative.

I. _____ Teachers in my district/school provide enrichment and acceleration in their classrooms.

J. _____ Only students who demonstrate achievement in the regular classroom should receive gifted program services.

K. _____ Some type of special learning opportunity should be available to students who may be gifted but who do not excel in the regular classroom.

MORE

2. In what area(s) (for example: general academic, a specific subject, social-skills development, community service projects, a visual or performing art) do you feel gifted students would benefit from having more challenging activities?

_____

_____

_____

_____

3. Please rank order the following methods for identifying gifted students, with 1 being the highest priority:

A. _____ standardized intelligence and achievement tests

B. _____ teacher nominations, recommendations, and anecdotal information

C. _____ parent checklists and anecdotal information

D. _____ student portfolios or work samples

E. _____ instruments that measure creativity and problem-solving ability

F. _____ interviews with students

G. _____ other: _____

4. Please rank order the following arrangements for meeting the academic needs of gifted students, with 1 being your strongest preference:

A. _____ in the regular classroom by their classroom teachers

B. _____ in the regular classroom, with occasional assistance from a teacher trained in gifted education

C. _____ in cluster groups of several gifted students

D. _____ in a pull-out program once or twice a week

E. _____ in a full-time classroom where all the children are identified as gifted

F. _____ in a resource room where children work independently

G. _____ other: _____

★ Administrator Survey: Improving Gifted Services (cont'd)

5. Please rank order the 5 gifted education inservice-training topics you believe would be of most benefit to teachers, with 1 being your highest priority:

A. _____ characteristics and identification of gifted children

B. _____ teaching strategies

C. _____ differentiation

D. _____ cluster grouping

E. _____ acceleration

F. _____ curriculum compacting

G. _____ Bloom's Taxonomy

H. _____ Internet activities

I. _____ service projects

J. _____ enrichment

K. _____ underachievement/undermotivation

L. _____ multiple intelligences

M. _____ twice exceptional (gifted students with LD)

N. _____ underrepresented student groups

O. _____ social and emotional needs

P. _____ creativity

Q. _____ intensity

R. _____ perfectionism

S. _____ student stress

T. _____ discipline/behavior issues

U. _____ other: _____

6. Additional comments:

_____

_____

_____

_____

_____

_____

_____

_____

2

Cast a Wide Net to Identify Students

Chip, a fourth grader, had never been considered gifted by any teacher or by virtue of his test scores. In fact, his only special placement was in the school's learning disabilities program, where he went daily for individual help in writing and reading. But the new reading specialist was amazed at Chip's advanced vocabulary and command of abstract concepts, especially about politics. He discussed Chip's knowledge base with the boy's mother, suggesting that Chip might be considered for gifted services. Chip's mother nodded in both agreement and surprise. "We've always known he was smart," she explained, "but we never figured anyone at school would see a kid with learning disabilities as gifted, too."

Then there is Jacqui. School didn't start off too well for her. In kindergarten and first grade, she would finish her work early and go around completing all the other children's assignments for them. Another source of trouble: Jacqui read aloud **with** the teacher during storytime—very distracting! Now in second grade, Jacqui is just as precocious as before, but her teachers don't want to label someone so young as gifted. They feel it's better to wait until fourth grade or so, thinking that what looks like high ability at this early age may even out over time.

★ ★ ★

And there's Kory, a seventh grader. From the start, it was easy for teachers to ignore Kory's giftedness because of his annoying sloppiness and disorganization. You could find Kory by following his trail of papers down the hallway. When he entered a classroom, all of his folders and books

appeared to spontaneously fall to the floor. Hidden beneath the disarray was an intense hunger for justice in the world. Kory led several classmates in being the force behind cleaning up a hazardous waste site near their school, a place where children played and rode bikes. To make sure that his neighborhood was protected, he organized a campaign to reelect a legislator who supported his views. While doing all this, Kory skipped a few math assignments, and his spelling remained creative, at best. These subjects weren't particularly important to him when compared to issues like children playing on piles of lead and toxic PCBs.

In each of these cases, a child's giftedness was initially disguised or overlooked because of one major factor: bias. This bias was not due to race or religion but rather to an unfounded and too-often unexamined assumption that students are gifted only if they are high-achieving teacher-pleasers whose giftedness is their most defining and recognizable trait. Often such bias stems from a lack of basic knowledge about giftedness. Many teachers receive no training about any aspect of gifted education, so it's not surprising that some wouldn't recognize gifted kids whose characteristics don't fit the standard simplistic view.

Not only teachers, but many parents, administrators, and kids, too, harbor this stereotypical picture of what a gifted student looks and acts like. Yet logic alone would dictate that gifted kids are multidimensional. We know that there are children of average intelligence and ability who are economically disadvantaged, lack facility with English, or have behavior disorders, psychological problems, physical impediments, learning differences, disabilities, or cultural backgrounds that distinguish them from the majority of students. It just follows that kids at the high end of the intelligence continuum will face the same challenges. Logic, though, does not always win out over habit of mind.

This bias is one that researchers, educators, and parents involved with gifted kids are working hard to address. An early place *you* can address it as you develop your gifted education program is through responsible identification. Survival Strategy 2 discusses ways to identify gifted children properly, what pitfalls (both philosophical and pragmatic) to avoid, and how to include teachers, families, students, and others in the identification process. Along the way, we'll also try to convince you (if, indeed, convincing is needed) that low grades, minimal achievement, weak skills in English, learning differences, uncontrolled behavior, and negative attitudes can disguise giftedness.

Defining Your Terms[1]

Before you can identify gifted children in your school or district, you will want to formally define what "gifted" means. There is no single correct or complete definition—it depends on the mission and philosophy you have in place. By listing and describing certain abilities and talents, a definition helps teachers identify children who would benefit from a gifted program. This means it's important for a definition to be broad yet specific, inclusive yet focused on particular qualities that set some children apart from their age peers and indicate the need for qualitatively different educational opportunities.

There are a number of existing definitions you can consider as you develop criteria for your school or district. The National Association for Gifted Children (NAGC) offers this broad statement:

*A gifted person is **someone who shows, or has the potential for showing, an exceptional level of performance in one or more areas of expression.** Some of these abilities are very general and can affect a broad spectrum of the person's life, such as leadership skills or the ability to think creatively. Some are very specific talents and are only evident in particular circumstances, such as special aptitude in mathematics, science, or music. The term **giftedness** provides a general reference to this spectrum of abilities without being specific or dependent on a measure or index.*

For state and local education agencies, one of the most widely used or adapted definitions of giftedness comes from the U.S. Department of Education's *Marland Report*. The 1972 report provided this definition:

Gifted and talented children are those identified by professionally qualified persons who by virtue of outstanding abilities are capable of high performance. These are children who require differentiated educational programs and/or services beyond those normally provided by the regular school program in order to realize their contributions to self and society.

Children capable of high performance include those with demonstrated achievement and/or potential ability in any of the following areas:

1. *general intellectual ability*
2. *specific academic aptitude*
3. *creative or productive thinking*
4. *leadership ability*
5. *visual and performing arts*
6. *psychomotor ability*

Since 1972, the U.S. Congress has twice revised the Marland definition, removing the reference to psychomotor ability. The reasoning here was that the category of visual and performing arts already included psychomotor talent, and having it as a separate category could lead to including, for example, athletically gifted students—who were already being well provided for in terms of funding and programming. Here is the 1978 federal definition of gifted and talented children:

. . . children and, whenever applicable, youth who are identified at the pre-school, elementary, or secondary level as possessing demonstrated or potential abilities that give evidence of high performance capability in areas such as intellectual, creative, specific academic or leadership ability or in the performing and visual arts, and who by reason thereof require services or activities not ordinarily provided by the school.

The 1988 definition is even shorter and more concise:

The term "gifted and talented students" means children and youth who give evidence of high performance capability in areas such as intellectual, creative, artistic, or leadership capacity, or in specific academic fields, and who require services or activities not ordinarily provided by the schools in order to fully develop such capabilities.

The Marland definition is sometimes criticized for being limiting. One limitation is that it does not mention all of the characteristics associated with giftedness. For example, it does not clearly include personality traits like sensitivity, passion, and focus. The result is that, on its own, this definition could prevent you from including in your gifted program a variety of gifted kids who don't exhibit their exceptional abilities in ways that are specifically cited in the federal definition. On the other hand, the definition is broad enough to include creative and artistic children, and it clearly indicates that specialized programming is justifiable and necessary for gifted students.

Pitfall 1: Creating a Definition That Isn't Inclusive

In thinking about how to define and identify giftedness, it's important to consider the range of students in your school or district—not just those kids who have already been identified as gifted or selected for an existing gifted program, but *all* students. Students from several groups are often overlooked.

Students from minority or nonmainstream groups. This is a big group, including kids from a range of cultural, racial, ethnic, and socioeconomic backgrounds that differ from what's considered mainstream. These kids' gifts may not be measurable by standard IQ and achievement tests, which are often biased to majority (white middle- to upper-class) students. Their gifts may lie in areas that are not celebrated or valued by society at large. If the students are immigrants or visiting foreign students, their English-speaking skills may be so limited as to mask high verbal ability or impede them in taking tests, writing, reading, listening, and speaking.

Of all the things we do in gifted education, perhaps our greatest failing is in locating gifted children who come from minority groups, who are poor or homeless, or whose first language is not English. This is not for want of attention. Educators and researchers such as Mary Frasier, Alexinia Baldwin, and Ernesto Bernal, among others, have all expressed concerns and ideas about finding the giftedness within these populations of children. In-the-trenches coordinators and teachers care about this issue as well, but are not always successful in finding ways to compel those who make decisions about student selection to look with a wider lens.

Even when minority students are identified for inclusion in gifted programs, they may not succeed. African American students, for example, may have mixed feelings about academic success. High-achieving black students may be accused of "acting white."

Some children's behavior may not fit with the teacher's beliefs about what giftedness means or how gifted students should behave. For instance, Native American kids are often taught to value interdependence, not independence, and to learn to make decisions collectively. Puerto Rican children typically learn to seek the advice of their family rather than act independently. Mexican American kids are taught to respect their elders, the law, and authority, not individual competition, initiative, and self-direction.

Poor and homeless children face additional biases when it comes to identification as well. If you've never seen or heard of a gazebo, never been to a zoo or read a book on African animals, and have spent more time worrying about whether the heat will be turned off than about global warming, you might not seem as engaged as kids who routinely learn, think, and talk about topics like these. Economically disadvantaged kids aren't as likely to correctly answer questions about these things on standardized tests, or to contribute to discussions about them in class. Because of this, in some cases neither teachers nor parents recognize these kids as candidates for a gifted program, meaning many highly able children are routinely left out at the identification stage.

Researchers have noted several reasons our identification procedures do not pick up on the abilities of children of color and those who are poor or have limited English skills. Among the reasons:[2]

- a too-heavy reliance on standardized tests, many of which are culturally biased in favor of the majority culture

- bias from teachers who don't recognize indications that children from diverse groups might be gifted

- too little attention to the challenges presented by nonintellectual barriers such as low teacher expectations, racism, and cultural conflicts regarding values and priorities

- narrow screening and selection processes that pay too little attention to visual learning styles due to the highly auditory nature of many tests and assessments

- a lack of family involvement in the educational process, as parents who themselves have few positive memories of school or who distrust the school bureaucracy are reluctant to become involved there

Students who perform poorly on tests. Some gifted kids aren't good test-takers. They may know the material backwards and forwards, but they find the test situation too stressful to perform at their best. Or, they may have personal problems that prevent them from concentrating. Since test scores are one of the main methods many professionals use to identify gifted students, this clearly puts kids with test anxiety at a disadvantage.

Troublemakers. Some teachers and administrators associate "good" behavior with being gifted and "bad" behavior with being unwilling or unable to learn. Parents may often (but not always) be more able to see beyond behavior issues and recognize their child's capabilities, but this won't help if parents aren't meaningfully included in the identification process. Defining and identifying giftedness in a way that ensures the selection process looks beyond these stereotypes can lead you to find the students whose acting out may be the direct result of boredom or frustration.

POSITIVE AND NEGATIVE ASPECTS OF GIFTED CHILDREN'S CHARACTERISTICS

Learn rapidly and easily.
+ Memorize facts and concepts quickly.
– Get bored easily and disturb others or daydream.

Possess an advanced vocabulary.
+ Communicate ideas well.
– Show off and invoke peer resentment.

Retain a vast quantity of information.
+ Are ready and able to give elaborate answers.
– Monopolize discussions.

Have a long attention span.
+ Stick with a task or project.
– Resist class routine and dislike interruptions.

Are curious about anything and everything.
+ Ask questions and get excited about ideas.
– Go off on tangents; seldom follow through.

Are alert and observant.
+ Recognize problems and inconsistencies.
– Correct adults, often in a way that is or seems impolite.

Are individualistic; challenge ideas.
+ Are assertive and self-assured.
– Stubbornness in beliefs can alienate classmates.

Figure 2.1

Students with disabilities. Gifted people with disabilities have been called an "unseen minority." Researcher Nicholas Colangelo has observed that when teacher and parent groups are asked to imagine a "gifted child," they rarely picture a child with disabilities. Physical, emotional, or learning differences or disabilities may hinder students' capacity to demonstrate their giftedness in accepted, recognizable ways. Think about it: the traditional methods used to identify gifted kids would have excluded Helen Keller, among others.

"The most universal quality is diversity"
—MICHEL DE MONTAIGNE

Young children. Most schools begin the identification process at third grade. There are a number of reasons kids in prekindergarten, kindergarten, and first and second grade are overlooked. With children of this age, a test will not necessarily measure what they know with any accuracy. Typically, too, gifted education specialists are not trained in early-childhood education; early-childhood educators are rarely trained in gifted ed, either. And more often than not, states provide little if any funding for programs geared to primary-aged gifted kids. Young children are adaptable; many can and do learn in these early grades to adopt average learning expectations and stop trying to reach beyond them. By the time some of these children reach third grade, they've squelched their talents to the point that their high ability can go unnoticed and undetected.

In her study of teachers' perceptions of giftedness in young children, researcher Jane Rohrer asked for short descriptors that came to mind when teachers thought of particular gifted kids they knew in kindergarten through second grade. The most overriding word was "spark," which got further subdivided into three related terms: "unusual," "bright," and "shining." As teachers spoke more of these able youngsters, more terms emerged: "creative," "powerhouse," "knowing laugh," "extreme worries," "hated," and "totally engrossed." Given the chance to reveal any qualities at all, teachers generally spoke to characteristics of personality, not just intellect.[3] How refreshing. Parents, of course, would follow on this same path in their thinking and, when asked to define their highly gifted children in just one word (not an easy task!), arrived at terms like "interested," "sensitive," "intense," "transcendent," and "wise."[4]

Limited by a definition focused on intellect or a program geared to older students, school officials may discount these apt descriptors of the unique qualities of all gifted children, unless the descriptions are supported by stratospheric test scores. Yet all the qualities of giftedness are not necessarily quantifiable.

Girls. Many girls have learned to cover up or deny their abilities in order to be popular, fit in, or feel "normal." This is especially true in middle school. A gifted girl in this situation might not receive a teacher's recommendation because the teacher may not see evidence of the girl's abilities; after all, middle school teachers have a lot of students. A girl who is recommended might purposely underperform on an achievement or ability test, too.

Boys. Boys are more likely than girls to rebel and question authority. Also, boys are on a different developmental schedule than girls. In general, they mature more slowly, particularly in the verbal and reading areas. They may be labeled hyperactive, distractible, or disorderly. Add to this the fact that most teachers are women who tend to value conformity and obedience, and you can probably see why some gifted boys aren't viewed by their teachers as potential candidates for the gifted program.

> *"Expecting all children the same age to learn from the same materials is like expecting all children the same age to wear the same size clothing."*
> —MADELINE HUNTER

Borderline cases. No matter what methods we use to identify and select gifted students, and regardless of how hard we try to be fair and inclusive, there are always some kids who fall between the cracks. To avoid or minimize this occurrence, an effective identification process allows teachers to recognize a student who goes through the core curriculum faster than anyone else in the class, or engages teachers in conversations they don't have with most other students that age, or shows a spark, a talent, or raw potential that just stands out.

Pitfall 2: Creating a Definition That Suggests All Kids Are Gifted

There are many ways to be gifted, and many lenses to use in looking for exceptional ability and talent. Take care not to let your definition of giftedness become so all-encompassing that, on paper, practically any child could qualify for some element of it. In the recent past, several researchers and educators have contributed to our understanding of intelligence, talent, and ability. While this research has offered us new ways to look at and understand giftedness, it has also led at times to a blurring of the difference between *learning styles or strengths* on the one hand and *abilities that are far*

beyond the norm on the other. Applied thoughtfully, these educators' ideas can help you define the characteristics your mission and services call for. Applied in a less disciplined way, they can create confusion and break the momentum and commitment you are working so hard to build. Here are some views of intelligence that currently influence the ways schools define giftedness:

IQ (intelligence quotient). In the 1800s, Sir Francis Galton investigated the concept of a fixed intelligence. In the early 1900s, Alfred Binet developed an intelligence scale, which Lewis Terman later revised to create the earliest version of the *Stanford-Binet Intelligence Scales*—an assessment that has since been updated and renormed and is still widely used. IQ is a measure of intellectual potential as demonstrated in performance and verbal ability in areas such as reasoning, knowledge, and memory. Although there are no standardized IQ levels for intellectual giftedness, many schools set an IQ cutoff point for acceptance into gifted programs at around 130. Further delineation can be made: highly gifted kids typically have an IQ of 145–159; exceptionally gifted, 160–179; and profoundly gifted 180+. IQ tests can be administered in a group or individually. Although individually administered tests are usually more accurate, they are costly and time-consuming and so not widely used. While IQ can serve as a sound baseline for screening students for an academic gifted program, IQ tests might fail to catch gifted students who do not read well, whose life experiences are different from the mainstream, or who are having a bad day.

A qualitative view of intelligence. The work of Howard Gardner, a psychologist at the Harvard Graduate School of Education, has expanded the meaning of intelligence and changed the way teachers think about teaching all students. Gardner believes that the brain can't possibly have all of its many capabilities measured by a one-time IQ test. He maintains that the brain actually contains eight different intelligences: linguistic, logical-mathematical, visual-spatial, bodily-kinesthetic, musical, interpersonal, intrapersonal, and naturalist.

Gardner's theory applies to all children, and among gifted educators, his ideas are controversial. There are some educators who perceive his theory as a relatively simplistic delineation of the various talents that many people possess. Of special concern is how Gardner's theory is being applied. Some districts and schools have interpreted his work as an argument that "every child is gifted at something" and as a rationale to do away with gifted programming—assuming that if a school teaches to multiple intelligences, it is automatically meeting the needs of gifted students. Keeping Gardner in perspective, his ideas can be useful in defining giftedness insofar as they help us discover how different highly able children absorb and use information.

Sternberg's dimensions of intelligence. Yale psychology professor Robert Sternberg has defined three types of intelligence: contextual (the intelligence you use when you adapt to your environment, change your environment, or choose a different environment that better suits your needs); experiential (the one you use whenever you build on your experience to solve problems in new situations); and internal (the one you use to approach a problem, then evaluate the feedback to decide if you should change your approach). This information is helpful in regard to all children, because every child will be stronger in some dimensions than in others. It has particular relevance in identifying gifted children when we see outstanding strengths in one or more of the dimensions.

Creativity and giftedness. Though educators have long known that creativity is a sign of giftedness, it's an ability that is difficult to measure, and therefore challenging to identify. E. Paul Torrance and Mary Meeker developed a view of creativity that focuses on divergent thinking through four facets: fluency (having a wealth of ideas and ways to express them), flexibility (being able to see various or uncommon ways of approaching situations or solving problems), originality (inventiveness), and elaboration (carrying out, expanding, and analyzing ideas).

The emotional realm. The concept of emotional intelligence gained national attention when Harvard Ph.D. Daniel Goleman wrote a book about it in 1995. Goleman identified several qualities that add up to "a different way of being smart," including self-awareness, impulse control, persistence, zeal, self-motivation, empathy, and social deftness.

Michael Piechowski, a professor emeritus of education and psychology at Northland College in Ashland, Wisconsin, coined the term emotional giftedness. Piechowski studied and translated the work of Polish psychiatrist Kazimierz Dabrowski (1902–1980). When Dabrowski studied a group of gifted children and youth, he discovered that they displayed something he called "overexcitabilities": They perceived things more intensely and thought about them more deeply than their age peers. They lived life to the fullest and experienced emotional highs and lows, joys and sorrows to extreme degrees. They were extraordinarily, exquisitely sensitive to everything around them. Today, overexcitability (OE) is one of the signs of giftedness that teachers who know about it look for.

In gifted children, we don't just look for linguistic intelligence, or adaptability, or the tendency to think creatively: we look for a level and intensity in these areas that sets the child apart from most other children. Taking care not to lose sight of this distinction as you discuss your definition and consider the characteristics you will look for will help you stay focused as you make plans for screening and selecting students.

With all these aspects in mind, what will your definition include? A report from the ERIC Clearinghouse on Disabilities and Gifted Education suggests considering the following in developing or revising a definition of giftedness for your program:[5]

- A definition should be the basis for decisions about identification procedures and program provisions.

- The concept of giftedness need not be limited to high intellectual ability. It also comprises creativity, ability in specific academic areas, ability in visual or performing arts, social adeptness, and physical dexterity. (Yet your definition will depend on the programming you will provide. See Pitfall 6, page 41–42.)

- Definitions of giftedness are influenced by social, political, economic, and cultural factors.

- Giftedness is found among all groups, including girls, minorities, handicapped persons, persons with limited English-speaking proficiency, and migrant students.

In addition, researcher Mary Frasier and her colleagues recommend using this set of ten core attributes, each of which applies to children in any social or economic group, in identifying gifted students:[6]

- communication skills
- humor
- imagination/creativity
- inquiry
- insight
- interest
- memory
- motivation
- problem solving
- reasoning

Identification: The Beginning Steps . . . and Missteps

Your definition is written, and now you're ready to move forward and find the students who will take part in your gifted program. Where to begin? You know that gifted kids are *not* always easy to spot: they don't arrive at school with a "G" conveniently emblazoned on their foreheads. Identification is, by nature and of necessity, a messy operation, analogous in many ways to conducting a scavenger hunt. As you move from the task of defining giftedness to the process of identification, potential pitfalls remain.

Pitfall 3: Treating Identification as an Event and Not a Process

Most school districts begin in the spring of each year to seek gifted candidates for the next school year, and this is fine. We need timelines and consistency for the sake of all parties involved in this procedure. It's important, though, to think of identification as an ongoing process, even if the bulk of the work is done in the spring. Have procedures in place for the evaluation and placement of gifted children at any time of the year. If identification is slotted to occur only once a year, there will be children who could benefit from gifted programming who will be automatically left out. For example, what happens if a teacher nominates a child who in midyear is showing intellectual or creative sparks that heretofore had not been noticed? Does the child have to wait until the next "gifted-go-round" to be considered for placement?

> *"Site-based and central office administrators need to reevaluate their gifted education programs to determine whether the criteria for admission consider all students or whether their programs promote exclusionary practices. The result should be a gifted program of which all factions of the school community will be proud."*
> —JAIME A. CASTELLANO

Consider, too, children who transfer from another school. It's not uncommon for gifted children who move from one district or state to another to find that they either cannot enter a gifted program midyear or aren't considered gifted under the new school's measures. Because screening and selection procedures vary so much from one locale to another, gifted children—and their parents—are often left shaking their heads in confusion. Here's how this situation transpired for one tenth-grade girl:

> *My family is in the military, so we move a lot. I was first identified as gifted in Germany, but when we moved back to the States I wasn't gifted anymore. Then we moved once more, to Missouri, and I **was** gifted again. When we got transferred back to Germany, I figured I'd just pick up where I left off, but I wasn't gifted there anymore. Now I live in Texas, where I've been for the past five years, and I've been gifted every year since we moved here. It's a little hard for me to understand how these "gifted" decisions get made!*

A scenario like this can be extremely stressful for the kids involved, and it makes us, as educators, look ridiculous. Take our advice: for the sake of both compassion and common sense, if a child who moves to your district was in a gifted program in the previous (or current) school year, make it a standard placement provision to include the child automatically in your school's gifted program, as long as the program fits the student's type of capabilities. Explain to all concerned that the assignment is a starting point to see if it's a comfortable fit for the student. Reexamine the placement after a few weeks, with input from teachers, the student, and the parent or parents. Then you will be able to make a more accurate assessment of whether gifted placement is in the student's best interests. The student, too, will have a chance to see whether this new gifted program is appropriate for him or her.

Of course, you don't want to admit someone into a program so limited that the student simply couldn't succeed. This might occur for a child who was in a creative writing program at the old school while your school's options focus on mathematics. Sometimes, too, a parent decides to opt out so a child can get used to the new school before facing the demands that gifted ed classes might bring. In these cases, take the time to talk to the student about the reasons he or she was included in the old school's program but not in this one. In no way does it mean that the student "isn't gifted anymore"; rather, it means that the options your school has in place aren't the right fit for the student's unique learning needs. Do all that you can to help the student find an opportunity somewhere else in the school program to pursue talents and interests not addressed in the available gifted programming or services.

Pitfall 4: Once in a Program, Always in a Program (and Vice Versa)

We're not sure which is more fruitless and frustrating for all concerned: denying a child the opportunity to participate because the student wasn't identified at the beginning of the year (or three years ago), although the child now qualifies, or keeping a child in a gifted program because she or he has always been in it, even if it's obvious the placement is no longer suitable. The ultimate goal of gifted identification is to open up to a child an appropriate array of educational experiences that best serve the child's present needs. An annual checkup, sometime midyear, of (1) the identified gifted students, (2) nonidentified kids who were "near misses," and (3) students who have transferred from other schools will help you maintain the integrity of your entire gifted program.

What if it's found that a child's needs are no longer being met adequately within your program? Let the interests of the student be your guiding light in both making and communicating this decision. In all such cases, be sure the children and the parents know that moving out of the program doesn't mean students are "not gifted anymore." The point to emphasize is that, among all the options available, opportunities outside the gifted program will serve a given student most effectively.

Will students or parents like this? Probably not. Yet every placement option in a school usually has an uppermost limit to the number of kids who can participate in it, and if that number is always maxed out (as it usually is in gifted programs), then the standard of "once included, always included" cannot be justified.

Pitfall 5: Using Limited Methods of Identification

Our field has gone 'round and 'round about what instruments can best be used to identify giftedness in children. The only advice that seems to come up again and again is to use "multiple criteria" and "reliable and valid measures." Both are sound ideas, except for two things: few people agree on what these multiple measures should be, and instruments that are truly reliable and valid with gifted students are extremely rare.

Then, of course, there is the matter of cost. The most reliable assessments are those that are individually administered, but few school districts have the financial capacity to give an individual IQ or achievement test to each gifted program candidate. And, because they are subjective, individual teacher recommendations carry their own set of problems.

So most districts go with a combination of objective data (test scores) and subjective data (teacher and parent input, portfolios) in the hope of locating as many gifted students as possible. This is okay as a start; indeed, at least it is realistic. Just be sure to remember these realities of testing gifted children:

- Most standardized tests were *not* standardized with gifted children in mind, so the high scores that you see may actually be the lower limit of what a child is capable of doing. As an analogy, think about all the teachers in your district. Probably every teacher would score 100 percent on a test of writing the alphabet sequentially. Still, this test would not differentiate which among them can write compelling essays and which struggle with constructing a coherent paragraph. When the ceiling of a test is too low, gifted children often bump their metaphorical heads on it.

- The most refined methods still need to be examined for bias. A good way around this is to compile a list of all the children found eligible for gifted services by whatever identification measures you have implemented. Then give this list to *teachers who know the kids* and ask if there are any students *not* on it who should be looked at more closely. Then, if even one teacher suggests a child not previously considered, go back and analyze this student's records. (In our experience, few names come up, and those that do are often cited by more than one teacher.) If the data you collect are inconsistent or contradictory—great teacher recommendations and low test scores, for example—*this* would be the time to administer individual assessments.

No matter how comprehensive you attempt to be in your identification procedures, there will always be kids who slip through the cracks; this is inevitable when we are dealing with human nature and our collective foibles. Still, you can mitigate these problems to some extent by always being willing to take a second look at a child.

Pitfall 6: Failing to Match Identification Criteria to Programming

Hard as it may be to believe, this does occur. It happens when those involved in planning fail to tie identification or program considerations—or both—to the gifted education mission and purpose statements. What happens when there is not a good match between identification and programming?

First, if your identification plan is based on exceptional performance across the board, even though your program options are varied or pinpointed, many gifted kids won't qualify at all—and will miss out on educational opportunities that address their specific learning needs. Gifted kids will be the first to tell you they don't have exceptional ability in every area. We know a young man who was denied access to the advanced English class in sixth grade because he did not meet the gifted program criteria of falling in the ninety-fifth percentile or above on *both* the language *and* math portions of a standardized achievement test. As far as we know, the ability to unscramble binomials has little to do with analyzing whether the life of Jonas in *The Giver* is a utopian existence. How silly (and wrong) to deny access to particular program options when the identifying tools in no way correlate with the curriculum that will be offered.

Second, a mismatch between identification and programming may result in enrolling a child with strengths and interests in one area (say, physics) in an option that focuses on skills and talents in another (say, fine arts). Another student we know dropped out of his gifted program because it was based entirely on Future Problem Solving—a highly language-based group-process program of considerable worth, but not to Matt. Matt was skilled and interested in anything mathematical and, since the program offering didn't fill this bill, Matt saw no need to be part of the gifted program for grades 4–6.

Do yourself and gifted students a favor: plan the approach to identification *in concert* with your programming options, and mesh the two as best you can. Indeed, in the upper grade levels, that may mean totally different criteria are used for specific classroom options. So be it.

Get Off on the Right Foot

Yes, there are many ways to identify gifted kids, some better than others, and some more equitable than any single test score can ever be. Here are our recommendations for doing it in the most effective way possible.

Establish a gifted education committee to examine possible identification tools and procedures. Don't put yourself (or someone else) in the awkward and vulnerable position of being *the* person who makes the decisions about who "gets in" to the gifted program. No single individual needs this much responsibility, or deserves the grief and angry phone calls that may ensue. Instead, form a committee of interested teachers from across the grade levels, a couple of parents who have no vested interest in the placement decisions (perhaps they have kids who are not yet of school age, or who have already graduated from the school system), a school counselor who is sympathetic to the needs of gifted children, and a school administrator who is committed to the process.

The issues the committee will grapple with are:

- a review of the state policies regarding identification of giftedness as well as any policies currently in place in your district or school (including the definition of giftedness)
- the weight that will be given to assessments both formal (tests) and informal (teacher recommendations, parent nominations, student portfolios, anecdotal evidence)
- methods of identification that will be culturally fair and will include students with disabilities and learning differences
- procedures for dealing with children who have widely discrepant data, such as strong test scores one year and weak ones the next
- the alignment of identification procedures with programming options

There will probably be more issues that emerge, but these five will certainly be enough to occupy a year of meetings, assuming you gather to meet once a month or so (hint: always provide cookies!). The bottom-line goal is to put together a set of identification guidelines that is precise, yet flexible. In other words, the plan you develop must be (1) justifiable to community members who ask, "Why are some children selected while others are not?" and (2) flexible enough to accommodate gifted children who are atypical in the ways they show their high abilities.

Familiarize yourself with the assessment tools that can be used to quantify giftedness. While you may or may not use every tool, you'll want to be aware of what is available to you and which methods will best help you identify students who will fit the gifted program and meet the definition you have developed. (See the next section for discussion of the tools you might use.)

Commit to casting a wide net. Gifted educator Joan Franklin Smutny talks about casting a wide net, and it's an apt metaphor. If you are to find giftedness in students from all backgrounds and all corners of the school community, this means you'll want to commit to a broad-based approach. Such an approach involves a number of elements that, while important in all identification efforts, are imperative if you are to find giftedness in diverse populations. These elements will let you "walk the talk" by demonstrating that your school or district:

- sees giftedness as a multifaceted phenomenon that is expressed in a variety of ways and contexts
- emphasizes the collection of data from an array of observable sources
- realizes that giftedness may be expressed at home in ways that are not evident in school
- seeks evidence of high abilities throughout the school year, not just on a specific day or with a one-time test

"If educators are really interested in identifying gifted and talented students in minority groups, they will direct their searches to those characteristics that are valued by the particular minority groups."
L. PAUL TORRANCE

Using a Range of Identification Methods

To make order out of the potential chaos identification can entail, you'll want to use a variety of screening and selection tools. The right type and quality of these tools will offer you the best chance of reaching out to all or most of the gifted children who can benefit from the your school's programming. Some of the most important tools in your toolbox will include the following:

- standardized intelligence and achievement tests
- checklists and nomination forms along with anecdotal information from teachers, parents, and students
- student portfolios or work samples
- individually administered ability tests and instruments that measure creativity and problem-solving ability
- interviews with students

Standardized Group and Individual Intelligence and Achievement Tests[7]

Though standardized test instruments not originally intended to identify gifted students are not an ideal selection tool, most schools use such tests as one way to screen students for gifted programming. Some of these tests are better for your purposes than others.

In most cases, your test options will be limited to the instruments that are given en masse to all children in your school district—for example, the *Iowa Tests of Basic Skills,* the *Stanford Achievement Tests (SAT),* the *Otis-Lennon School Ability Tests,* or the *Cognitive Abilities Test (CogAT).* If you know this is the case, it is probably a waste of your time to explore other instruments that you won't be able to use. (Lobbying district administrators for the opportunity to use more effective, tailored testing instruments may not be a waste of time, though. See pages 116–120 for more on this type of advocacy.)

If you do have a chance to look for other test instruments, it might be a good idea to invite in a local or national expert who specializes in either assessment in general or gifted-child assessment in particular. This person can go over the pluses and minuses of the assessment tools you are considering. Beyond standardized, group-administered ability and achievement tests there are an array of other assessment items that can be used to complement the initial measures, to serve as secondary sources if data are discrepant or inconclusive, or to assist in identification of nonmainstream gifted kids.

Teacher Recommendations

A more difficult task will be arriving at decisions regarding the teacher nomination and recommendation forms you wish to use. There are some such forms available for purchase, yet most are devised at the local level. Depending on your definition and programming plans, you may wish to use a form similar to the "Teacher's Gifted Student Recommendation Form" provided on page 52. The form we have provided is for a general academic gifted program. You can also use it as a model to adapt or develop a form tailored to your specific definition and program. To use the data from the completed form, compute the sum of the numbers in the first eight boxes and write that number in the ninth box in the bottom left-hand corner. Then compare that number to the range or cutoff score your district or school has set, based on the size and scope of your gifted program.

A preferred way to gather relevant information from teachers is to consider the characteristics that your gifted education committee thinks will be necessary for children to succeed in the gifted program, perhaps similar to those on the "Teacher's Gifted Student Nomination Form" (pages 53–54). Then collate these characteristics and gather your teachers together for a one-hour meeting. Describe each trait with a possible example ("This is the child who asks questions that other children don't get, but you do") and ask teachers to write the names of up to three students from their class who come to mind. It's best to seat teachers together by grade level or team for this activity, and have their class lists readily available.

Another way to help teachers identify giftedness (and to make some good allies, to boot) is to ask if you can do a lesson in a teacher's classroom while the regular teacher sits back and observes the students. If your lesson is big on higher-level or abstract thinking, the observing teacher can take notes, using the "Teacher's Gifted Student Observation Form" on page 55 or something like it, and collect some evidence of giftedness *in situ*. Also, this gives teachers an opportunity they too seldom have: to observe how their students respond to the curriculum being offered to them.

Parent Checklists

An efficient way to get parent input is in the form of a checklist of characteristics with space for comments. We've provided one form you might use ("Parent Checklist of Child's Traits," pages 56–57). Again, you may prefer to adapt the form or create something that uniquely fits the definition you've established and the services you plan to offer.

Make a general announcement inviting parents to complete the checklist if they'd like a child to be considered for gifted programming. As part of this announcement, state the date when placements will be finalized and when parents of students who qualify for services will be notified. Make it clear that parents of nonqualifying students will not be notified; those families not contacted by the scheduled date will know that their children were not selected for the program. Explain that parents will have a specific period of time, typically two weeks past this date, to appeal the committee's decision. (For more on this appeals process, see page 47–48.)

Don't assume that a parent who does not respond by returning a completed checklist isn't interested in having his or her child take part in the gifted program. If, through test results and/or teacher recommendations, children whose parents haven't responded appear to be strong candidates, make additional efforts to get input from the parents. You or someone on the committee might call individual parents and ask if there is any interest. If there is, you might go over the checklist with the parent by phone, arrange a time for the parent to come in for an interview, or schedule a time when several parents can come in and sit down with school staff or volunteers to complete the form.

Student Nominations

Anyone should feel free to nominate a student for gifted programming, so it's appropriate to invite students to nominate themselves for consideration. This invitation can be made in the daily announcements, in class, or in the student newspaper. You might invite students to write a statement about why they should be considered or to schedule an interview with the gifted coordinator, where the student can explain (rather than write) why she or he should be considered to participate in gifted programming. The student can address any or all of the following:

- specific strengths that make the student a good gifted program candidate (including grades, honors, interests, talents, or experiences)
- a rationale explaining the ways in which the student's current program in school is not a good fit
- a specific teacher who might speak on the student's behalf regarding this request
- specific learning and performance goals, should gifted program admission be granted

It will be pretty rare that a student will go this extra mile to self-nominate, yet when it happens, it may also be interpreted as a sign of keen interest and (perhaps) high ability. Should a student follow through, treat this nomination as an important part of the identification process for the identification committee to consider.

Other Methods for Identifying Gifted Students

There are a number of other approaches you can take to identify children who qualify for your gifted program.

Portfolio assessment. Student portfolios allow the selection committee to look at a body of work (what Mary Frasier calls a "package of evidence"[8]) demonstrating high ability or talent. Samples of students' products—such as stories, essays, poems, mathematical problems, science experiments, reports, inventions, drawings, or photographs of projects—can be compiled by teachers, often with input from parents and students. (You'll especially want to involve parents when identifying younger students, who might have more samples at home than in school.)

Anecdotal evidence. Ask teachers to provide anecdotal examples of a child's abilities, too—for example, unusual or astute questions or comments kids make in class, a noticeable depth of interest or understanding, extraordinary memory, or inventiveness. As your program continues year by year, it will be helpful if teachers can keep a notebook or journal where they make quick entries about these things; a pattern of evidence may emerge for some students. Ask parents, too, about their children's passions and interests now and in the past. Look for evidence of gifted characteristics that aren't necessarily readily identified through testing, such as curiosity, intuitiveness, long attention span, abstract thinking ability, a strong sense of justice, or inquisitiveness beyond what most children of the same age exhibit.

"Curiosity is one of the permanent and certain characteristics of a vigorous mind."
—SAMUEL JOHNSON

Interviews. Interviews with individual students are time-consuming, so this is a tool you will probably use quite selectively. Interviews can, however, be very helpful in identifying students who might otherwise be missed. Interviews can be especially useful for:

- resolving concerns administrators, parents, or teachers may have about a child's participation in a gifted program

- making decisions about kids whose testing has them teetering or who show certain gifted characteristics but not others

- learning more about a student who is not fluent in English (with the assistance of a translator/interpreter)

- offering another opportunity for consideration of students who have high test anxiety

- giving kids a chance to argue for their own admission into a program

Individually administered ability tests. In assessing intelligence, individual intelligence tests are generally more accurate than group tests—particularly as the mainstream culture defines intelligence. Typically administered by a trained psychologist, these tests compute scores based on age rather than grade. The ceiling of difficulty is likely to be higher than on a group test. They often include several *scales* (testing areas to be measured) that provide broad scores as well as more detailed subtests, which can give clues to a child's strengths and weaknesses in different areas. Individual testing is costly and time-intensive, so

school personnel are not always able or willing to administer one-on-one ability tests. In this case, you may want to ask a school psychologist who works in the district for recommendations of outside testing agencies or psychologists. Sometimes these can be found at universities in the psychology or education departments. Also, state gifted education associations can be a source for such services.

Creativity tests. Creativity tests are usually fun for kids and show promise as a tool for identifying students who think creatively or approach problem solving in original ways. Many of the published tests are based on or influenced by E. Paul Torrance's research on fluency, flexibility, originality, and elaboration.

Nominations from the community. It's also appropriate to invite members of the community at large to nominate individual students for gifted programming. Youth leaders, coaches, grandparents, and other adults who know and work with kids often see exceptional talents, abilities, performance, interests, and leadership qualities outside the school setting. An effective way to seek this kind of input is by putting an announcement in the local newspaper, along with dates and locations where people can obtain a form for nominating a student (such as the school office or the district Web site). In your announcement, explain that the nominator will not be personally informed if the child is selected, but that he or she can call the individual school after a stated date to find out. You can use the "Gifted Student Nomination Form" on page 58, create your own form, or simply ask people to write a brief nomination with the following information:

- the name and contact information of the person making the nomination

- the name of the student being nominated

- reasons the student should be considered for gifted programming

The Next Steps

Once all the data have been gathered, the selection committee should meet to consider which children will be the best fit for the gifted program and make plans for follow-through.

Make Selections

How straightforward or complicated this process is depends in part on the parameters set by the state, the district, and the program itself. Some issues you will likely grapple with include:

- Does state or district policy dictate the weight that is to be given to particular measures, such as IQ versus achievement or a specific instrument versus more informal supporting evidence (for example, teacher recommendations or student products)? Or, will it be up to the committee to make these determinations?

- If these choices lie with the committee, will you go strictly by the numbers (test score and grade cutoffs)? Will other information, gathered more informally (for example, teacher, parent, or self-nominations), carry extra weight if test scores are relatively low?

- Will you accept a certain number of children each year (for example, fifteen kids per grade level), or will you let the identification data determine how many children qualify from one year to the next? (Although the latter may appear to make more sense to the interests of students, it can mean that the number of children chosen could vary considerably from year to year, leading to a program with too many kids one year and not enough the next.)

- How will issues like amount of staff time, materials budget, and teacher training opportunities affect the number of children the program can serve?

- When using multiple criteria to determine eligibility, how can you efficiently evaluate and compare student data?

You need to raise these questions with your selection committee, and decide which direction makes the most sense for your particular school or district. In some programs, any child with an exceptionally high IQ—say, 140 and above—is included automatically, despite results on achievement tests. In others, you need a "package" of high IQ and achievement (often 130 IQ and ninety-fifth percentile on a math and/or reading composite score). And in some cases, every child is looked at individually, all nominations and recommendation forms are read, and the committee makes a decision based on the holistic information available for each child.

Though rare, this comprehensive approach is the ideal. More realistic is a process that relies on at least three or four different types of measures which match the program you're developing. Such an approach holds a sound chance for openness and fairness. You might, for example, consider students based on:

- a nonverbal ability test (which attempts to be nondiscriminatory in screening underrepresented students)

- an achievement-based instrument (such as the *SAT* or an *Iowa Test*)

- a recommendation from a teacher or teachers

- a product, such as a student's portfolio, work samples, project, or essay

When looking at multiple criteria, a visual tool can help make selections efficient and fair. An overview ranking form or organizational sheet such as the one illustrated in Figure 2.2 can serve this function, allowing you to view students' qualities and compare their strengths.

Even if you cannot follow this comprehensive process for *every* child, it is a fine way to examine the records of children who have discrepant data—low test scores and high teacher nominations, for example, or vice versa. In fact, in these instances, even more data may

Student's Name	NNAT	RC	MA	TR	Score	Other Comments

Figure 2.2 This sample from an overview form is intended to help in the selection of students who are academically talented. The form allows for comparison of students' scores on the *Naglieri Nonverbal Ability Test* (NNAT), the reading comprehension (RC) and math application (MA) portions of the *Stanford Achievement Tests,* and teacher recommendations (TR). It is adapted from a form used by the Park City School District, Park City, Utah, and is used with permission.

need to be compiled—classroom observations of the student, perhaps, or a one-on-one interview with the child.

The reality is that if your state or district guidelines prohibit you from choosing one child over another based on a variety of diverse information, and you *must* stick to test scores, the job of the selection committee is basically one of number crunching. In this situation, do what you can to make the fairest determinations possible, and then take steps to advocate for broader, more inclusive identification and selection (and programming) to meet the academic needs of a more diverse group of gifted students. (Program planning is addressed in Survival Strategy 3; pages 116–120 discuss advocacy.)

Review Close Cases with the Committee

It's not necessary to review every case, every child. But when you have discrepant data about particular children, the committee should make one of three decisions:

1. Admit the child, or

2. Do not admit the child (with justification for this decision), or

3. Gather more evidence (perhaps an individual IQ test, an interview, or additional information from teachers or parents).

If you don't discuss the close cases now, at the committee level, you may regret it later. Parents may contact you expecting a thorough explanation of why their child was not included in the gifted program. With notes from your discussion in hand, you will be able to say, "Our gifted education committee considered many factors as to whether your child's educational needs would be best met in the gifted program. Let me explain how we arrived at the decision we did." Doing your homework thoroughly can really minimize unhappiness.

Share the Results

The most well-thought-out and inclusive selection process won't be complete without follow-through. Get back to the people who were involved with the results of your identification process. When we seek out input for gifted identification and then keep the results from the teachers, parents, administrators, students, and others who took the time to complete your forms, participate in interviews, gather supporting materials, and nominate students—or at least neglect to report those results—we show a disrespect for the process and the people involved. The conse-

quence of this oversight can be charges of elitism and loss of buy-in. It not only can leave people feeling sour about the gifted program but also can result in losing the dedication and vision of many folks who could contribute greatly to your program.

As soon as you have compiled a list of students who will be included in the gifted program, show the list to the superintendent, the principal, or other key administrators. This allows you to respond to their questions about specific selections and ensures support if parents or teachers challenge any decisions the committee has made. Occasionally an administrator will question a selection or request that a child not on the list be included. In this case, share your student rankings to make clear why the student does or does not fit the program. Perhaps the superintendent or principal will insist on placing a child in the program anyway (politics do happen—something we've come to accept, even if we don't fully understand it), but it's equally likely that seeing the data will help the person see this differently or allow you to take a second look at a student the committee had considered borderline.

With administration sign-off, your next step is to inform the individual parents of children who qualify for gifted services and share the list of students with the teachers. You can create a form letter similar to that in Figure 2.3 (page 48) to send to parents.

We do not recommend that you send a letter to parents of children who were not selected, as long as you made it clear when you invited nominations and recommendations that notification would be made to parents of selected students only. It is also important, however, to invite any parent who wishes to challenge the committee's decision to meet privately with the gifted coordinator or another official the district designates. Allow ten or fifteen minutes for this meeting. Show the parent the selection criteria and how his or her student ranked. (Never show the scores of other students—this violates privacy. Just show the ranking.) Most parents who see that the process has been fair and that there isn't the right fit between child and program will accept the committee's decision. Typically this is not a burdensome task for the coordinator.

If a teacher is astute and committed enough to nominate a child, get back to this teacher as soon as a decision has been made about the child's placement. This shows that you are taking the teacher's recommendation and insight seriously, even if the child nominated has not been selected for the gifted program. If there are particular students you weren't able to admit despite avid teacher campaigning, write a personal note to the teachers involved, saying something like, "Everyone appreciated the effort you made to nominate Mariah. Can we get together soon to talk about the reasons she wasn't included in the program?" Most teachers, upon hearing a sound rationale, will accept the decision of the gifted education committee.

Your goal is for parents (or others who question the outcome) to understand the rationale behind your decision. And, if they still disagree, let them know the procedure for appealing this decision. (Usually, it is a meeting with the superintendent or another central office administrator, so be prepared to give this individual all the information needed to make an informed decision.) If you are invited to participate in an appeal hearing, we advise you to go. Why? More than anyone else, you can try to ensure that the final decision is made on the basis of a child's needs rather than the political expediency of just saying yes to get an assertive parent or an influential teacher off the superintendent's back.

Sometimes a parent, an administrator, a teacher, or someone else has valuable evidence to show that the student should be in the program. For this situation, have in place a back-up test, individually administered ability assessment, or some other reliable source of information that will let you take a second look at this child. In our experience, there may be cause to include a few children after this step who otherwise would have been overlooked. But the evidence that is gathered must support the fact that the student qualifies and meets the criteria established. This is an ideal time to use a school psychologist who is qualified to administer an individual ability test.

Once you are as confident as you can be that all the placements are final, let the students who will

---

APRIL 6, 2003

Dear Parent/Caregiver:

As you may be aware, the Rendon School District has a program designed for students identified as intellectually gifted in grades 3–6. A selection committee composed of teachers, administrators, and community members has met to consider candidates for the gifted education program for the coming school year. Based on a variety of data compiled from test scores, student products, and recommendations from teachers and parents, your child, _MIKAEL ROSOLOV_, has been selected to participate in the gifted program at _WINDFALL ELEMENTARY SCHOOL_.

You are invited to attend a meeting at _7:00 P.M._ on _TUESDAY, APRIL 30_, at the Windfall Elementary School cafeteria so that we can discuss the program with you. The gifted coordinator and resource teacher will present an overview of the gifted program and answer any questions you may have about the program and your child's participation. We will also distribute permission forms for you to sign if you wish to have your child participate in this opportunity.

A child's participation in the gifted program requires written permission from a legal guardian; the school must have this permission on record on or before _MAY 15, 2003_. If you are unable to attend the scheduled meeting, please contact my office to arrange a time to meet and go over important information about the program.

Sincerely,

Margo Gogetter

Margo Gogetter, Gifted Coordinator

(513) 555-8383

gogetter@rendondistrict3gt.org

Figure 2.3

take part in the program know about their selection. Make sure you have signed parent permission forms for every child before making this announcement. You might do so through a letter or a group meeting, possibly even an evening meeting for both kids and parents. Be prepared to answer kids' questions about what the program will involve and how it will work. Last but not least, those few students who risked nominating themselves but did not fit the program criteria should be told in person about the decision. A sensitive discussion focused on what will best meet the child's unique learning needs is in everyone's best interests. And, as with adults, stay receptive to the possibility that there may be a situation where a student might legitimately challenge not being placed in the gifted program.

Plan an Exit Policy

Despite your best efforts, there will be some gifted students whose needs cannot be met by the school's gifted program. This is not an indictment of your guidelines or of the children's abilities. Rather, it's a reminder that, in the world of people, there are no "perfect fits." For this reason, it is essential to take as much care in designing an exit policy—formal criteria and procedures for removing a child from the gifted program—as in developing the program entrance requirements.

There are some reasons *not* to recommend that a child exit a program. You may find yourself dealing with requests from teachers or parents like the following:

- There may be a teacher or two who wants the child out because of poor performance or bad attitudes in class. Yes, poor grades and bad attitudes are problems, but they are seldom solved by removing a student from a setting where the child is succeeding.

- There may be a student who presents behavior problems within the gifted class. Again, it is unpleasant for a teacher to be at the receiving end of student negativity, but there's almost always a reason behind it. Get to the root of these issues and plan procedures for dealing with them, or the gifted program will be seen as a place that is only open to do-gooders.

- Sometimes, too, a parent may not be happy when a child's grades in the regular classroom take a dip when the child begins taking part in the gifted program. This does not happen frequently, but when it does, it is often because the student has not turned in required assignments or homework that was missed while she or he was in the out-of-class gifted program. This is not necessarily

a sign that the student has a too-full plate; it could simply be a cue that a lesson or two in "Organization 101" is called for. Or, if a student is involved in a high-power calculus class with other gifted students, grades may drop (often temporarily) because the level of academic competition has become more intense. If the class is challenging in a way that meets the student's needs, this drop in grades may not be as big a problem as the parent (or student, or teacher) believes it to be. Though the parent has the final say about placement, it would be worth your while to explain to the parent that a drop in grades is not unusual and is often temporary. Encourage the parent to wait it out.

How can you determine that a student may be misplaced or simply may not be a good fit for the program? Indicators might typically include situations where a student:

- is anxious in class

- is absent often

- routinely does not complete assignments that are attainable

- voices dissatisfaction with the whole "gifted thing" ("This program is stupid!")

- simply cannot keep up because the material is too difficult

If there are various combinations of factors like these, it's time to have a meeting among the involved parties—the program coordinator, the gifted teacher, the classroom teacher, the child, the parent, and perhaps the school counselor.

At this meeting, it's imperative to make it clear at the outset that you are all in search of the same thing: the best fit between a child's needs and the school placements. If the situation within the gifted program can be rectified or improved, great. If not, then other options will need to be considered.

You may want to use the "Gifted Education Program Action Plan" form (pages 59–61) to compile information from the various parties about the specifics of the situation. Then, use this completed form (all parties should have copies available to them) as a basis for discussion about possible solutions.

We would advise allowing at least three weeks before scheduling a second conference—more if you agreed to a longer time frame. When the second conference takes place, the meeting can be a bit more informal, with the goal of resolving whether the child's placement in the gifted program should be continued. If you conclude that it should, be sure to set parameters for the child's ongoing participation and agree on goals or standards he or she will be expected to meet. If you decide the student should step out of the program, let the decision stand for a set length of time. Generally, we tell the student that readmission into the gifted program will not occur before the next school year, at the earliest. However, flexibility should always be the rule here.

A situation of this nature is a rare occurrence. When it happens, it's important to take the time to explore all the possibilities for an individual student's success. If you don't do this, what message does this send to parents and kids?

One final recommendation: If you want to get even more serious about making your program successful, for this student or others, you may wish to wait several weeks after a student exits the program and then meet with the child and parent. Ask the student the following questions:

- Are you satisfied with your decision to exit the gifted program?
- Do you feel your views were respected?
- Can you think of any other ways we could have resolved this issue?
- How are things going for you in school now that you are not involved in the gifted program?
- Can you offer suggestions for making our gifted program better?

Ask similar questions of the parent:

- Are you satisfied with the decision to have your child exit the gifted program?
- Do you feel your views were respected?
- Can you think of any other ways we could have resolved this issue?
- How are things going for your child in school now that she or he is not involved in the gifted program?
- Can you offer suggestions for making our gifted program better?

Keep in mind that your program can only be improved by examining the reasons why it works better for some students than others.

Keep Your Perspective

If you are involved in identification decisions for your school district, you may lose sleep over the child who almost "made it," but just fell short. You will question each decision to place a gifted child with learning disabilities in a highly academic program, hoping that his teachers will see beyond the problems and locate the hidden talents. You will ask yourself how to engage the bright young first grader who is doing fifth-grade math, but since she just moved her from Croatia, can't tell you in English how she arrived at her answers. And you will have the perfect answer to the parent who called you at home to complain that her child was disliked by her classroom teacher and, therefore, was not given due consideration for the gifted and talented program—except, you will have that perfect answer only after the angry parent hangs up.

Just remember to do the best you can with the information available to you, both quantitative and qualitative. And get used to a fact that we all live with each day: We sometimes make mistakes. We're sometimes short-sighted. Because we're human, this is unavoidable.

Notes

1. This section includes some material adapted from *When Gifted Kids Don't Have All the Answers: How to Meet Their Social and Emotional Needs* by Jim Delisle and Judy Galbraith (Minneapolis: Free Spirit Publishing, 2002), pages 14–21 and 68–69. Used with permission.

2. Donna Y. Ford and J. John Harris III, *Multicultural Gifted Education* (New York: Teachers College Press, 1999) and Mary M. Frasier, et al., "Educators' Perceptions of Barriers to the Identification of Gifted Children from Economically Disadvantaged and Limited English Proficient Backgrounds" (Storrs, CT: The National Research Center on the Gifted and Talented, University of Connecticut, 1995) (RBRD 95216).

3. Jane Rohrer, "Primary Teacher Conceptions of Giftedness: Image, Evidence, and Nonevidence," *Journal for the Education of the Gifted* 18:3, 269–283 (1995).

4. Jim Delisle, "Profoundly Gifted Guilt," *Gifted Education Communicator* 32:1, 17–19 (2001).

5. Elizabeth McClellan, "Defining Giftedness" (Reston, VA: ERIC Clearinghouse on Disabilities and Gifted Education, 1985) (ERIC Digest ED 262519).

6. Mary M. Frasier, et al., "Core Attributes of Giftedness: A Foundation for Recognizing the Gifted Potential of Economically Disadvantaged Students" (Storrs, CT: NRC/GT, 1995) (RBRD 95210).

7. For information on finding assessment tools and on some of the instruments available, see page 51.

8. Mary M. Frasier, "Issues, Problems, and Programs in Nurturing the Disadvantaged and Culturally Different Talented." In K.A. Heller, F.J. Monks, and A.H. Passow, *International Handbook of Research and Development of Giftedness and Talent* (New York: Pergamon, 1993), pages 685–692.

Resources

The following resources apply specifically to topics addressed in this strategy's chapter. For a complete list of gifted education resources, see pages 146–154.

"How Can My School Better Serve Diverse Gifted Students? Frequently Asked Questions" by Donna Y. Ford (Washington, DC: NAGC, 1997). Hints on identification.

"National Association for Gifted Children Pre-K–Grade 12 Gifted Program Standards" (*www.nacg.org*). This Web page features a document that cites five guiding principles along with both minimum and exemplary standards for appropriately assessing gifted learners.

Total Talent Portfolio: A Systematic Plan to Identify and Nurture Gifts and Talents by Jeanne H. Purcell and Joseph S. Renzulli (Mansfield Center, CT: Creative Learning Press, 1998). This book offers a step-by-step approach to gathering and acting on identification information, including often overlooked traits of giftedness. Also discusses which enrichment and acceleration options will best develop each young person's talents.

National Research Center on the Gifted and Talented (NRC/GT)
University of Connecticut
2131 Hillside Road, Unit 3007
Storrs, CT 06269
(860) 486-4676
www.gifted.uconn.edu/nrcgt.html

NRC/GT is a nationwide cooperative of researchers, practitioners, policymakers, and other persons and groups that have a stake in developing the performance and potentials of young people from preschool through postsecondary levels. The following reports can be accessed via the Web site:

"The Coincidence of Attention Deficit Hyperactivity Disorder and Creativity" by B. Cramond; research monograph 9508.

"Educators' Perceptions of Barriers to the Identification of Gifted Children from Economically Disadvantaged and Limited English Proficient Backgrounds" by M.M. Frasier, et al.; research monograph 95216.

"Instruments Used in the Identification of Gifted and Talented Students" by C.M. Callahan, et al.; research monograph 95130.

"Project START: Using a Multiple Intelligences Model in Identifying and Promoting Talent in High-Risk Students" by C.M. Callahan, et al.; research monograph 95136.

"The Recruitment and Retention of Black Students in Gifted Education Programs: Implications and Recommendations" by D.Y. Ford; research monograph 9406.

"Square Pegs in Round Holes—These Kids Don't Fit: High-Ability Students with Behavioral Problems" by B.D. Reid and M.D. McGuire; research monograph 9512.

"Talents in Two Places: Case Studies of High-Ability Students with Learning Disabilities Who Have Achieved" by S.M. Reis, T.W. Neu, and J.M. McGuire; research monograph 95114.

Tests for Identifying Giftedness

There are dozens of assessment instruments that are or can be used in the screening and selection of gifted students. Some of the most commonly used tests include (but are not limited to) the following:

GROUP AND INDIVIDUALLY ADMINISTERED IQ TESTS

Cognitive Abilities Test (CogAT), Riverside Publishing (1-800-323-9540; *www.riverpub.com*)

Slosson Intelligence Tests, Slosson Educational Publications (1-888-756-7766; *www.slosson.com*)

Stanford-Binet Intelligence Scales, Riverside Publishing (1-800-323-9540; *www.riverpub.com*)

GROUP AND INDIVIDUALLY ADMINISTERED ACHIEVEMENT TESTS

California Achievement Tests (CAT), CTB McGraw-Hill (1-800-538-9547; *www.ctb.com*)

Iowa Tests of Basic Skills (ITBS), Riverside Publishing (1-800-323-9540; *www.riverpub.com*)

Metropolitan Achievement Tests (MAT), Pearson (1-800-328-5999; *www.pearsonassess.com*)

Stanford Achievement Tests (SAT), Pearson (1-800-328-5999; *www.pearsonassess.com*)

INSTRUMENTS DESIGNED TO BE ECONOMICALLY AND/OR CULTURALLY BIAS-FREE

Culture Fair Test, Institute for Personality and Ability Testing (1-800-225-4728; *www.ipat.com*)

Discovering Intellectual Strengths and Capabilities while Observing Varied Ethnic Responses (DISCOVER), University of Arizona (1-520-622-8106; *www.discover.arizona.edu*)

Kingore Observation Inventory (KOI), Professional Associates (1-866-335-1460; *www.professionalassociatespublishing.com*)

Naglieri Nonverbal Ability Tests, Pearson, (1-800-328-5999; *www.pearsonassess.com*)

Otis-Lennon School Ability Tests, Pearson (1-800-328-5999; *www.pearsonassess.com*)

Peabody Picture Vocabulary Test, Pearson AGS Globe (1-800-328-5999; *www.pearsonschool.com*)

Raven's Progressive Matrices, Pearson (1-800-328-5999; *www.pearsonassess.com*)

INSTRUMENTS THAT ASSESS CREATIVITY

Group Inventory for Finding Talent (GIFT), Educational Assessment Service (1-800-795-7466; *www.sylviarimm.com/creativity.htm*)

Khatena-Torrance Creative Perception Inventory (KTCPI), Scholastic Testing Service (1-800-642-6787; *www.ststesting.com*)

Screening Assessment for Gifted Elementary Students (SAGES), Riverside Publishing (1-800-323-9540; *www.riverpub.com*)

Torrance Tests of Creative Thinking, Scholastic Testing Service (1-800-642-6787; *www.ststesting.com*)

FOR MORE INFORMATION ABOUT TESTS AND TESTING

Talented Children and Adults (Piirto) includes an appendix with a detailed comparison of standardized tests. Two other good sources of information on assessment include *Being Gifted in School* (Coleman and Cross) and *Reaching New Horizons* (Castellano and Díaz). See pages 146 and 148 for facts of publication.

Buros Institute of Mental Measurements
University of Nebraska-Lincoln
21 Teachers College Hall
Lincoln, NE 68588-0348
(402) 472-6203
www.unl.edu/buros

If you don't have access to an expert who can evaluate the tests you're considering, this site may be a helpful alternative. Publisher of the *Mental Measurements Yearbook* and *Tests in Print* series, the organization offers comprehensive information about more than 10,000 published tests, including links to descriptions and reviews of standardized intelligence and achievement tests.

★ Teacher's Gifted Student Recommendation Form ★

Student _____

Teacher _____ Grade _____

School _____ Date _____

Characteristics

For each of the seven characteristics described beneath this box, select the one choice that **best** describes the student's performance within the group of students you teach. Mark the number for your choice in the space provided.

1. below average (bottom third of students)

2. average (similar to most students)

3. above average (top 20% of students)

4. outstanding (top 5% of students)

5. exceptional (top 1% of students)

Learns new material quickly .... ☐

Grasps the essentials .... ☐

Completes assignments efficiently .... ☐

Creates his/her own learning activities and/or becomes absorbed and involved in topics and problems .... ☐

Asks penetrating questions .... ☐

Makes interesting connections .... ☐

Shows unusual independent thought .... ☐

Overall

Considering everything you know about this student's academic strengths (intelligence, ability, motivation, school performance), and comparing the student to other students in your class, how strongly do you recommend the student as a candidate for our school's program for academically gifted students? Mark the number for your choice in the space provided.

1. I do not consider this student academically talented and **do not recommend the student** as a candidate for the gifted program.

2. I am uncertain about the student's level of academic talent and **have doubts about recommending the student** as a candidate for the gifted program.

3. I consider this student academically talented. The **student might be a candidate** for the gifted program.

4. I consider this student one of only one or two extremely academically talented students and **strongly recommend the student** as a candidate for the gifted program.

5. I consider this student the most academically talented student I teach and **urgently recommend the student** as a candidate for the gifted program.

Write the number of your recommendation ...... ☐

Do not write in this space. ☐

If you would like to make additional comments, please **circle the arrow to the right** and write your comments on the back of this paper.

➡

★ Teacher's Gifted Student Nomination Form ★

Teacher _____ **Grade** _____

School _____ **Date** _____

Please use this form to identify students who are strong candidates for the school/district gifted education program. For each description, write the first and last names of **up to 3 students** who **first** come to mind. The same student may be listed multiple times. You need not fill in every space if no students, or fewer than three, come to mind for a particular quality. Thank you for your help.

1. Learns rapidly and easily

_____   _____   _____

2. Offers original, imaginative responses

_____   _____   _____

3. Is widely informed on many topics

_____   _____   _____

4. Is self-directed and has a long attention span

_____   _____   _____

5. Is inquisitive; skeptical

_____   _____   _____

6. Has an extensive vocabulary

_____   _____   _____

7. Constantly asks questions

_____   _____   _____

8. Seeks out challenging work

_____   _____   _____

MORE ➔

9. Associates often with other smart children

_____   _____   _____

10. Has an advanced sense of humor

_____   _____   _____

11. Is easily bored

_____   _____   _____

12. Has intense emotions

_____   _____   _____

13. Understands concepts readily

_____   _____   _____

14. Challenges the teacher's knowledge base

_____   _____   _____

15. Does not accept things at "face value"

_____   _____   _____

16. Dislikes arbitrary decisions

_____   _____   _____

17. Is seen by other children as "smart"

_____   _____   _____

18. Produces original ideas and projects

_____   _____   _____

19. Uses logic to solve problems

_____   _____   _____

20. Is intrigued by abstract ideas

_____   _____   _____

★ Teacher's Gifted Student Observation Form ★

Teacher _____ Grade _____ Room _____

School _____ Date _____

Please list **up to three students** who, in your observation, **best** fit the following categories in today's lesson. The same student may be listed multiple times.

1. The students most interested or excited by today's activity:

_____   _____   _____

2. The students who presented the most unusual ideas or responses:

_____   _____   _____

3. The students who provided the greatest number of relevant responses:

_____   _____   _____

4. The students who assumed a leadership role in the activity:

_____   _____   _____

5. The students who appeared to have the best grasp of abstract concepts:

_____   _____   _____

6. The students who needed things done perfectly:

_____   _____   _____

Any additional observations or comments:

_____

_____

_____

_____

_____

★ Parent Checklist of Child's Traits ★

Name of Student _____ Grade _____

Classroom or Homeroom Teacher _____

Please answer the following question by checking yes or no:

I believe my child is or may be gifted and would like to have him/her
considered for participation in the school/district gifted education program. _____ **Yes** _____ **No**

If you checked yes, please check the **10 items** that **best describe** your child's traits or that **most usually or often**
apply to your child:

_____ **1.** Is curious—wants to know how and why, asking lots of questions about a variety of subjects.

_____ **2.** Questions rules.

_____ **3.** Likes to pretend and has a vivid imagination.

_____ **4.** Makes up stories and has unique ideas.

_____ **5.** Invents games, toys, and other devices.

_____ **6.** Uses many different ways of solving problems.

_____ **7.** Solves problems in unusual ways.

_____ **8.** Shows uneven development—may be "super smart" in some areas while age-appropriate or
even somewhat delayed in others. (*Example:* An eight-year-old who understands and can avidly
explain the role of chlorophyll in the process of photosynthesis, but struggles with reading all the
words in a picture book.)

_____ **9.** Is sensitive; responds intensely to noise, pain, frustration.

_____ **10.** Empathizes with others' feelings, worries about their troubles.

_____ **11.** Expresses concern about world problems such as endangered animals, racism, pollution, war,
and poverty.

_____ **12.** Tends to rebel against what is routine or predictable.

_____ **13.** Is easily bored.

_____ **14.** Has a wide range of interests.

_____ **15.** Chooses difficult problems over simple ones.

_____ **16.** Has many unusual hobbies or interests.

_____ **17.** Knows a good deal about many subjects.

_____ **18.** Sticks to a project once it is started.

_____ **19.** Has a long attention span for things that interest her/him.

MORE →

Adapted from *The Survival Guide for Parents of Gifted Kids*, rev. ed., by Sally Yahnke Walker, Ph.D. (2002), pages 26–27, and *Stand Up for Your Gifted Child* by
Joan Franklin Smutny (2001), pages 21–23. Used with permission of Free Spirit Publishing. From *The Survival Guide for Teachers of Gifted Kids* by Jim Delisle, Ph.D.,
and Barbara A. Lewis, copyright © 2003. Free Spirit Publishing Inc., Minneapolis, MN; 800-735-7323; www.freespirit.com. This page may
be reproduced for individual, classroom, or small group work only. For other uses, contact www.freespirit.com/company/permissions.cfm.

★ Parent Checklist of Child's Traits (cont'd)

_____ **20.** Resents being interrupted from something that interests him/her.

_____ **21.** Has a well-developed sense of humor.

_____ **22.** Has an amazing memory.

_____ **23.** Learns quickly and applies knowledge easily.

_____ **24.** Sees patterns and connections that others don't see, even among things that are apparently unrelated.

_____ **25.** Is aware of problems other often do not see.

_____ **26.** Has a high activity level.

_____ **27.** Is extremely focused and intense.

_____ **28.** Talked early and in complex ways.

_____ **29.** Has an extremely large vocabulary.

_____ **30.** Talks or thinks like an adult.

_____ **31.** Discusses or elaborates on ideas in complex, unusual ways.

_____ **32.** Likes to discuss abstract ideas like God, love, justice, and equality.

_____ **33.** Shows intuitive sensitivity to spiritual values and beliefs; ponders philosophical issues.

_____ **34.** Gets others to do what she/he wants.

_____ **35.** Sets high standards for himself/herself.

_____ **36.** Is strong willed.

_____ **37.** Shows leadership in organizing games and activities and in resolving disputes.

_____ **38.** Is frustrated with imperfection in others and herself/himself.

Other special talents or skills your child has, or other factors you feel are important in understanding your child's abilities:

_____

_____

_____

_____

Parent/Caregiver Signature _____

Date _____ **Phone Number** _____

Adapted from _The Survival Guide for Parents of Gifted Kids_, rev. ed., by Sally Yahnke Walker, Ph.D. (2002), pages 26–27, and _Stand Up for Your Gifted Child_ by Joan Franklin Smutny (2001), pages 21–23. Used with permission of Free Spirit Publishing. From _The Survival Guide for Teachers of Gifted Kids_ by Jim Delisle, Ph.D., and Barbara A. Lewis, copyright © 2003. Free Spirit Publishing Inc., Minneapolis, MN; 800-735-7323; www.freespirit.com. This page may be reproduced for individual, classroom, or small group work only. For other uses, contact www.freespirit.com/company/permissions.cfm.

★ Gifted Student Nomination Form ★

Name of Person Completing Form _____

Address _____

Telephone _____ **Email** _____

What is the name of the student you are nominating for participation in gifted education programming?

_____

Why are you nominating this student? Please give details you have observed about the student (academic abilities, talents, social skills, sensitivities, other personal traits) or other anecdotal information that demonstrates the student's exceptional qualities.

_____

_____

_____

_____

_____

_____

_____

_____

_____

_____

_____

_____

_____

_____

_____

_____

_____

★ Gifted Education Program Action Plan ★

Student _____ Grade _____ Date _____

Person completing form

_____ Gifted education teacher (complete items 1, 2, 3, and 7 prior to meeting)

_____ Parent (complete items 1, 2, 4, and 7 prior to meeting)

_____ Student (complete items 1, 2, 5, and 7 prior to meeting)

_____ Other (please specify) _____ (complete items 1, 2, 6, and 7 prior to meeting)

Items 1–7 are to be completed prior to a group meeting.

1. Situation or concern:

_____

_____

_____

_____

_____

_____

_____

2. Any actions taken thus far in relation to situation or concern:

_____

_____

_____

_____

_____

_____

_____

_____

MORE ➜

★ Gifted Education Program Action Plan (cont'd)

3. Teacher comments:

_____

_____

_____

_____

4. Parent comments:

_____

_____

_____

_____

5. Student comments:

_____

_____

_____

_____

6. Comments from _____:

_____

_____

_____

_____

7. Signatures:

Teacher _____

Parent _____

Student _____

Other _____

MORE ➤

★ Gifted Education Program Action Plan (cont'd)

Items 8–12 are to be completed at the group meeting.

8. Steps teacher will take to attempt to resolve the situation:

_____

_____

_____

_____

_____

9. Steps student will take to resolve the situation:

_____

_____

_____

_____

_____

10. Other steps that will be taken by _____ :

_____

_____

_____

_____

11. Date of next scheduled conference: _____

12. Signatures:

Teacher _____

Parent _____

Student _____

Other _____

Lay the Groundwork for a Well-Structured Program

Before considering new K–12 gifted programming options, the G/T planning committee for Beulah Consolidated Schools decided to take a systematic look at opportunities currently in place for gifted kids. Their offerings at the elementary level included a poet-in-residence, cluster grouping for reading and math, a lively student-created school newsletter, essay contests, and a popular monthly spelling bee; the district's two elementary schools were also beginning to implement differentiation inservices for all of its teachers. Beulah's middle school had a strong writing program with visiting authors and produced an annual student-scripted one-act play. High school students were able to take honors English and humanities classes as well as video-based courses in calculus and trigonometry in collaboration with the state university. Ninth- through twelfth-graders with a B average or better were also invited to participate in full-day seminars three times a year; the last three seminars had been in architecture, Web design, and government.

Justifiably, the committee and the school community took a good deal of pride in the many distinctive options the district had to offer its students. At the same time, they saw gaps and inconsistencies in the offerings. A look at the gifted mission and philosophy statement, which called for serving the diverse academic and social/emotional needs of all gifted students, confirmed that gifted education opportunities were out of balance and that some needs were going unmet. A needs assessment underlined the existence of gaps, particularly the lack of individualized services in math and science at the elementary and middle school levels. The needs survey also highlighted a demographic change that had not been addressed in terms of gifted programming: Over the past five years, several

dozen immigrant families had settled in the Beulah district. Many of the new children were still learning English and were not yet well served by current G/T initiatives.

The committee agreed that what was needed was a set of specific goals along with a broad structural model they could use to start planning ways to comprehensively and continually give support to all identified gifted kids at all grade levels.

There are a host of ways that gifted children can be served, both in specific programs offered exclusively to them and via additional services that exist in any comprehensive K–12 school district. Ideally, the components you plan will be carefully structured to provide both range and breadth within a continuum of offerings that meet the diverse needs of the gifted students you serve. Key concepts here are *structure* and *continuum*. Planning your program and choosing its elements depend on several factors:

- the gifted program's established philosophy and mission

- your school or district's definition of what it means to be gifted

- the goals you set for both the program and its participants

- learning opportunities that are already in place for gifted students in your school or district

- key information gleaned from the needs assessment process

- present and anticipated staffing and funding levels

Getting Started with Program Planning

This book discusses program planning after presenting information on identification; in reality, however, these tasks will (indeed should) overlap. At least some of your planning will need to take place prior to and in conjunction with the identification and selection process. Understanding all the ways students can be gifted and having a grasp on the number and types of students you will serve will guide your program planning. At the same time, as noted in Survival Strategy 2, nominations, recommendations, and selections must lead to a fit with the programming itself. Thus, you may need to revisit your identification process and criteria once your programming alternatives begin to solidify. Issues of programming and identification are more cyclical than linear.

Within this fluid framework, there are concrete steps you can follow as you begin your broad program planning. As a prerequisite, the gifted education committee will need to do some research and preparation. Invite gifted coordinators from other districts—ideally, districts with demographics similar to those of your own—to make presentations to the full committee about the programming in their schools. Try to learn as much as possible about both the content of the programs that are being offered and the implementation processes that have been followed. You'll also want to establish subcommittees by content area and/or grade level. These subcommittees can gather additional input from outside and in-school experts and then take responsibility for making recommendations to the full committee.

The steps that follow are some of the most important ones the committee and subcommittees should take.

Step 1: Take the Inventory of Excellence

If you are beginning or expanding services for gifted children in your school district, there may be an assumption that there is not enough going on *now* that benefits their learning. In all but a few rare cases, this is probably not entirely true.

For example, if asked about services for K–3 students, many people might respond, "Our pull-out program doesn't begin until fourth grade." Yet, consider your district's present opportunities for cultivating excellence at the primary level. Ask:

- Does the school participate in any artist-in-residence programs?
- Are children ever ability grouped in basic subjects, once their achievement levels are documented?

- Are hands-on learning centers, with open-ended projects, a part of classrooms?
- Can students be grouped occasionally by interest or ability, rather than grade level or age, to work on a common project?
- Do teachers or parent volunteers facilitate a Future Problem Solving or Junior Great Books Program? Can advanced primary-aged students participate?
- Are special workshops ("Writing Wizards" or "Science Sleuths") offered as enrichment opportunities?
- Are students allowed to read books at the level that is appropriate for them, rather than stick with a grade-level book list when they can read beyond it?
- Is multiage grouping (sometimes called looping) available to students?

If even half of these opportunities exist in your elementary school, you are already on track for appropriate programming for young gifted students (and upper-elementary kids as well). Another case in point: the local high school. In answer to the question "What sort of gifted program do you have for gifted secondary-level students?" the most common response may be, "Oh, our gifted program only serves children up through grade 8." But, as with the answer about programming for primary-aged children, this response is incomplete. Options that exist for gifted secondary students in many high schools may include:

- Advanced Placement (AP) or honors-level classes
- dual enrollment at local colleges on a part-time basis
- Internet-based courses for credit
- a mentorship program offered through the guidance office
- interest clubs (math, chess, drama, technology)
- newspaper and yearbook committees
- competitions (debate or decathlon, physics Olympics, talent show)
- independent study courses
- community service projects
- advanced foreign language instruction
- summer opportunities abroad or at local colleges

Few would contend that these options should limit their enrollment to identified gifted students. Yet, clearly, they offer opportunities for gifted kids to be served and challenged.

Looking at the ways your school or district currently meets these kids' needs, whether in the name of gifted education or not, lets you take an "Inventory of Excellence." To do this inventory, sit down with a few members of the various school staffs. This is the time to boast, brag, and roll out the many options that exist from kindergarten through grade 12, documenting everything your district does—within the curriculum as well as in clubs and other extracurricular activities—to support or enhance students' learning opportunities. What you'll find is that a vast number of these options benefit identified gifted students who have the interest, passion, or creative wherewithal to participate actively in them.

It limits your vision to equate terms like *services for gifted kids* or *gifted programming* with *resource room, pull-out program,* or *gifted class.* Instead, think of *gifted programming* and *G/T services* as "umbrella" terms, overarching a broad continuum of options that can serve gifted children and, at times, other students as well.

Step 2: Note the "Gifted Gaps"

After finishing your excellence inventory, the next question is: "Despite all of our existing efforts, what gaps still exist in our educational options for gifted students?"

Depending on your situation, you may find gaps related to:

- content areas for academic programming (such as an emphasis on math and science rather than language arts)

- opportunities outside of academic programming (such as creativity or the arts)

- ways to extend gifted students' learning within the existing required curriculum

- perceived grading penalties (for example, an A in Basic English carrying the same weight as an A in Honors English)

- unintentional exclusion of gifted kids from minority or nonmainstream groups, including obviously bright kids whose other learning needs carry the focus (perhaps students categorized as ESL, LD, or EBD)

- meeting the needs of smart kids who get poor grades

- social and emotional concerns related to gifted kids (including perfectionism, poor social skills, stress, low self-esteem, and negative behavior, among others)

Look at these gifted gaps alongside the results of the needs assessments you've already conducted (see pages 12–14). You're likely to see broad areas that require addressing through a variety of means: program services, curriculum, training, and policy.

In Survival Strategy 6 we'll take a closer look at issues related to training and policy (see pages 122–124). The remainder of this chapter and Survival Strategy 4 address the kinds of programming arrangements and instructional methods that can help you develop a well-rounded gifted education program.

Step 3: Set Your Program Goals

Goals are essential. They give meaning to the vision articulated in the mission, allowing you to form a framework and parameters that clearly state what benefits you want and expect your gifted program to provide for the students it serves. Goals also set a baseline for future evaluations of how the program is fulfilling its purpose.

One of our favorite examples of goals tied to mission and philosophy comes from Ohio's Alliance City Schools' IPESI gifted education program. Here are the program's mission, philosophy, definition of gifted children, and goals:[1]

The word "ipesi" is a South African word meaning, "Where are you going?" The letters of this word have been assigned symbolic representations which we use as a basis for where we hope our gifted children are headed.

Imagination	We seek to encourage divergent thinking and to stimulate the characteristics which develop creativity.
Persistence	We present students with challenges at their ability levels and guide them as they work through these problems.
Excellence	Students are encouraged to strive toward excellence in all areas.
Synthesis	Synthesis involves the creation of a new product utilizing fluency, flexibility, and originality. We assist students in finding a suitable market for their products.
Inspiration	One purpose of IPESI is to assist students in the realization of their abilities and to guide them in the selection of goals which are challenging.

Figure 3.1 This mission statement establishes the basis for the direction Alliance wants to set for its gifted students.

PROGRAM PHILOSOPHY

In accordance with the stated philosophy of the Alliance City Schools, and in recognition of the differentiated needs of gifted students, the program for gifted and talented children will provide opportunities designed to broaden and extend the learning process. Learning will be enhanced by materials, tasks, and experiences differentiated in content, process, and products and/or performances.

Figure 3.2 The IPESI philosophy statement is directly tied to school-wide philosophy.

DEFINITION OF GIFTED CHILDREN

"Gifted" means students who perform or show potential for performing at remarkably high levels of accomplishment when compared to others of their age, experience, or environment and who are identified under division (A) superior cognitive, (B) specific academic, (C) creative thinking, or (D) visual and performing arts, of the Section 3324.03 of the Ohio Revised Code.

Figure 3.3 IPESI's definition of giftedness, tied to the state code, establishes the kinds of gifts and talents children served by the gifted program will have.

PROGRAM GOALS

- In the education of the gifted individual, considerable emphasis should be placed upon developing higher-level thinking skills using in-depth content as demonstrated by a variety of products and/or performances.
- In the education of the gifted individual, considerable emphasis should be placed upon developing affective and social-behavioral skill using in-depth content as demonstrated by a variety of products and/or performances.

PROGRAM OBJECTIVES

1. CONTENT

1.1 Services for gifted will present content related to broad-based issues, themes, or problems incorporating and/or combining a variety of subject areas.

2. PROCESS

Services for gifted will emphasize:

2.1 Logical reasoning
2.2 Critical thinking
2.3 Divergent thinking
2.4 Creative problem solving strategies
2.5 Research
2.6 Communication
2.7 Affective development

3. PRODUCTS/PERFORMANCES

Services for gifted will emphasize products/performances that:

3.1 Refine or challenge existing ideas
3.2 Integrate concepts
3.3 Use techniques, materials, forms, and knowledge in innovative ways
3.4 Use a variety of evaluation techniques

Figure 3.4 The IPESI goals are divided into broad goals and more specific objectives. Together, these two elements serve as a ready guide for planning programs and services.

The IPESI program's framework is one example of how goals can be set. There are other ways to go about this as well, depending on your school or district's particular situation and gifted focus. One useful approach is to establish separate goals for the students and for the program. Figures 3.5 and 3.6 provide examples of complementary student and program goals.

GOALS FOR GIFTED STUDENTS

1. To develop positive self-concepts and an appreciation of giftedness, which will enable the students to be successful in their interactions with others.

2. To develop critical, creative, and evaluative thinking processes so that students will be able to address complex issues with the necessary tools of problem solving.

3. To develop in students a love for lifelong learning by giving them the technical and personal skills necessary to achieve success, both inside and outside the classroom.

4. To provide students with opportunities to "learn how to learn," which requires organizational skills, study skills, and persistence in the face of difficulty.

5. To develop the academic abilities of students so that they will be able to master new and difficult curriculum challenges.

6. To provide students with opportunities to learn alongside intellectual peers so that they might gain a realistic appraisal of their own abilities.

Figure 3.5 These goals reflect an emphasis on academics and critical thinking, balanced with the need to address students' social and emotional well-being.

GOALS FOR GIFTED EDUCATION PROGRAMMING

1. To integrate, wherever possible, learning opportunities provided in the gifted program with objectives of the regular classroom curriculum.

2. To develop an awareness in all staff members that gifted students have unique cognitive and affective needs which can sometimes be best met outside of the regular classroom setting.

3. To increase efforts meant to maximize the potential of gifted children sometimes "left behind"—such as underachievers, children of color, children with learning disabilities who are also gifted—and to provide them with appropriate enrichment experiences.

4. To provide staff development opportunities for K–12 staff on the characteristics of gifted children and methods they can use to challenge these children throughout the curriculum.

5. To develop liaison relationships between gifted children and community members so that students can learn from practicing professionals about areas of mutual interest.

6. To develop criteria and policies regarding acceleration, including (but not limited to) grade skipping, early admission to kindergarten, and dual enrollment in college.

Figure 3.6 Much is accomplished by creating these program goals in support of the student goals. Specific direction for programming can be found here (services in the regular classroom, enrichment activities, mentorships, and accelerated learning opportunities). Objectives for staff development (understanding giftedness, teaching methods) are established. Also documented are the intent and broad means for meeting the needs of gifted children from underrepresented populations.

One reason these dual goals are useful is because goals for programming can often be more directive and discernible than those for students. For example, it would be easy to determine the success of program goal 6—the district will either arrive at an acceleration policy or it will not. Still, all of the goals can, to a larger or smaller degree, be measured, either by direct observation or through more ambitious evaluative efforts. For example, for student goal 3, the development of technical and personal skills can be documented and, while a lifelong interest in learning cannot be guaranteed, a student's broad love of learning in and out of the classroom can be documented over time.

Considered together, the goals in Figures 3.5 and 3.6 present a road map for planning gifted education

services for a program with an emphasis on diversity, academic excellence, and meeting gifted children's social and emotional needs.

It's possible that someone—a parent, a teacher, or an administrator—will respond to your goals with the legitimate question, "But aren't these goals good for *all* children?" Your answer can be a simple one: "Yes, but it's our responsibility to articulate specifically the ways that we want the gifted children in our program to benefit from the services we offer." The truth is that very few classroom teachers, and very few schools in general, have a set of written goals to which all staff members ascribe. If goal setting for your gifted program serves as a catalyst for other programs to do the same, so much the better.

Step 4: Establish Your Program Structure

In its "Pre-K–Grade 12 Gifted Program Standards," the National Association for Gifted Children (NAGC) sets forth clear criteria for program administration, management, and design. Among the guiding programming principles are the requirements (1) that gifted education be integrated into the general education program and (2) that there be a planned range of services to provide both continuity and diversity in the offerings available to support all gifted students' education. (For more information on the NAGC standards, see page 68.)

Planning a structure that . . .

- delivers a continuum of offerings
  - for diverse gifted students
    - across all grade levels, and that is
      - tied to the school or district's stated objectives
        - and integrated into the general curriculum

. . . can seem like a very tall order. One concept that could make the process more manageable might be to think of gifted programming in terms of a pyramid of service options. Such a pyramid was first described by June Cox, Neil Daniel, and Bruce O. Boston. In the 1980s, this University of Texas research team surveyed every U.S. school district and asked about the programming options available for gifted students. The original survey was sent to more than 16,000 superintendents, with more extensive follow-up (including some on-site visits) conducted in more than 4,000 districts. Cox and her fellow researchers wanted to know how comprehensive gifted services were and what could be done to improve opportunities for gifted children.

What they found was no surprise: a national crazy quilt of provisions here and there, with very few efforts to plan for a comprehensive K–12 program. Also, a "one size fits all" approach was used most often, with the part-time pull-out program (the resource room) the most common option at the elementary level and the availability of honors-level classes the provision of choice in high schools. Middle school appeared sorely underserved for giftedness, as very few direct efforts were made toward supporting the unique learning needs of gifted students in grades 6–8. Provisions for the arts or for counseling services were minimal at best. Splintered and sporadic, the programs for able students provided a slapdash approach to a need that called for structure and depth.

After publishing the results of their survey, the Texas researchers put together and tested a series of recommendations for change. Through this initiative they set forth a model for excellence in gifted education programming, still valid today, called the Pyramid Project.

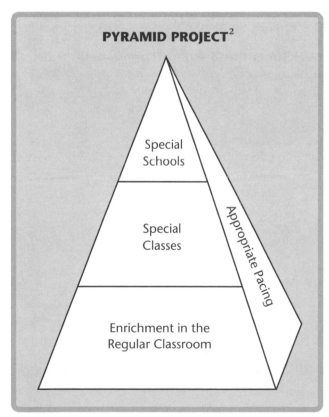

PYRAMID PROJECT[2]

Special Schools

Special Classes

Enrichment in the Regular Classroom

Appropriate Pacing

Figure 3.7

The widest section of the pyramid, its base, is labeled "Enrichment in the Regular Classroom." From our more recent perspective, this category can be broadly thought of as "Gifted Services in the Regular Classroom." Within these services, a large number of students can benefit from lessons structured on

Bloom's Taxonomy, differentiated instruction, creative processes, in-class grouping, and independent study related to the curriculum.

The pyramid's second tier, its narrower dimensions representing the smaller number of students to be served by it, is called "Special Classes." Under this heading fall the pull-out classes and honors-level courses, as well as self-contained classes for gifted students where this option is feasible in a school district.

The top level of the pyramid, "Special Schools," represents a provision to serve those students whose talents are so exceptional that they need to learn full-time in a distinctly different setting. Examples of these include magnet schools, Governor's Schools, and school-within-a-school programs.

Spanning the side of the pyramid and encompassing each option is "Appropriate Pacing." This provision provides that students will be able to tackle academic content when they are ready to do so, rather than in a prescribed, grade-level sequence that may not be in sync with the individual student's learning needs.

From the perspective of nearly two decades after the Pyramid Project, we would add one more element along the pyramid's side: "Social/Emotional Support." Although research shows that gifted kids may not have more emotional problems than other children, their problems are at times different, and they may need special guidance. Many gifted children experience high degrees of perception, involvement, sensitivity, and perfectionism. Tending to have extreme and intense expectations of themselves, they may also face high expectations from parents, teachers, and other students. It's not unusual for gifted young people to struggle in peer relationships. They may experience rejection, isolation, alienation, and even ridicule from other kids their own age. They may also have a deep sense of helplessness in the face of social problems and feel overwhelmed by their own capabilities. Added to these pressures, highly able children's cognitive development is often uneven: one gifted child may be a math whiz but struggle with reading; another may have strong spatial skills but find computation difficult. For these kids, affective and physical development may be out of sync with many of their highly developed academic abilities, leading to frustration, confusion, and a lack of confidence.

 "One test of the correctness of educational procedure is the happiness of the child." –Maria Montessori

Responsible gifted programming must integrate ways for gifted kids to have these kinds of social and emotional needs met. Training for teachers, a chance for G/T students to interact both socially and academically with peers who share their abilities, and opportunities for gifted kids to discuss concerns in a safe environment should be built into the gifted education model.

With that added emphasis on the emotional dimensions of giftedness, the plan set forth in the Pyramid Project still stands as the best of the comprehensive programming models that you will find. Not only does it suggest that both acceleration and enrichment options are necessary for adequate services, it also illustrates that providing only limited or one-dimensional programming in response to gifted students' educational needs can do no more than partially meet and fulfill those needs.

Of course, this model is an ideal example. It shows what can be done when a district is committed—both philosophically and financially—and when a community of people come together to turn people's ideas into reality. In the next chapter, we'll look broadly at a variety of programming options that exist in gifted education today and see how these offerings tie to the elements of the pyramid. As you consider your choices, you may find it helpful to use the "Gifted Programming Planner" form on page 69. If you need more writing space, make an enlarged (17" x 11") photocopy. (For an example of a completed form, see Figure 4.4 on page 85.)

Notes

1. The IPESI program examples are from the Alliance City Schools' (Alliance, Ohio) *IPESI Gifted Education Handbook for Parents* and are used with permission.

2. From *Educating Able Learners: Programs and Promising Practices* by June Cox, Neil Daniel, and Bruce O. Boston, copyright © 1985. By permission of the University of Texas Press.

Resources

The following resources apply specifically to topics addressed in this strategy's chapter. For a complete list of gifted education resources, see pages 146–154.

Aiming for Excellence: Annotations to the NAGC Pre-K–Grade 12 Gifted Program Standards edited by Mary S. Landrum, Carolyn M. Callahan, and Beverly D. Shaklee (Waco, TX: Prufrock Press, 2001). An excellent source for determining goals for your gifted program, this book reviews and expands on the gifted education program standards set by NAGC (see below).

"National Association for Gifted Children Pre-K–Grade 12 Gifted Program Standards" *(www.nagc.org/webprek12.htm)*. Find here tables for program design and program administration and management. These tables cite guiding principles along with both minimum and exemplary standards for systematically planning, developing, implementing, and managing comprehensive programs and services for gifted children.

★ Gifted Programming Planner ★

	SPECIAL SCHOOL(S)	SPECIAL CLASSES	REGULAR CLASSROOM	
PRIMARY				
UPPER ELEMENTARY				
MIDDLE SCHOOL				
HIGH SCHOOL				

Appropriate pacing?

Provisions for social and emotional needs?

Plan Programming You Can Build On

At Idawaso Middle School, a group of sixth-, seventh-, and eighth-grade gifted students meets twice a week, once during the math block and once during the science block, to work on projects for the state science exposition, held each year in April. The students are working under the supervision of teachers from the science and math departments and two visiting scientists, one from the local university and one from a private manufacturing business. Students not identified as gifted also have an opportunity to participate in the state exposition; all projects from all students are entered in the Idawaso Science Fair in February, where visiting state judges select projects that will be included in the exposition. For the gifted student scientists at Idawaso, the projects provide a stimulating and challenging ongoing forum for working with peers and mentors while they solve complex science- and math-related problems.

★ ★ ★

All winter, upper-elementary students at the Summit Ridge Fine Arts Academy have been spending the last two hours of every day plus one after-school hour rehearsing and building sets for a student-launched production of **The Lion King.** With the support and guidance of school staff and community dramatists, students have been in charge of every aspect of the production: acquiring the rights to present the musical, planning and constructing sets, making costumes, holding auditions and casting, and even conducting, choreographing, and directing the show. In the spring, the students will do several performances for kids from area schools and for the community. They have also arranged to have the musical taped and replayed over the local cable outlet.

★ ★ ★

Children in Juana Perez's kindergarten classroom are learning about geometric shapes. Juana has previewed students' knowledge and experience and has grouped the children for learning. Of her twenty-one students, six need help identifying different shapes; each day, Juana goes over the names of the shapes with them and has them work with actual shapes and with shape puzzles. A second group of seven children is using matching cards to distinguish among shapes. Five children look at books about shapes and discuss which shapes are parts of the buildings, vehicles, and tools pictured. The other three students are using similar books and are creating a chart that shows which shapes occur in vehicles like bicycles, cars, buses, and airplanes. Twice a week, these three students meet with a resource teacher and with gifted students from the other kindergarten classroom to discuss questions about the properties of vehicles and their shapes—questions like "Why are wheels round?" and "What if the bus door was shaped like a triangle?" This group is also doing a building project, inventing a vehicle using different shapes.

★ ★ ★

McCafferty High School is a small school located far from any urban center. For several years, gifted writing students at McCafferty have participated, via satellite hookup, in a three-day intensive writing seminar at a college 100 miles away. This year, thanks to an increased budget for high school gifted programming, the district arranged to send the students to the workshop so they could work firsthand with other students from across the state and have one-on-one *critiques of their work from visiting published authors who participate in the program.*

ifted education will never languish for want of creative programming ideas. Nonetheless, for many schools and districts, it is unrealistic to expect to be able to implement wide-ranging and diverse options that fulfill every provision of the Pyramid Project's plan (see page 67), at least in the short run. Within a district, though, over time, it is possible to develop a span of offerings to provide a depth, scope, and continuum of services to tailor your own version of such a pyramid.

In the next few pages, we outline many of the programs and services that fit within each of the pyramid's three delivery categories and highlight some of the strengths and weaknesses of each option.

"Gifted programming that is blended effectively with the total school program does not 'just happen.' It must develop deliberately and gradually."
—DONALD TREFFINGER

Gifted Services in the Regular Classroom

There are a variety of ways gifted elementary, middle school, and high school students are and can be served in the regular classroom. Some of the most common approaches include acceleration, inclusion, in-class grouping, and differentiation.

Early Entrance and Acceleration

Starting kindergarten early and grade acceleration in elementary school are standard approaches to meeting the needs of young, highly able children. Early-childhood gifted specialist Joan Franklin Smutny and her colleagues note that:[1]

Early entrance to kindergarten or first grade may be the best acceleration option for young gifted children. This allows for the child's intelligence to be better accommodated and for a peer group to be established. It saves the student the later disruption of skipping a grade. By being more academically challenged in the earliest grade, a bright child is likely to have fewer of the emotional problems that typically result from facing academic challenges after years of "coasting" along. Early entrance can set the stage for

many young gifted children to continue to thrive and excel throughout their school experience, to participate in more activities, to feel secure within a peer group when they express their ideas, and to experience more interdependence and cooperation.

Early entry into kindergarten is only one form of acceleration that can take place within a regular classroom. Others include skipping a grade, completing two grades over the course of one school year, skipping grades in a given subject, and early entrance into college.

For early entrance and grade acceleration to succeed, children's social and emotional readiness needs to be carefully considered, with an eye to avoiding both inappropriate "pushing" and the discouraging and decelerating effects of "holding a child back." It's also important that everyone involved in an acceleration decision—the child, the parent, the teachers, and the administration—be invested in the process. And, of course, for acceleration options to be viable, district policy must allow for their implementation, classroom teachers must be open to them, and institutions (elementary and middle schools, middle schools and high schools, high schools and post-secondary schools) must be able to work effectively together. The reality is that, regardless of when a child starts kindergarten or what grade or grades a student skips, every gifted child will continue to have special needs that must be accommodated. This is true for all gifted kids in any kind of setting or program.

Parents and teachers are often very concerned about having made a possible wrong decision in grade-skipping a child, especially in the earliest grade levels. From fears about the future ("Will he be big enough to play sports in middle school?" "Will she feel odd when every other eleventh grader has a driver's license?") to anxieties about the present ("Will teachers expect my child to be equally advanced in all areas of learning and development?"), parents and educators often forget that the choice to accelerate does not have to be a permanent one. Our advice? Regard *every* acceleration as provisional. Make sure that all involved, especially the child, understand this. Let the child know that she or he can try the placement and that it may be changed it if it doesn't seem to be the best approach. When this is handled in a matter-of-fact way with a focus on seeking the right situation for the student, most kids, parents, and teachers find themselves reasonably at ease with the arrangement. Then, if the placement doesn't seem to fit from one or more important vantage points (intellectual, emotional, or social), there is always the option of returning the child to the previous placement or arriving at a totally new decision alto-gether. Acceleration is meant to be an enjoyable experience, not a punishing, irreversible sentence!

The Inclusive Classroom

Back in the 1980s, some educators involved with the Council for Exceptional Children (CEC) began a push to get children with special learning needs out of their self-contained or pull-out programs and place them in the regular classroom. There, special educa-tors would work with these students in a more natu-ral setting, approximating the larger community outside of school, where people with differing abili-ties and conditions live and work side by side. The term Regular Education Initiative (REI) was coined to identify this social experiment.

The REI eventually came to be called *inclusion,* denot-ing the fact that special-ed students were no longer outside of education's mainstream. And who could argue with the premise? Inclusive classrooms had the look of democracy at its best, with all students treated as equals. Parents of children with special needs were among inclusion's most vocal advocates, as it removed some of the stigma of having a disability and recog-nized at last that *all* kids are capable of learning more than is often expected.

In a perfect world, inclusion would mean that students with special learning or behavioral needs would spend their days in regular classrooms, accom-panied by a special education teacher or an aide who would assist them in acclimating to this setting. Unfortunately, this ideal world remains just that—an ideal—as a shortage of both money and special education-certified personnel dictates that, in the real world, students with special needs are often "on their own" in the regular classroom. More often than not, the teacher in charge of the real-world classroom works valiantly and relatively independently to juggle the learning needs of as diverse a group of children as could ever be assembled: kids with special needs ranging from language barriers and learning differ-ences to physical and emotional disabilities, students with abilities that span from low to average to high.

Initially, gifted children were not a part of the inclusion movement, just as gifted children are often not really considered a part of special education (sadly, for their needs are often as extreme, just in dif-ferent ways). Eventually, though, many of gifted edu-cation's most prominent proponents—such as Joseph Renzulli, Susan Winebrenner, John Feldhusen, and Carol Ann Tomlinson—concluded that the future of gifted education lay in providing services to gifted children within the regular classroom. These educa-tors' research, publications, and conference presenta-tions became focused toward what regular classroom teachers could do to serve gifted children and toward how the gifted education specialist could be a catalyst in making this happen.

Today, in many school districts, the regular class-room is the primary setting for delivering gifted ser-vices. Within the classroom, gifted children's academic needs are met through grouping provisions and other methods of differentiated instruction.

In-Class Grouping

In the regular classroom, gifted children may be grouped in any of a number of ways:

- cluster grouping (five to ten students at the top of one grade level are placed together in one classroom)
- ability grouping (students are grouped based on their performance in specific curricular areas)
- like-ability cooperative grouping (students are grouped based on their performance levels to work together on specific projects or assignments)
- mixed-ability cooperative grouping (kids of varying abilities are placed together in small groups to work on tasks or create products together)

Which grouping methods to use should depend on the structure of the school and on students' personal characteristics, levels of cognitive functioning, learn-ing preferences, and interests.[2] For example, cluster grouping requires a school community that supports differentiated instruction and a trained gifted teacher at each grade level; gifted students most likely to suc-ceed in this arrangement need to like academic chal-lenge, enjoy small group work, and be willing and happy to work outside of the regular classroom rou-tine. As another example, mixed-ability grouping calls for a group of reasonably well-behaved kids who like the curricular area of focus and are social, moti-vated to learn, and willing to learn from each other; the classroom teacher must also be comfortable with the idea of peer learning.

Many in-class grouping arrangements take place in classrooms where teachers differentiate instruction (see the next section) to meet the needs of all stu-dents. In schools or classrooms where this kind of instruction is not emphasized, or where class size and the number of identified gifted students is small, another grouping choice is to pair two highly able students to work together on a project or cooperative assignment.

Differentiated Curriculum and Instruction

Though inclusion has become a widely accepted model for schools in the United States, gifted students do not always benefit from this classroom arrangement. Fast learners can languish in the classroom, rehashing skills and material they've already mastered. Research conducted by the National Research Center on the Gifted and Talented revealed that "approximately 40–50% of traditional classroom material could be eliminated for [gifted] students in one or more of the following content areas: mathematics, language arts, science, and social studies"[3] because gifted students have already mastered the grade-level curriculum.

What can be done in this situation? How can gifted kids have their needs met within an inclusive classroom? *Differentiation* provides a process that allows teachers to better serve both gifted students and the rest of the class. Teachers differentiate—modify—the curriculum and their instructional methods in response to the needs, strengths, learning styles, and interests of individual students so that all students have an opportunity to learn at their full potential.

Differentiation typically involves modifying instruction in terms of the following:

- **Content.** Content concerns the curricular material: facts, ideas, generalizations, principles, and theories. With gifted kids, this content can stem from the basic curriculum, but it should go far beyond it in depth and complexity. It should allow for flexible pacing and the skipping of material fast learners already know.

- **Process.** This refers to the teacher's instructional methods and strategies and the thinking skills, learning styles, and strengths that children bring to the table. Process can be differentiated by adding depth or complexity to students' research and analysis and by fostering creative and critical thinking.

- **Product.** Products are the outcome of instruction, the student's response to learning. The student's interest and learning style might dictate the choice of a product, which can definitely go beyond the standard assessments of tests, quizzes, and book reports.

All kids in a classroom can benefit from differentiation when it is well implemented. For gifted students, G/T curriculum specialists focus on both employing and developing several qualities:

- **Flexibility,** so that shifts of ideas can safely take place. For example, when studying the U.S. Constitution, a student might research the laws and government of Russia or France, looking for a wealth of specific types of details regarding each legal system.

- **Fluency,** so that students can have many choices and generate large numbers of answers to open-ended questions. In this case, the same student could examine the many different types of governments around the world, looking for patterns that allow the student to compare, contrast, and evaluate different legal systems or governmental organizations.

- **Elaboration,** so that students can improve, embellish, or add to an idea. In this arena, the student who is exploring the U.S. Constitution might focus on particular kinds of changes in a foreign legal system over time, perhaps describing how children who broke laws were treated in eighteenth-century France.

- **Originality,** so that students can generate a unique product or experience. The same student might look for a different point of view here, perhaps researching how present-day youth offenders are treated when incarcerated.

- **Abstraction,** so that students can work with "fuzzy" problems or ambiguity. The gifted student in our example might, for instance, work with a problem where the boundaries are not clear or where ethical questions are involved: What conditions for incarcerated youth would be fair? Unfair? Who should decide? What would have to be done to make changes?

- **Risk taking,** so that students can push the boundaries and stretch their imaginations. Our student might develop an emotional connection to or empathy for incarcerated youth and could come up with ways to challenge some of the conditions for youth who are incarcerated.

- **Complex thinking,** so that students can meet more difficult challenges and develop problem-solving skills for answering difficult questions. Here, the student might contact a legislator and lobby to design some legislation that will improve conditions for youth offenders who are incarcerated.

- **Curiosity,** so that students can continue to pursue depth in their study. In this case, the student might become interested in the way laws are passed and then follow the process through, learning the rules and language of lawmaking.

"Gifted students have specific learning differences that call for specific differentiation techniques. Simply increasing challenge and variety may not be enough."
—DIANE HEACOX

In-class grouping has already been mentioned as a method for differentiating learning for gifted students. Schools and teachers have at hand a variety of other differentiation strategies as well:

- Curriculum compacting, which allows the student who shows expertise to skip known material and work on more advanced instructional options. This involves pretesting or assessing for competency.

- Independent study, providing for some choice of independent investigation.

- The use of advanced texts and materials, which might include those available from a university, library, or professional organization or from the Internet.

- Working with experts, such as visiting scientists, mathematicians, business leaders, or writers from whom a student or group of students might learn.

- Tiered assignments that create different levels of challenge, growing in complexity.

- Variety and choice of assignments and homework, to add scope and interest. Within the same curricular unit, students could be asked to write poetry, speak, draw, create a chart to compare and analyze facts, compose a song, conduct an interview and write a newspaper article, and so forth.

- Challenging and complex learning centers that broadly extend and expand students' opportunities to explore a subject in depth. Possibilities could include a center on the Holocaust with exploratory, open-ended assignments or a center that includes examples, information, and materials that will encourage children to make tessellations or design a board game.

- Advanced computer programs that allow the student to design and solve problems or provide services.

- Advanced, real-life tasks in which students work to solve complex problems. For example, a group of students can explore what might be done to improve a traffic problem around the school and then present their information to the faculty or administration.

- Support for goal setting and designing products, so that students can gain respect for their own work and find ways to meaningfully share it with others. For example, a student who has worked with a legislator to learn how laws are made could report his or her legislative experience to other students or to the student council or school board.

Gifted in the Regular Classroom: Benefits and Drawbacks

There are many benefits to serving gifted children within the regular classroom, including the following:

- Students interact with other kids their own age.

- There are opportunities to group students in different ways, adding variety and helping all kids recognize their own unique gifts and appreciate those of others.

- Planners can more readily ensure that gifted students' programming fits within the established curriculum, as recommended in the NAGC standards.

- The social stigma of being labeled "a giftie" is lessened when children are grouped heterogeneously in the same classroom.

- Instances of assigned makeup work and added homework due to placement in a pull-out program are eliminated.

- When gifted kids' "home base" is a regular classroom, it's clear that the job of reaching and teaching the gifted students belongs to the classroom teacher.

- Charges of elitism raised when gifted kids are placed in separate classes can be circumvented.

While the ideas for serving gifted children within the regular classroom are many, what actually happens to the education of highly able kids in an inclusive setting? Are these students served as well and as thoroughly as they may be in separate classrooms? To a large degree, this is dependent on the philosophical commitment of the district, school, and teachers and on the support that programs like differentiation are given in terms of ongoing funding, teacher training, and evaluation. Based on the Pyramid Project plan, carefully planned and implemented educational opportunities for gifted children within the regular classroom are desirable and necessary. In looking at this option for your gifted program, you'll want to weigh the depth of commitment and support presently and potentially available.

FUNDING ISSUES

Serving gifted children in the regular classroom often involves having a gifted specialist come into the classroom to work with students. The same specialist who can work with groups of gifted kids in a resource room will more than likely not be able to reach all those students as efficiently when traveling from classroom to classroom. For example, consider a district with a resource teacher operating pull-out programs that serve sixty gifted second through fifth graders in two schools. Each school has two classrooms per grade: sixteen classrooms. If the teacher brings the students into the resource room at each school, he or she might conduct sessions with four groups of children (one group per grade level) at each school. Such an arrangement will readily accommodate two full days each week at each school. If, instead, the same teacher needs to work with groups of gifted kids within sixteen classrooms, teaching time will be fragmented and it might not be possible to see the students with the same regularity. Additional gifted specialists will need to be hired. Were the teacher going into middle-school subject-area classes, the picture would be even more complicated and expensive.

Staffing costs for running an effective inclusion-based gifted program can triple those of a comparable pull-out program. One district we know instituted an exemplary in-class program—and went from employing 1.5 gifted staff members for pull-out programming to having 6 full-time staff members working with gifted kids in the regular classroom. The 4.5 new staff members added approximately $160,000 annually in staff salaries and benefits. The district's superintendent and board of education realized that the addition of new staff members was the only way to assure that the level of services to each gifted child would remain as high as it had been under the pull-out system. While this is an exceptional example—one as rare as it is extraordinary—it serves to illuminate the ever-present issue of funding and its impact on the programming decisions you will make.

"All schoolchildren are hostages to red tape and fiscal insufficiency."
—ROSELLEN BROWN

The cost of inservice training must also be considered. In an inclusion program, regular classroom teachers share the responsibility for providing appropriate learning opportunities for gifted kids. This means the teachers need training in recognizing and understanding giftedness, differentiating instruction, working with parents of gifted students, and dealing with the unique social and emotional issues (such as perfectionism and intensity, among others) that are part of gifted territory. To be effective, such training must be in-depth and ongoing. One or two inservice days with no follow-up won't give teachers the support they need to work successfully with gifted children in their classrooms.

PEOPLE ISSUES

Differentiation will be one among many topics seeking the attention of already-overworked, overstressed teachers. There may also be a literacy initiative, a five-year technology plan, changing guidelines for serving children with limited English proficiency, new policies regarding kids who don't pass the state-ordained competency tests . . . the list goes on—as well you know. Even if the district provides funds for teacher training and appears to be philosophically supportive of inclusion for gifted education, teachers, like everyone else, must make choices during their day about what concerns will receive emphasis and attention. In many cases, it's human nature to put the needs of kids who are struggling or not succeeding ahead of those of children who readily catch on and do well. To varying degrees, teachers' and schools' performance is measured based on how many children pass subject-area competency tests. Part of the challenge of inclusion, then, goes back to buy-in—helping teachers see and embrace the value of making gifted children's needs a priority. It also means looking realistically at district goals and administrative and teaching emphases, and then balancing the kinds of services you want to provide in class so that the regular classroom teacher's responsibility fits what can realistically be managed.

As noted, bringing a gifted specialist into the classroom is one key element of an inclusion program. In this regard, some regular classroom teachers are more flexible than others. A few will gladly invite the teacher in, and when they do, will be delighted to work with this specialist. However, there will also be teachers who would prefer to teach alone and who won't welcome another professional on the scene. Some teachers, too, may be reluctant about this, believing that the visitor is there to evaluate their teaching.

A third issue: How will underrepresented gifted kids be served? In many ways, a differentiated classroom offers a model for fostering children's learning in the styles, modes, and pacing that work best for them. When a teacher differentiates with each individual student in mind, talents and abilities have a chance to emerge and blossom. Yet what is likely to happen for the gifted student with very limited English skills? Will the teacher always group that student with other LEP kids or with the ESL teacher? What about the gifted girl who is intimidated working with boys on a mathematical problem or an architectural design and so doesn't contribute her ideas? And what about the child whose behavior becomes an issue in cooperative groups? Where will the teacher's focus go?

The nonacademic needs of gifted students present another important consideration. Gifted kids are, in a word, intense—they tend to be extra perceptive, highly involved, super-sensitive, and perfectionistic. At the same time, their physical and affective development may be out of pace with intellectual development. Cognitive development is also often uneven for gifted kids, who may have strong computational skills but weak spatial skills, or be highly verbal yet have a reading disability. In many cases, gifted children also face super-high expectations from adults and other kids, are overwhelmed by all they are capable of doing, worry deeply and feel helpless in the face of world problems, feel different and alienated, and have trouble finding friends who understand them. Some classroom teachers may not be sensitive to these needs. And though many teachers *are* supportive, their role is to teach, not to counsel. In a responsible gifted program, the social and emotional aspects of growing up gifted must be addressed; even the best inclusion program cannot stand completely on its own in serving gifted children. (For more on this subject, see pages 125–128.)

An unfortunate truth is that some schools use inclusion for gifted students as a way to curtail both staff and budgets, stretching the remaining human resources so thin as to make the situation untenable for the gifted staff and an ineffective option for the gifted students. Understanding the issues involved can help you avoid this kind of situation. Not to overstate the point, but inclusion alone does not a gifted program make! As you plan your programming options, take care not to overemphasize the in-classroom component of gifted services.

Special Classes for Gifted Students

There are a number of interesting ways to provide specialized instruction and learning for gifted students outside of the regular classroom setting. Here, we'll look at six options: pull-out classes, self-contained gifted classes, ability-grouped classes, honors and Advanced Placement programs, weighted grades, and seminar series.

Pull-Out Classes

Though some schools offer pull-out programs in middle school, the majority of pull-out classes for gifted students take place at the elementary school level. Typically, the gifted teacher in a pull-out program (also referred to as a resource-room program or send-out classes) will meet with anywhere from ten to thirty kids at a time, generally for a half or full day each week. Monday may be allotted to third graders, while Tuesday and Wednesday have cross-age groupings of fourth–fifth or fifth–sixth graders. Thursday might be a day where the pull-out teacher goes into regular classrooms and conducts some model lessons, and Friday might be reserved for more administrative tasks.

While the structure of a pull-out program is generally consistent, the focus of the learning that goes on there is quite varied. Three different ways of implementing this provision that we often see include the following:

- **A multiyear curriculum.** In some of the best-managed pull-out programs, gifted education teachers construct a multiyear curriculum that weaves topics from one year to the next. Thus, working under a multiyear theme of Change and Adaptation, fourth graders might focus on environmental changes; fifth graders may consider politics and the changes brought about under democracy, monarchy, and oligarchy; and sixth graders could investigate the changing roles of the family in various regions of North America. Though such multiyear linkages can provide a very rich experience for students, this type of programming is not the most commonly used approach for the pull-out provision.

- **Regular classroom extensions.** With this approach, the pull-out teacher relates the content of the pull-out program to the classroom curriculum. For example, if the fourth-grade science coursework deals with the solar system, a more in-depth exploration of space science may become a part of the pull-out program's focus.

- **Regional and national enrichment programs.** A number of enrichment programs (such as Odyssey of the Mind, the Future Problem Solving Program, and the Science Olympiad) can serve as the basis for a pull-out program's curriculum and structure. Additional activities may then center on the logical- and creative-thinking skills that underlie student success in these programs. (For more on enrichment and support programs, see pages 84–86.)

It's also quite common to see a fourth programming approach, in which the focus of the pull-out program becomes whatever the resource teacher decides it will be, usually based on the teacher's own interests and passions. In the hands of a competent, dynamic, well-versed teacher, the program content may be excellent. In the hands of someone less skilled or worldly, this type of pull-out focus ends up based more on whim than design.

When the study that led to the Pyramid Project plan was conducted, researchers found that pull-out classes were the most common way to serve gifted children at the elementary level. Even today, in an era of inclusion-based teaching, various forms of pull-out programs are very visible nationwide.

This is good . . . and this is bad. This option, as all the others that serve gifted children, has its benefits and drawbacks.

BENEFITS OF PULL-OUT CLASSES

Pull-out classes present benefits to both gifted students and to the schools that offer this programming provision:

- The classes provide gifted students a weekly opportunity to get together with intellectual peers and share "adventures" that capitalize on their individual strengths. (Many kids in our pull-out classes would never miss school on the day of their gifted class, even if they were coughing, wheezing, and miserable!)

- The pull-out class's curriculum is often open-ended enough to allow for individual talents and interests to be explored. The freedom to design interesting and worthwhile projects invokes the imagination and skill of the pull-out teacher and the gifted students who take part.

- Hiring a pull-out resource teacher yields a good deal of economic value for the school district. Generally, the teacher sees every identified gifted student in multiple grade levels and handles a good deal of parent phone calls, which many principals are only too happy to hand over to someone else. Also, the pull-out teacher often conducts inservice presentations or in-classroom lessons and handles myriad other functions that require heavy communication with a variety of audiences.

- The teacher in the pull-out program generally sees the same children over a number of years, getting to know them and their families on a highly personal level. This often proves very helpful in times of crisis or change, when the teacher is able to work knowledgeably and effectively with kids and parents alike.

DRAWBACKS OF PULL-OUT CLASSES

The pull-out program's drawbacks are many and well documented, and they begin even before children have left their regular classroom for the first time. For instance:

- Thoughtful coordination between the classroom curriculum and the pull-out program experiences may be lacking, causing some teachers to ask questions like, "What does model-airplane building have to do with fourth-grade science?"

- Because there is generally no assigned curriculum for the pull-out class, the teacher needs to be very conscious of not just providing fun, engaging activities that have very little relation to advanced levels of learning. Certainly, there is no shortage of curriculum materials and guides that teachers can access (see "Resources," pages 86–90), but some teachers fall back on doing projects that tap into their personal interests rather than capitalize on student strengths.

- There may be classroom teachers who resent that the gifted kids leave for one day a week. Occasionally, a teacher may take this resentment out on the students. The teacher may require the children to make up *every* page of missed homework, schedule major tests or introduce important new topics on the day the kids are gone, or plan classroom parties or field trips on pull-out days, causing the gifted students to make a choice that they should not have to make. Though rare, this very nonprofessional behavior does occur, and can lead to unhappy outcomes for students, teachers, and your gifted program.

- Since the children have a day set aside for a gifted class, some classroom teachers may not provide other advanced learning options for their gifted students over the rest of the week. Particularly because they are pulled in so many directions, teachers may feel that gifted kids have been "taken care of" and thus decide to focus on the needs of other students in the classroom.

"Gifted students must have their academic needs addressed every day in almost every academic area. A send-out experience once or twice a week will not, by itself, suffice."
—KAREN B. ROGERS

As with teaching gifted children in the regular classroom, there are ways to overcome some of the pull-out provision's drawbacks, including the distribution of a newsletter to teachers that explains what the resource teacher is doing in the program and how it ties in with the curriculum. Another useful strategy is for the resource teacher to switch places with a willing classroom teacher for a day (or part of one). This gives the classroom teacher an opportunity to work with the group of gifted students on a project the teacher chooses and offers the gifted specialist a window into the issues the teacher grapples with. The resource teacher could also offer to conduct a lesson with or for the classroom teacher. Pull-out programs can wither or bloom on the basis of sound communication, mutual understanding, and friendly overtures.

The Self-Contained Gifted Classroom

For many parents of elementary-aged gifted children, it sounds like a dream come true: a classroom where all the children are identified as gifted and they stay together day after day, year after year. And, in some ways, this situation can be the best possible way to prompt high achievement among a group of intellectual peers.

Districts that support self-contained gifted classes usually provide them during the elementary level only. In middle and high school, there may be *de facto* self-contained classes, if ability grouping (see page 79) is used to place students in their academic subjects, but the idea of a true self-contained class for all subjects is foreign once the school structure becomes a departmentalized one.

Like other gifted programming options, there are pluses and minuses to self-contained gifted classes. On the positive side, there are the following advantages:

- Instruction can more often be geared to higher levels of thinking and more challenging content.

- There is evidence that the achievement levels of students who participate in self-contained gifted classes are higher than those of gifted children who participate in pull-out type programs.

- In all but the smallest school districts, there is no additional cost involved with a self-contained class. For example, if the typical fourth-grade classroom in your district has twenty-eight kids, you would fill the gifted class with a similar number of kids who just happen to be gifted. These children would have to be placed *somewhere*, so placing them together is an economical choice for districts strapped for cash.

- The children are grouped with intellectual peers, so it is easier for them to discuss issues related to growing up gifted—peer pressure, perfectionism, unrealistic expectations of adults, and so forth.

- For identified gifted students who might hold back or whose gifts lose the teacher's focus in a regular classroom, the self-contained gifted class provides space and time where these students can blossom. The teacher has a daily chance to observe, work with, and get to know these children. There is also an opportunity for the class itself to become an environment of support and encouragement—for the gifted ESL student whose skills in math and visual imagery are remarkable, for the gifted girl who doesn't speak up as often or as loudly as some of her more loquacious classmates, and for the gifted boy who has a learning disability in writing yet has a way of relating a story orally that keeps the other kids on the edges of their seats. Frequently, these children shine more brightly and more consistently in a self-contained gifted class than in other settings.

The weaknesses of the self-contained option are both educational and political:

- If the self-contained class exists for three or four years, the children in it interact with few other children in their grade level. This can be ameliorated by arranging for all kids to spend time together in other situations (physical education, art, music, lunch), and these opportunities should be pursued. Some districts address this issue by making the self-contained class part of a team of two to four classrooms. Then, the gifted students interact with other kids on a daily basis.

- A logistical nightmare can occur if there are too few (or too many) gifted kids identified in a grade level in a particular year. We know of one district that had a dilemma of qualifying only fourteen children for the self-contained class in a particular year. The choices were to keep the class size to fourteen (and risk creating ill will with other teachers who had twenty-five or more kids in their own classrooms) or to place nonidentified children in the class to make up for the shortfall. If this were your district, what would your decision be? On the other hand, there could also be a "bumper crop" of kids identified as gifted in one grade level during a particular year—for example, thirty-five children when there is room for only thirty. Then the gifted committee is faced with having to decide who will *not* be enrolled in the class. Not many coordinators want to make the phone call to a parent that begins, "Hello. I'm sorry to have to tell you that, while your child qualifies for the gifted class, there isn't enough room for him."

- There may be the feeling on the part of some teachers, parents, and students that the school is selecting an elite group of children and isolating them from other kids. And the self-contained classroom can have a kind of "hothousing" effect on the gifted kids themselves, sometimes bringing about feelings of superiority. The division between "gifted" and "non-gifted" becomes crystal clear to everyone.

- Teachers may be unhappy about having all the high-achieving students removed from their classes, leaving few academic role models for other children to follow. While there is no evidence that other students languish in the absence of the most highly able ones, this perception will still exist in the minds of many. Related to this, occasionally a teacher will conclude that without gifted students in the classroom, there is no longer a need to differentiate the curriculum for the remaining students. This reflects a lack of understanding of the purpose of differentiation, which is to tailor instruction to meet the needs of *every* child.

Academic rigor is the greatest potential advantage of most self-contained classrooms for gifted students. This is subject, however, to the strength of the curriculum itself and how it is delivered. There is minimum value to a self-contained class where *every* student is reading the *same* book at the *same* time and taking the *same* tests and quizzes. If this occurs, the arrangement is not taking full advantage of the abilities and needs the students bring in as individuals. In the end, a self-contained class is only a placement decision. Beyond that, the curriculum and teaching methods still need to be modified to meet specific needs of the kids.

Ability-Grouped Classes

Ability-grouped classes generally occur in middle and high schools. The two most common subject areas for ability grouping are math and language arts. Based on previous high performance or on high potential, students are "channeled" into classes with other kids who share high ability in those subjects. Most often, the teachers are not trained in gifted-child education, yet many often have high expectations for their students and allow more diverse and complex ways for students to show what they know.

For years, there has been an active controversy about the merits of ability grouping for students, especially at the middle school level. Critics like Hank Levin, Robert Slavin, Jeannie Oakes, and Linda Darling-Hammond attest that it is unfair in a democratic society to separate some children from others on the basis of perceived intellectual ability. They state that when children are grouped in classes based on high ability, teachers of the "slower" classes tend to lower their expectations for their students, while the high-achieving students are pushed to their academic limit. Also, critics of ability grouping cite the lack of role models for children when the brightest kids are all assigned to different classes. Too, these critics (especially Levin) contend that if all children were given the type of instruction and curriculum that the gifted students receive, most students—not only those who are gifted—would succeed at much higher levels than they do currently.

There is much evidence, nonetheless, that gifted children *do* benefit when they are grouped together academically. The work of Karen Rogers (see page 87) is most prominent in this regard, as is the research of James and Chen-Lin Kulik. In study after study, the range and depth of knowledge of gifted students in ability-grouped classes has been found to increase when compared with those gifted kids who are not grouped in this way.

A key point on which opponents and proponents of ability grouping seem to agree is that it is wrong to "track" students in an inflexible arrangement. For example, students in an English class for highly able young people should not automatically be included in the highest-level math or science courses. These latter subjects may not be an individual student's strength areas, and they may be strengths for students not selected for the advanced English class. Herein lies an important distinction: *ability grouping* is a flexible arrangement that is practiced based on students' talents in particular subjects, while *tracking* is the inflexible placement of students in either all-honors-level or no-honors-level courses. You aren't likely to find many educators who promote tracking. Ability grouping, though, makes eminent sense to many.

**IS ABILITY GROUPING
CONTROVERSIAL IN YOUR DISTRICT?**

Within a range of other services, ability grouping is a useful and often essential tool. If it is controversial in your district, here are steps you can take:

1. Read the research of Karen Rogers and share its highlights with school board members. Her book *Re-Forming Gifted Education* has an excellent chapter on grouping. The Winter 2002 issue of *Tempo* from the Texas Association for the Gifted (TAGT) is also devoted to the issue of grouping, and includes an article by Rogers along with many others.

2. Raise the very real distinction between tracking and ability grouping.

3. Recruit an articulate student who has benefited from ability-grouped classes to address the school board on their importance.

4. If the question is raised, stress that services for kids of lower ability is a separate issue from the matter of ability grouping gifted kids. Your concern in this time and place is in developing and sustaining options for gifted young people. Gifted students are *not* "better" than anybody else, and offering them instruction geared to their known levels of intellect or ability is *not* special treatment. It is a legitimate and necessary effort to do what we strive for with *all* students: to match their needs with programs and classes that address these needs.

5. End with the Felix Frankfurter quotation (see below).

Figure 4.1

"It was a wise man who said that there is no greater inequality than the equal treatment of unequals."
—Felix Frankfurter, U.S. Supreme Court Justice, 1939–1962

High School Honors and Advanced Placement (AP) Classes

There are three general types of specialized offerings to serve gifted high school students. *Honors* classes are advanced courses with an accelerated and challenging curriculum provided by the school. (Honors classes are present in both middle and high schools.) *Concurrent enrollment* offers college-level classes to high school students, who receive both high school and college credit. *Advanced Placement (AP)* is an internationally formalized system that gives students an opportunity to take college-level courses and exams while attending high school. Around the world, 13,000 secondary schools participate. There are thirty-three specialized AP courses offered in nineteen subject areas. (See "Resources," page 87, for more information about the Advanced Placement Program®.)

Much of the emphasis of such offerings is on preparing for college. Gifted kids should begin planning for college somewhere between fifth and eighth grade. The students and their parents should be provided with the latest guides to college selection, information about private scholarship sources, and a list of recommended courses to take through middle and high school. This is also a time to encourage students to begin keeping a portfolio of activities and accomplishments and to develop and routinely update a résumé.

Many of the same arguments you may hear against self-contained and ability-grouped classes in elementary and middle school are likely to come up in regard to advanced courses in high school, so we won't repeat them here. However, the controversy is not typically as electric when it comes to high school, for several reasons:

- There exists at the high school level a long history of providing options to address various future-oriented needs of students on the cusp of adulthood. In this environment, the presence of vocational classes, advanced courses, intensive arts programming, and other opportunities is usually readily accepted.

- There is generally quite a degree of flexibility and choice built into high school students' schedules, especially in the junior and senior years. Indeed, it is now common to see advanced-level students taking "college in the schools" or Internet-based university courses during the regular school day.

- Colleges and universities, especially selective or highly competitive institutions, rely heavily on the presence of honors and AP classes to determine admission. In addition, scholarship money is often tied to a student's ability and willingness to carry a heavy load of difficult coursework. Thus, *not* offering advanced classes puts *all* college-bound students at a disadvantage, and this will remain true until colleges alter their admissions requirements.

The question of who should be admitted to honors or AP courses is sometimes an issue, but the majority of schools are willing to give the benefit of the doubt to students who express a desire to stretch their academic wings. In fact, the most common criterion for admission to advanced classes is that the student has satisfactorily completed (with a grade of C or better) any prerequisite coursework. Again, this is similar to the system used at most universities. The only time to have strong concerns about student placement in advanced courses is if the push is coming from the parent while the student has expressed no interest in accepting the challenge.

AP classes conclude with a nationally based test of content. Colleges nationwide may award students academic credit based on the results of these tests, and it is not uncommon for a highly able high school senior to enter college as a sophomore, having collected thirty or more credits through AP programming.

Two of the more common foibles we see in high schools involve AP coursework and testing.

The first concern relates to the curriculum. By design, AP courses are highly structured. For example, a teacher handling an AP biology course must follow a curriculum that is similar for anyone, anywhere taking that course. Some teachers deviate from the curriculum and teach what they believe is important in the chosen subject. While these might be fine teachers who enjoy working with facile young minds, they do a disservice to the students enrolled in the AP options, for when it comes time to take the AP tests, the students will likely be ill prepared.

This issue can become political, because AP courses are often awarded to teachers who have been at the school the longest. While tenured teachers may feel they have earned the chance to teach the top kids, it's appropriate for them to teach AP classes only if they agree to prepare the AP students for the test that lies ahead in May. A win-win solution here is to offer two types of high-level classes: (1) AP courses that follow the AP curriculum closely and (2) honors-level courses that are not AP based. Teachers who feel stifled by the AP curriculum can then be assigned to the non-AP honors classes.

Another issue: Some schools are not forthcoming in letting students know about the AP tests. The tests are optional, but students cannot earn college credit without taking them. AP tests cost money (presently about $75 each), and financial assistance is available in most states. It is incumbent upon high school teachers and counselors to clearly urge students to take the AP tests and to provide information on getting help with testing costs. Whether paid by the student or through financial aid, the fee is a small price to pay for earning three or four college credits, tuition free.

Weighted Grades

Consider this: You are a high school student who is intent on graduating at the top of your class. You look at the course schedule, and you see a class called Advanced Chemistry and another class called Everyday Chemistry. Knowing that it will be difficult to get an A in Advanced Chemistry (you know others who have taken it, and they say it's really tough), you opt for Everyday Chemistry, where you may not learn anything more than the restorative properties of gelatin, but at least you'll earn an A.

In a school with weighted grades, this scenario would probably not take place. Weighted grades give credit—literally and figuratively—to students willing to accept the challenge of a difficult class. Although all kinds of numerical formulas are used to arrive at the actual weight, essentially it boils down to this: a grade of B in Advanced Chemistry gets the same amount of credit as an A in Everyday Chemistry; a B in the advanced course earns a 4.0, and an A in that course earns a 4.5 or a 5.0.

There is some bias against weighted grades. First, there are educators who believe students should not be rewarded for doing their job; if a young person is smart, the student belongs in advanced courses and shouldn't receive special grading considerations because of the workload. These critics will say that lower-level classes are just as hard for someone without exceptional intellect, and that it's wrong to give added advantage to a gifted student for working up to potential.

A second concern comes in regard to determining which courses should receive the added weight. Most people would probably agree that advanced calculus or physics should qualify, but what about the school's most arduous art course, or that physical education elective that makes boot camp look like playschool? We've found that a reasonable way around this issue is to leave it up to each department (English, History, Math, and so forth) to decide which courses should qualify for weighted credit, with a rationale provided for each course selected.

Another question involves the difficulty in interpreting transfer students' transcripts when weighted grades are involved. In fact, there have been lawsuits filed when a student from a weighted-grade high school transfers into one without weighted grades. In determining a final grade point average (GPA) for scholarships and for naming the valedictorian, a newly arrived student's grade credits of 5.0 create an imbalance in a system where 4.0 is the top. What is called for here is a policy, written by a high school committee of educators, explaining how this situation will be handled. Because transfer-student transcripts can introduce this dilemma, it's important to have a policy in place regardless of whether your school does or does not have weighted grades.

Despite some glitches, we believe in the utility of weighted grades—and so do colleges and universities. Although many institutions of higher learning are now computing their own GPAs for students, counting only those courses that they see as solidly academic, the presence of advanced classes and the high commitment of excellence they require is more visible with a weighted-grade structure. More important, weighted grades encourage gifted kids to choose classes that will stimulate and challenge them rather than to coast through courses that basically just fill their time.

Seminar Series

With the operation of gifted programs in middle school or high school, scheduling presents a large challenge. It's a rare secondary-level classroom teacher who wants to be interrupted every week with the imposition of a pull-out program, as this wreaks havoc with scheduled tests, group projects, and assemblies. Also, students get caught in the very real bind of having so many responsibilities and so much makeup work that they question their commitment to the gifted education option.

One way that some school districts have addressed this concern is through a series of scheduled all-day seminars. In Twinsburg, Ohio (Jim's school district), Project Plus is the program for identified gifted students in grades 7 and 8. As part of Project Plus, for two days each academic quarter, thirty to forty gifted students spend the entire day enmeshed in learning about a career-related topic or one of general interest. For the first two hours of each day, students are introduced to the topic through lectures, films, Internet searches, guest speakers, or simulations. The remainder of the day typically involves a stimulating field trip. As students participate in more and more seminars, discussion centers around the many unique facets of life that encompass our world.

Teachers are asked at the beginning of the school year if they would like to attend a specific trip that ties in with their interests or area of teaching expertise—and the list of volunteers is always longer than the available trips! Since teachers know the schedule of seminars for the entire year and since students know it is their responsibility to coordinate any missed assignments or class projects ahead of time, logistical problems are minimal. In fact, in four years only one student chose to drop out of this optional gifted pro-

gram, proving its success in terms of both content and operation.

An additional benefit is that the Twinsburg seminars tie in with the school's commitment to community service. For example, prior to visiting a homeless shelter, items of need are collected for distribution there. Following a visit to the burn unit of a local children's hospital, a fund-raising evening of poetry and song is held at the local library, bringing in enough money to send several children recuperating from severe burns to a unique summer camp.

Project Plus provides only one example of how seminar series can be incorporated into a school or district's gifted education program. Often, they provide a low-cost adjunct to other gifted services offered through secondary schools. Tapping into both student interest and community resources, everyone wins.

EXAMPLES OF PROJECT PLUS MIDDLE SCHOOL SEMINARS IN TWINSBURG, OHIO

**Having Your Day in Court:
The Career of Law, and Its Practice**

The day begins with a visit by an FBI agent, who speaks to students about crime detection and the problem-solving processes used to solve crimes. Then students visit two different courthouses, observing trials, arraignments, and/or jury selection. The students also have the opportunity to speak directly to judges about the law profession and to take a brief tour of the Akron Police Museum.

**Computers, Model Ts, and Cessnas:
Understanding Math and Technology
Through Inventions**

It's Math Day at the Western Reserve Historical Museum. Through hands-on exploration of antique cars and historic aircraft, students apply principles of algebra, probability, and other mathematical concepts. A brief visit to the Federal Reserve Bank of Cleveland follows.

To Have or Have Not: A Study of Contrasts

Does where you live determine your importance? On this day, students visit two of Akron's treasures: The Stan Hywet Mansion (home of a former rubber baron) and the Haven of Rest Shelter for the Homeless. In both places, students learn of the history of each residence and the people who called or call these places home.

Figure 4.2

Special Schools for Gifted Students

There are a variety of special public schools for gifted students, known by names like *magnet schools* or *Governor's Schools* or by the individual school's emphasis (fine and performing arts, science and technology, and so forth). Sometimes, these schools are entirely separate (for example, a public school in a large city or county that is dedicated to arts education), but just as often there will be a school-within-a-school. Both

---

EXAMPLES OF MAGNET SCHOOL PROGRAMS

Stargate Charter School, Thornton, Colorado
This K–8 school for intellectually gifted children relies on a strong teacher-parent partnership to foster core values that include continual improvement, lifelong learning, diversity, self-esteem, love of learning, personal responsibility, and role models. Programming is based on the districtwide curriculum and uses innovative instructional strategies tailored to intellectually gifted students. Highlights of the program include Montessori kindergarten, individualized learning plans for each student, foreign language instruction at all levels, multiage classrooms, continuous progress, portfolios, checklists, frequent field trips and speakers, and direct parent involvement. Stargate students are highly involved in community service and can also enroll in before- and after-school enrichment programs, Destination ImagiNation, Club Amigos (a Spanish-language support program), and additional extracurricular activities. Throughout the year the school also offers several Parents' Nights Out—evenings with planned activities for children so dads and moms can have a needed break.

Whitney M. Young Middle School, Cleveland, Ohio
Ohio's only coeducational public school for gifted and talented students in grades 6 through 8 offers its students extensive academic experiences appropriate to the levels and learning styles of gifted children while also developing creativity, critical thinking, and leadership. Following the middle school concept, students are arranged into four teams, moving through their classes together and sharing the same core teachers. Whitney Young students participate in numerous charitable programs and activities, including fund-raisers for the Special Olympics and the United Negro College Fund. Peer mediation and tutoring are also strong components of life at Whitney Young. Upon graduation, students frequently attend either one of Cleveland's magnet high schools or various private schools throughout Ohio and the U.S.

Samuel Morse Middle School, Milwaukee, Wisconsin
A U.S. Office of Education "School of Excellence," Samuel Morse states that its mission is to "assure that the special needs of gifted and talented students are understood and accommodated." This is done through a diverse curriculum that includes among its offerings honors courses, a project-oriented math/science/technology lab, foreign language immersion classes, and FAVE (Fine Arts, Vocational Education), which covers everything from study skills to dance to Junior Great Books. The student body of nearly 1,100 is representative of Milwaukee's varied ethnic, cultural, and socioeconomic backgrounds. Approximately one-third of the students come from the district's elementary magnet schools for the gifted, while the remaining students are from throughout the district's other schools.

Distinguished Scholar Program (DSP), Belleville, Illinois
Housed within Belleville Township High School West, DSP meets the needs of identified gifted ninth through twelfth graders. Providing a four-year curriculum developed specifically for these students, DSP guarantees all students access to all honors classes without schedule conflicts. Comprehensive personal and college counseling services are offered, and a weighted grade structure is used in the extensive DSP offerings in math, history, the sciences, and the humanities. Teachers are selected for both their content knowledge and their interest and expertise in teaching gifted students. Twenty-five students per year are invited to become Distinguished Scholars.

Robert A. Millikan High School, Long Beach, California
The QUEST Program (Questioning, Understanding, Engaging Success through Technology) provides a curriculum that integrates the disciplines through a thematic, problem-solving approach to learning. QUEST engages students in real-world activities and experiences and enables them to use technology for research and to produce multimedia presentations. Individual, ongoing projects are required each year, as are internships and apprenticeships. During grades 9 and 10, half of each day is devoted to interdisciplinary instruction in flexible time blocks with other QUEST students. The other half of each day is spent in foreign language instruction, the arts, physical education, and other activities that place QUEST students in touch with other students at Millikan. In grades 11 and 12, honors and AP courses are the norm, with extended time available to pursue individual interests and internships. Student success is judged through portfolios, exhibitions, written tests, self-evaluations of work, evaluations by community members, and exit interviews.

Figure 4.3

structures have much to offer, especially for urban or large suburban school districts.

The term "magnet schools" is an apt one, as these schools are designed to "attract" students to them because of the variety and intensity of special programs offered. Not all magnet schools or specialty schools are strictly for gifted students. Generally, the magnets are open to all students, although there may be a portion of the school program open exclusively to those identified as gifted. Some elementary magnet schools house within them *all* of the community's gifted and talented classes (often, self-contained), so parents must agree to send their kids to this school if they want their children enrolled in a full-time gifted program.

A downside of the magnet concept is that in order for students to attend, some have to be bused long distances to reach it. An upside is that this kind of voluntary busing helps promote diversity within the school.

The quality of education found in most magnet programs and schools is often superior and the cost to run them is minimally more than it would cost to operate a typical comprehensive elementary, middle, or high school. Of course, the magnet concept works best in larger communities, where the numbers of students make this concept feasible. For those who live in rural communities, a different option may suffice: independent study. See "Resources," page 87, for a description of the Independent Study High School, whose programming is available worldwide.

There are other opportunities for gifted students to participate in advanced study programs, either in a separate school or a school-within-a-school arrangement. A widely accepted form of the latter is the International Baccalaureate Organization (IBO). The IBO is growing in popularity all over the world. There are approximately 1,200 authorized IBO world schools (often called IB programs) in over 100 countries. Descriptions of these programs for elementary, middle school, and high school settings are also described on page 87.

Other Options for Serving Gifted Kids

Within and outside of the pyramid for gifted services lie two other opportunities for gifted students: mentorships and a variety of enrichment and support programs. These might take place during school or after school and in the regular classroom, a pull-out class, or a specialized class or school. In addition, summer and off-track programs offer yet another forum for continued learning.

Mentorships. You can find special expert mentors to hook up with your students and provide expanded educational opportunities. A teacher who has an active interest in poetry or has published a book might mentor a student who is a gifted writer. A local legislator may become a mentor for a student interested in law. Depending on specific interests and inclinations, a mathematically gifted student might be paired with an actuary or an architect.

Often, parents or the guidance office can assist with or facilitate a mentor program. From the school and community, they can solicit volunteers who are interested in and willing to take the time to do this. They must take care to work with people and agencies that are known to the school.

Mentors might do any or all of the following:

- help individual students advance their skills, talents, and knowledge

- provide feedback on projects

- introduce students to real-life applications within their areas of interest

- answer students' questions

Enrichment and support programs. Although enrichment or support programs do *not* constitute a gifted program, there are many challenging and competitive experiences available that can strengthen and enrich your gifted education plan. Some are focused on math, literature, the arts, or sciences, sometimes combined with social problem solving and ethical decision making, like this program in Barbara's district:

> *Students aboard the spaceship **Voyager** at the Christa McAuliffe Space Education Center in Pleasant Grove, Utah, are struggling with an ethical question. Should they allow Rool, a slave from another quadrant of the galaxy, to board their ship? Should they risk the safety of their crew in order to defend Rool's civil rights? Suddenly **Voyager's** scanner officer detects another ship approaching through the wormhole. It is the **Pennou** pursuing the escaped slave, Rool. The security officer grows alert, ready to seize any intruder who might attempt to sneak aboard the ship, while the ambassador and captain ask for advice from the twenty-eight crew members. They haven't much time. "Raise the shields!" the captain shouts.*

There are many enrichment programs that encourage student service as well. Service can be a powerful tool for use with the gifted student, if it is problem based. Such service supports character development, helping students learn about compassion,

	PRIMARY	UPPER ELEMENTARY	MIDDLE SCHOOL	HIGH SCHOOL
REGULAR CLASSROOM	• Early entrance, grade acceleration • Learning centers • Curriculum compacting • Cluster grouping (critical and creative thinking) • Differentiated curriculum • Math and music go round • High-interest focus units (animals, natural world, culture) • Arts focus • Writing lab • Genre reading	• Grade acceleration • Curriculum compacting • Accelerated coursework • Cluster grouping • Differentiated curriculum • Resident expert • Independent study • Invent America!	• Curriculum compacting • Accelerated coursework • Cluster grouping • Ability grouping • Independent study • Differentiated curriculum • Distance learning • Learning centers • Science fair	• Accelerated coursework • Distance learning • Independent study • Differentiated curriculum • District "Scholar Track" option • Math/science/technology fair
SPECIAL CLASSES	• Math/science pull-outs • Field trips • Wonder of words • World band • FPSP • Older buddy groups (K-2 with grades 3-5) • Community service groups	• Pull-out classes • Science Olympiad • FPSP • National written and illustrated by awards contest • Band, orchestra, chorus, art club • Math contest • Older buddy groups (int - 2) • Community service groups	• Math Olympics • Debate teams • Scholastic writing awards • Foreign language (at Bridge High School) • Performing arts productions • District & mentor program • College prep and planning groups • All-school activities and clubs	• AP classes • Concurrent enrollment • Mentorships • PSAT/SAT prep classes • Mock trial • All-school activities, clubs, organizations
SPECIAL SCHOOL(S)	• Excelsior performing arts magnet school • District 8 school for the highly gifted	• Spanish immersion school • Excelsior performing arts magnet school • District 8 school for the highly gifted	• District 8 school for the highly gifted	• Semester abroad • IB program (Bridge High School) • Performing arts high school

Appropriate pacing?

Provisions for social and emotional needs?

Figure 4.4

understanding, responsibility, decision making, and leadership. Both through enrichment and as part of the regular curriculum, gifted children need a range of problem-based educational experiences that aid and promote sound character traits. Adults should function as facilitators of student service experiences. In a well-administered problem-based program, students should identify a problem based on community need or as an extension of the curriculum, research different sides of the issue, choose a solution and implement their plan of action, and reflect on and evaluate their experience. You will find descriptions of many support and enrichment programs beginning on page 87.

Summer and off-track programs. Summer and off-track programs offer opportunities for additional challenges during the time that students are not attending school. To design these programs:

- Survey local schools to see what challenging experiences are being offered.

- If you are near a university or a college or junior college, contact the institution for programs and classes that they might offer.

- Check for educational programs offered by community organizations, such as Boys and Girls Clubs, scouts, and 4-H. Sometimes these organizations offer challenging experiences.

- Contact your State Board of Education or any professional organizations for suggestions.

- Contact your state organization for gifted children and ask for suggestions for appropriate programs.

- Contact district gifted program coordinators to glean their suggestions.

- Check the NAGC Web site (page 7) for national summer programs for gifted students.

In weaving together the elements of your gifted program, you may wish to use the "Gifted Programming Planner" form on page 69. (Make an enlarged copy if you need more writing space.) As you discuss and plan provisions, keep in mind the Pyramid Project plan discussed in Survival Strategy 3.

Figure 4.4 (page 85) shows an example of a completed planning form, one that is representative of an established program developed over time in a large school district. If you are beginning from scratch, or from a few existing offerings, plan to build gradually, a bit at a time. Start by identifying a few opportunities that will offer the most meaningful support you can both afford *and* physically manage in order to address the needs you have identified, the students you want to serve, and the mission and goals you have set.

Notes

1. The quote on page 71 and some additional information in the "Early Entrance and Acceleration" section are from *Teaching Young Gifted Children in the Regular Classroom: Identifying, Nurturing, and Challenging Ages 4–9* by Joan Franklin Smutny, Sally Yahnke Walker, and Elizabeth A. Meckstroth (Minneapolis: Free Spirit Publishing, 1997), pages 176–178. Used with permission.

2. These considerations are highlighted in "Making Wise Choices in Grouping the Gifted" by Karen B. Rogers, in *Tempo* (a publication of the Texas Association for the Gifted and Talented) 12:1 (Winter 2002).

3. Sally M. Reis, et al., "Why Not Let High Ability Students Start School in January? The Curriculum Compacting Study" (Storrs, CT: NRC/GT, 1993) (RBRD 93106).

Resources

The following resources apply specifically to topics addressed in this strategy's chapter. For a complete list of gifted education resources, see pages 146–154.

Grouping and Differentiation

Curriculum Compacting: The Complete Guide to Modifying the Regular Curriculum for High Ability Students by Sally M. Reis, Joseph S. Renzulli, and Deborah H. Burns (Mansfield Center, CT: Creative Learning Press, 1992). This book offers a practical, step-by-step approach to compacting. Find out how to modify curricula, pretest students, and prepare enrichment options for grades K–12.

The Differentiated Classroom: Responding to the Needs of All Learners by Carol Ann Tomlinson (Alexandria, VA: Association for Supervision and Curriculum Development, 1999). This basic introduction to differentiation describes its primary elements and offers ways to incorporate its methods into the classroom.

Differentiating Instruction in the Regular Classroom: How to Reach and Teach All Learners, Grades 3–12 by Diane Heacox (Minneapolis: Free Spirit Publishing, 2002). Presents a menu of strategies including differentiating discussions, creating tiered assignments, matrix plans for designing curriculum units, and lesson plans that encompass content, process skills, and evidence of learning. Individual chapters focus on evaluation in a differentiated classroom and how to manage both behavior and work tasks. Includes a wealth of reproducible templates and forms.

It's About Time: Inservice Strategies for Curriculum Compacting by Alane J. Starko (Mansfield Center, CT: Creative Learning Press, 1986). This book provides step-by-step guidelines for conducting inservice presentations on curriculum compacting. Topics include methods for compacting the regular curriculum, techniques for assessing mastery, simulation activities, and more. If you can't find this book in your bookstore or library, contact the publisher toll-free at 1-888-518-8004 or at *www.creativelearning press.com*.

Leadership for Differentiating Schools & Classrooms by Carol Ann Tomlinson and Susan Demirsky Allan (Alexandria, VA: Association for Supervision and Curriculum Development, 2000). A practical guide for school leaders developing differentiated classrooms that address the needs of individual learners, this book offers techniques that can be used on a schoolwide basis.

Re-Forming Gifted Education: Matching the Program to the Child by Karen B. Rogers (Scottsdale, AZ: Great Potential Press, 2002). This book is a fine resource for your committee and for parents and teachers interested in honing in on the best options for individual children. Grouping practices and acceleration and enrichment options are discussed with a rundown of the benefits and set-up procedures for each.

Teaching Gifted Kids in the Regular Classroom: Strategies and Techniques Every Teacher Can Use to Meet the Academic Needs of the Gifted and Talented by Susan Winebrenner (Minneapolis: Free Spirit Publishing, 2001). This revised, expanded, and updated edition of a gifted classic is an invaluable resource on differentiating instruction in the inclusive classroom model. The book offers strategies and techniques for meeting the needs of the gifted without extra planning or preparation of lesson plans.

Teaching Young Gifted Children in the Regular Classroom: Identifying, Nurturing, and Challenging Ages 4–9 by Joan Franklin Smutny, Sally Yahnke Walker, and Elizabeth A. Meckstroth (Minneapolis: Free Spirit Publishing, 1997). A comprehensive resource for developing programming and curriculum for young children, this guide offers practical strategies and techniques for compacting the curriculum, documenting student development, teaching to multiple intelligences, and more.

Davidson Institute for Talent Development
9665 Gateway Drive, Suite B
Reno, NV 89521
(775) 852-3483
www.ditd.org

The Davidson Institute seeks out profoundly gifted young people and supports their educational and developmental needs. The Institute's Web site is an excellent tool for educators, providing comprehensive information on all aspects of giftedness. Specifically, find information on grouping by gifted expert Karen Rogers by visiting the site and searching for her name under the "PG Cybersource" listing.

Advanced Placement, Concurrent Enrollment, and College Planning

College Planning for Gifted Students by Sandra L. Berger (Reston, VA: Council for Exceptional Children, 1989). Directions and information for careful college preparation for the gifted.

Think College? Me? Now? A Handbook for Students in Middle School and Junior High School (Washington, DC: U.S. Department of Education, 1998). This online government publication explains to students the benefits of secondary education, the many options available, an analysis of college costs, and courses and activities that offer preparation for secondary education. Find it located at *www.ed.gov/pubs/CollegeMeNow.*

National Alliance of Concurrent Enrollment Partnerships
www.nacep.org

This Web site provides information about concurrent enrollment as well as a listing of colleges and universities in the United States and Canada with available programs.

College Board
45 Columbus Avenue
New York, NY 10023-6992
(212) 713-8000
www.collegeboard.org

Contact College Board for information on the Advanced Placement Program®.

Specialized Programs and Schools

Independent Study High School (ISHS)
P.O. Box 839400
Lincoln, NE 68583-9400
1-866-700-4747
www.nebraskahs.unl.edu

In 1929, fourteen high school students from Crookston, Nebraska, enrolled in correspondence courses at the University of Nebraska. Today, this correspondence program has grown to include students in every U.S. state and 135 nations. Currently, more than 6,000 students enroll in more than 15,000 classes annually, making ISHS one of the world's largest high schools—without a campus! Communication takes place through fax, mail, and the Internet. While some students enroll for only a course or two, others enroll in ISHS as their full-time high school. A fully accredited high school, ISHS provides a diverse offering of courses. Each course costs about $300, with limited scholarships available.

International Baccalaureate Organization (IBO)
IBO North America
475 Riverside Drive, Suite 240
New York, NY 10115
(212) 696-4464
www.ibo.org

The IBO offers three programs to schools:

• Diploma Programme: A rigorous pre-university course of studies. It is a comprehensive two-year curriculum for secondary students, available in English, French, and Spanish, that allows students to meet requirements of various national education systems. Students who earn IB diplomas gain admission to universities around the world. Highly respected, the program is for ages 16–19.

• Middle Years Programme (MYP): This program provides a thorough study of various disciplines, with an emphasis on their interrelatedness. Authorized schools are evaluated regularly to ensure that IBO programs meet assessment standards. The program is for ages 11–16.

• Primary Years Programme (PYP): This program provides an opportunity for students to learn through concept-driven inquiry. Traditional academic subjects are part of the program, which emphasizes the interrelatedness of knowledge and skills. The program is for ages 3–12.

Enrichment Programs

Following are several examples of enrichment programs. The book listed directly below offers information on programs from a variety of topic areas. Thereafter, programs are broken into main curriculum areas.

Academic Competitions for Gifted Students: A Resource Book for Teachers and Parents by Mary K. Tallent-Runnels and Ann C. Candler-Lotven (Thousand Oaks, CA: Corwin Press, 1996). This guide provides information on challenging competitions for gifted children. Useful for directing enrichment projects, the book has criteria to help educators decide on programs and competitions best suited to students' strengths.

LANGUAGE ARTS

National Federation of State High School Association (NFHS)
P.O. Box 690
Indianapolis, IN 46206
(317) 972-6900
www.nfhs.org

Description: The NFHS Speech, Debate, and Theatre Association provides opportunities for creating high school speech, drama, and debate programs, with inservice training available.

Purpose: This organization works toward the establishment of a strong network of educators to work with students participating in speech, drama, and debate.

Audience: Secondary students.

National Forensic League
P.O. Box 38
Ripon, WI 54971
(920) 748-6206
www.nflonline.org

Description: The NFL provides competition opportunities for high school students to continue on from local, regional, and state competitions to compete in the national tournament in a number of areas that include debate, impromptu speaking, and poetry and prose reading.

Purpose: The purpose of the contest is to encourage proficiency in the forensic arts of debate, public speaking, and interpretation.

Audience: Secondary students.

National Language Arts League
P.O. Box 2196
St. James, NY 11780
(631) 584-2016
www.continentalmathematicsleague.com

Description: Designed by language arts teachers, this program can be held in school on any day during a two-week period. The contest consists of multiple-choice questions covering spelling, vocabulary, reading comprehension, analogies, grammar, and other topics.

Purpose: This program seeks to strengthen language arts skills in students. High school contests can be a benefit toward student preparation for the SAT, ACT, or achievement tests.

Audience: Grades 2–12.

Scholastic Art & Writing Awards
557 Broadway
New York, NY 10012
(212) 343-6100
www.artandwriting.org

Description: All students may enter the competition, with or without official school sponsorship. Entries must be original, with judges evaluating the imaginative content and form of projects. A number of categories for both writing and art are open to competition. More than 600 art awards and 300 writing awards are presented each year on the national level. Winners may receive cash awards, certificates, scholarships, and publishing and exhibition opportunities.

Purpose: These awards are intended to encourage talented and dedicated young writers and artists.

Audience: Grades 7–12.

MATHEMATICS

American Mathematics Competitions
Mathematical Association of America
P.O. Box 81606
Lincoln, NE 68501-1606
1-800-527-3690
www.unl.edu/amc

Description: The Mathematical Association of America offers many programs for secondary students. One of these programs is the USA Mathematical Olympiad (USAMO), a two-day competition that includes six questions. Students must undergo a very challenging qualification process to participate in the program. Contact the Mathematical Association of America for information on this and the many other programs available.

Purpose: This organization's programs serve to strengthen the mathematical capabilities of the nation's youth, providing them with opportunities to compete with other students around the country and world.

Audience: Secondary school students.

American Regions Mathematics League
711 Amsterdam Avenue
New York, NY 10025
www.arml.com

Description: This organization's annual contest includes both team and individual competition. Often called the "World Series" of mathematics, the contest consists of rounds of short-answer questions. The Power Round encourages mathematical analysis and proof. Participants must expand and generalize; their conclusions are put together in the form of a report. Students participate at a host college, where local, state, and national competitions are held.

Purpose: This program aims to promote excellence in mathematics. For the highest-achieving math students, it offers a wonderful challenge.

Audience: High school students.

Continental Mathematics League
P.O. Box 2196
St. James, NY 11780
(631) 584-2016
www.continentalmathematicsleague.com

Description: This organization offers a series of math meets for students in grades 2–9, a calculus league for high school students, and a computer programming contest.

Purpose: Meets are intended to inspire students toward excellence in mathematics and related subjects.

Audience: Grades 2–12.

Mathematical Olympiads for Elementary and Middle Schools
2154 Bellmore Avenue
Bellmore, NY 11710-5645
1-866-781-2411
www.moems.org

Description: This program provides contests involving math concepts, strategies for problem solving, creativity, resourcefulness, and ingenuity. It consists of five contests during the school year. Students can prepare ahead of time from the curricular materials contained in the program, which provide different strategies for solving similar problems. The Math Olympiads program doesn't overtake a regular math program, but extends it. Some schools have incorporated the program with an investment of just one hour per week during the five contest months. Teams may consist of thirty-five students.

Purpose: This challenging program teaches students to think, to reason, and to understand mathematical concepts and strategies. It also increases interest and enthusiasm for math.

Audience: Grades 4–8.

The Stock Market Game
120 Broadway, 35th Floor
New York, NY 10271-0080
(212) 313-1350
www.smgww.org

Description: This game provides teachers with a tool to introduce students to principles of economics, finance, and capital formation. It can be used with a national or global focus and employs an interdisciplinary approach involving social studies, language areas, economics, science, and mathematics. The competition lasts for ten weeks during the fall and spring of each year.

Purpose: To motivate students and to increase their knowledge of the stock market as it applies to all areas of life. The program recognizes excellence of achievement through the competition.

Audience: Grades 4–12.

TIVY—Home and Classroom Activity
TIVY Games
8205 Brownsville Lane
Bethany, OK 73008-3038
(405) 491-9706

Description: TIVY is a home and classroom activity for two to four players. Players move their Tivots across a game board, using strategy and critical-thinking skills to create the highest-scoring math problems. Players solve the math problems to determine a winner.

Purpose: This game will motivate and challenge your best math students, and help them to improve their problem-solving and critical-thinking skills.

Audience: Grades 4–9.

SCIENCE

Intel International Science and Engineering Fair
Society for Science & the Public
1719 N Street NW
Washington, DC 20036
(202) 785-2255
www.societyforscience.org

Description: The Intel ISEF is a science competition that brings together over 1,200 students and 40 nations to compete for scholarships, tuition grants, scientific field trips, and a grand prize trip to the Nobel Prize Award Ceremony in Stockholm, Sweden. Intel ISEF is both a competition and an enrichment program, creating opportunities for students to create science projects. Fairs are conducted at local, regional, state, and national levels.

Purpose: This program enhances accomplishment in science through competition. It provides incentive for scientific investigation, motivation, and excellence for participating students.

Audience: Grades 9–12.

Invent America!
United States Patent Model Foundation
P.O. Box 26065
Alexandria, VA 22313
(410) 489-2802
www.inventamerica.org

Description: Invent America! is an exciting program that helps students find creative solutions to everyday problems through the process of inventing. Students can compete in local, state,

and national competitions. Contact Invent America! for free program materials.

Purpose: Students discover new ways to use skills they are learning in math, science, art, language, library science, and other topic areas.

Audience: Grades K–8.

Science Olympiad
2 Trans Am Plaza Drive, Suite 415
Oakbrook Terrace, IL 60181
(630) 792-1251
www.soinc.org

Description: This organization offers a series of individual and team interscholastic competitions held on local, state, and national levels. The competitions, which follow the formats of popular board games, TV shows, and athletic games, encourage learning in biology, earth science, chemistry, physics, and technology.

Purpose: Programs and competitions are dedicated to improving the quality of science education, increasing student interest in science, and recognizing outstanding achievement in science education by both students and teachers.

Audience: Grades K–12.

Trinity College Fire-Fighting Home Robot Contest
Trinity College
300 Summit Street
Hartford, CT 06106-3100
(860) 232-0435
www.trincoll.edu/events/robot

Description: Participants are challenged to build a robotic device that can move through a model of a single-floor house, find a fire (a lit candle), and extinguish it. The participant whose robot extinguishes the candle in the shortest time is the winner. Cash prizes are offered to the top finishers in four divisions of competition.

Purpose: The competition encourages creativity, problem solving, and enthusiasm for science and its applications.

Audience: Grades K–12.

SOCIAL STUDIES

Future Problem Solving Program International (FPSPI)
2015 Grant Place
Melbourne, FL 32901
1-800-256-1499
www.fpspi.org

Description: The Future Problem Solving Program is a complex problem-solving experience for students. It has the following categories:

• Team Problem Solving: Teams of four students in grades 4–12 use a six-step problem-solving process to solve complex, futuristic problems. At regular intervals teams mail their work to evaluators who return it with suggestions for improvement. The highest scoring teams may attend regional and national competitions.

• Individual Problem Solving: Affiliates of FPSP that choose to administer their own programs offer opportunities for students to work individually instead of with a group.

• Action-Based Problem Solving: This yearlong, non-competitive component is designed for the regular classroom and introduces students to creative problem solving in a hands-on environment. Teams work in groups of four to six in three divisions: Primary (grades K–3), Junior (grades 3–6), and Middle (grades 6–9).

• Community Problem Solving: Teams apply their problem-solving skills toward solving real problems in the community.

• Scenario-Writing Contest: Students are encouraged to write a futuristic short story (1,500 words or less) about an important topic in the present.

Purpose: This program helps students think creatively and critically, work cooperatively, and develop research skills.

Audience: Grades K–12.

National Social Studies League
P.O. Box 2196
St. James, NY 11780
(631) 584-2016
www.continentalmathematicsleague.com

Description: The NSSL is a national event consisting of six contests where students participate with other students at their grade level from schools throughout the United States. Contact the Continental Mathematics League for more information on available programs that cover topics like American history, current events, and geography.

Purpose: This organization aims to encourage and motivate students toward strengthening their social studies skills.

Audience: Grades 2–12.

National History Day Contest
University of Maryland
119 Cecil Hall
College Park, MD 20742
(301) 314-9739
www.nationalhistoryday.org

Description: The National History Day Contest encourages the study of historical subjects related to an annual theme. Students produce dramatic performances, imaginative exhibits, multimedia documentaries, and research papers. The projects are evaluated at local, state, and national competitions.

Purpose: This program encourages the discovery and interpretation of historical topics as well as an appreciation of history and its impact on the present.

Audience: Grades 6–12.

Service Projects

The Kid's Guide to Service Projects: Over 500 Service Ideas for Young People Who Want to Make a Difference by Barbara A. Lewis (Minneapolis: Free Spirit Publishing, 1995). This book has hundreds of ideas for service projects, from simple projects to large-scale commitments. It also serves as a step-by-step guide for creating flyers, petitions, press releases, and other documents.

The Kid's Guide to Social Action: How to Solve the Social Problems You Choose—and Turn Creative Thinking into Positive Action by Barbara A. Lewis (Minneapolis: Free Spirit Publishing, 1998). This book outlines a step-by-step process for solving community problems, from brainstorming the problem to evaluating your experience. It includes complete instructions for writing letters, Internet research, interviewing, speechmaking, fund-raising, working with the media, and pushing through local, state, and national laws.

President's Volunteer Service Award
P.O. Box 189
Wilmington, DE 19899-0189
1-866-545-5307
www.presidentialserviceawards.gov

Description: Full-time students in grades K–12 who contribute at least 100 hours of service to the community in a twelve-month timeframe are eligible for the President's Student Service Award. Students in grades K–8 who perform at least fifty hours of service are also recognized. High school juniors and seniors may also be eligible for scholarships.

Purpose: This program encourages students to solve real problems in the community, motivating them to care about others and the world. Problem-based projects provide opportunities for students to use critical thinking, demonstrate leadership, share their gifts and talents, and examine different perspectives.

Audience: Grades K–12.

Plan and Conduct Ongoing Evaluation

Ramón Vasquez, the gifted coordinator of a small school district, was responsible for all G/T programming at two schools, K–8. Programming included several pull-out programs (two of which he taught himself). His time and that of the part-time gifted teachers was spread thin. When the superintendent asked for an evaluation of gifted programming, Ramón inquired about hiring an outside consultant. The answer was a regretful but unqualified no. The evaluation request came because of upcoming budget reductions, which would require weeding out programs that weren't quantifiably effective in order to support those that were; spending additional money on the evaluation was out of the question. Ramón knew that no gifted staffers were trained to conduct a professional evaluation. He gathered together an evaluation committee made up of a parent, a classroom teacher, a gifted pull-out teacher, and a building principal he knew to be an advocate for gifted ed. The committee learned that the school psychologist had training in evaluation and found a way to convince the superintendent that this professional, already on salary, would be the logical person to help. With the psychologist's guidance, the committee surveyed kids, parents, and classroom teachers. They were able to present a report to the district administration showing that gifted students were being challenged, particularly in pull-out classes and the science enrichment program, and that the grades of nearly all gifted students participating in these programs were being maintained or were improving. As a result, the district did not cut gifted funding, but directed the gifted advisory board to implement ongoing program evaluation.

★ ★ ★

The gifted program of a fast-growing school district in a suburb of a large metropolitan area had been in place for five years. In that time, the district had grown from having three elementary schools, one middle school, and one high school to five elementary schools, two middle schools, and one high school. The district was committed to providing quality services to its gifted students. The gifted advisory committee recognized that the program needed to grow along with the district. All areas of service—staffing, funding, student screening and selection, program structure, and instructional methods—needed attention. The committee was determined not to be overwhelmed by the scope of the challenge it faced. They knew that thoughtful, competent planning based on experience held the most promise for guiding the program's path. So they proposed that the school board hire a reputable team of outside consultants to spearhead and direct an evaluation of present programming and to recommend a plan for implementing changes and improvements over time. They were able to effectively present the case for this approach, and the school board agreed. The result was a thriving program continually refreshed and improved through a thorough ongoing evaluation process.

The part of gifted program operation that is most often neglected—indeed, sometimes forgotten or ignored—is that of program evaluation. In a setting where human and financial resources are spread thin, funding for evaluation can mistakenly seem like a less-critical "extra." At times, too, people who have fought long and hard for gifted programming can't help but fear that evaluation will reopen a door to questions and possible criticism of services or even the idea of gifted education itself.

Yet, ongoing evaluation is essential. Much as keeping a car tuned up can save the driver money and time and the vehicle wear and tear, systematically evaluating gifted programming can ensure savings, too—savings of money for the school and of time and effort on the part of teachers and parents. Effective evaluation can provide valuable information to share with administrative teams and school boards—those who control the purse strings and make district-level decisions. It can shape decisions about identification and programming and can foster and sustain buy-in from all of the stakeholders in gifted services. Most important, it can help ensure that gifted students have their unique educational needs met.

Ongoing Program Evaluation: What Does It Look Like?

The National Association for Gifted Children (NAGC) defines program evaluation as "the systematic study of the value and impact of services provided."[1] In its guiding principles and standards, NAGC recommends that evaluation be purposeful, efficient, and ethically conducted and that a written report of evaluation results be made available to all interested parties.

If this sounds high-minded, that's because it is—and rightly so. There's little point in evaluating programs and services in a haphazard way. In fact, as educator Jan Hansen notes:[2]

> . . . poorly done evaluation can do damage. Superficial judgments regarding the quality of services for gifted learners can gloss over deep underlying problems, squelch constructive criticism, serve political but not educational purposes, and can actually stunt the growth of services.

There are a variety of means to ensure an evaluation process that's honest, comprehensive, and useful. At the outset, a commitment to ongoing evaluation, rather than a once-at-the-end-of-the-year approach, can help you be sure that neither problems nor successes are slipping through the cracks. With ongoing evaluation, you continually collect information that builds upon itself, allowing for a dynamic look at all aspects and elements of programming and services. Investigating the gifted program's strengths and weaknesses throughout the school year should yield information about what's working and what's not as

well as ideas for changes and improvements. It's still critical, of course, to take a broader look at the quality of services annually and over several years. A more sweeping evaluation, perhaps annually, should yield a report with specific recommendations for future programming.

NAGC addresses this issue by recommending two types of evaluations:

- *summative*—assessing the quality of programming or success in reaching its stated goals

- *formative*—geared toward improving programming and services

At a minimum, you'll want to conduct a summative evaluation every five years (though state or local policies may dictate doing this more often), and a formative evaluation once a year. These formal evaluations always call for a written report of the findings.

Figure 5.1 (page 93) presents a step-by-step outline, developed by Jan Hansen and Karen Rogers, for evaluating gifted programming and services. While it may seem that this outline represents the ultimate in terms of best evaluation practice, for the most part it delineates the means of meeting minimum standards for evaluation as set by NAGC. Yes, the task can seem overwhelming, yet getting started may be your primary challenge; with key planners in place and the groundwork laid, your evaluation process can evolve systematically.

That said, we recognize certain realities and limitations many gifted education programs face. As noted earlier, barriers—particularly those of time and money—can make this kind of comprehensive evaluation seem like a pipe dream. If you are in this situation, start small, but start well. You might, for example, convene a meeting with teachers who have taught gifted students in their classrooms during the past two or three years and ask for their perspective on what's working well and what could be improved. You could then conduct a similar meeting with school administrators from the same school district and develop a report, based on the teachers' and administrators' input, about the themes that emerged in these informal discussions. Perhaps teachers feel the need for some staff development sessions on curriculum differentiation with gifted students, and principals see a similar need and are supportive of after-school workshops. Is this an ideal evaluation plan? No. Is it a reasonable starting point? Yes.

Another "small step" approach would be to consider evaluating services every other year at first, and work toward doing this once or twice a year later. Or, you might start by evaluating one element of your

HOW TO EVALUATE YOUR GIFTED PROGRAM: A STEP-BY-STEP PLAN[3]

STEP 1: Build an Evaluation Steering Committee

    A. Hire 2 Evaluation Leaders/Consultants

    B. Select 1 Administrator/Gifted Learner Advocate

    C. Select 2 Central Office Administrators or

        1 Central Office Administrator & 1 School Board Member

    D. Select 2 Teachers of Gifted & Talented Students

    E. Select 1 Teacher of a Regular Classroom

    F. Select 1 Parent of a Gifted Student

STEP 2: Identify Purposes of the Evaluation

    A. Determine the Evaluation Questions

    B. Determine Which "Stakeholders" Will Be Surveyed/Interviewed

    C. Determine How You Will Question "Stakeholders"

    D. Determine Timeline

    E. Determine Format(s) of Recommendations

    F. Determine Audiences for Recommendations

STEP 3: Collect Information

    A. Interview "Stakeholders"

    B. Survey "Stakeholders"

    C. Focus Groups of "Stakeholders"

    D. Observation

    E. Collect Literature on Program

    F. Collect Test Data & Results

STEP 4: Analyze Information

    A. Identify Themes from Interviews

    B. Tabulate/Analyze Survey Responses

    C. Identify Themes from Focus Groups

    D. Analyze Observational Data

    E. Analyze Literature on Program

    F. Analyze Test Data and Results

STEP 5: Deliver Evaluation Recommendations

    A. Recommendations Gain Approval of Steering Committee

    B. Steering Committee Makes Recommendations (Steps 2E and 2F)

    C. Evaluation Leaders Work with Steering Committee "As Needed"

    D. Steering Committee Produces Action Plans (Recommendations)

Figure by Jan B. Hansen and Karen B. Rogers

Figure 5.1

programming (such as a grouping approach you have been using or a pull-out program that involves many gifted kids) at a time. Like Ramón Vasquez, you may need to look within the school or district for expertise.

PROGRAM EVALUATION BASICS

Whatever level of evaluation you wish to conduct, the keys that will help you ensure integrity are these:

✔ Involve an administrator, a G/T teacher, a regular classroom teacher, and a parent in planning the evaluation.

✔ Define the purpose of your evaluation.

✔ Commit to objectivity.

✔ Look at both how your program is doing and how it can be improved.

✔ Keep individual data confidential.

✔ Make your results available in a written report.

Figure 5.2

One helpful way to frame your evaluation process is by answering a series of questions. Like an investigative reporter, by finding the answers to tried-and-true journalistic questions you can determine an effective form and procedure for your school or district's program evaluation to follow. The questions to ask include:

- Why are you conducting your evaluation?
- Who will take part in it?
- When and how will you gather information?
- How will you report the evaluation's results?
- What will you do to follow through on the recommendations?

Why Are You Conducting Your Evaluation?

This "why?" question gets to the purpose behind your program evaluation. What do you want to learn? In the most basic of terms, your evaluation needs to demonstrate that students are being served, that they are being challenged appropriately, and that the means for growth and improvement of services are built into the program structure. Broadly, you'll want to find answers to two questions:

1. Are we delivering quality programming that meets the needs of our gifted students? (summative evaluation)

2. How can we better serve gifted students and staff in the years ahead? (formative evaluation)

The answers you seek will be closely related to the mission and goals that are in place for gifted programming. Consider, for example, the following gifted program goals:

GOALS FOR THE DISTRICT 11 GIFTED PROGRAM

- Meet individualized learning needs for all identified gifted students, including those in LEP and ESL programs and those with learning disabilities.

- Differentiate instruction to provide a range of educational learning opportunities and accommodations in core curricular areas (language arts, math, science, and social studies) that are tied to the schoolwide curriculum and that continually challenge gifted students in their specific areas of ability.

- Provide students with opportunities to learn alongside intellectual peers so that they might gain a realistic appraisal of their own abilities.

- Develop critical-thinking processes so that gifted students will be able to address complex issues with the needed problem-solving tools.

- Provide staff inservice training on the characteristics of gifted children and methods teachers can use to challenge these children throughout the curriculum.

- Ensure that gifted students have ongoing guidance and support for understanding and managing the social and emotional challenges they face.

Figure 5.3

The purpose of evaluating a gifted program with these particular goals will be:

EVALUATION PURPOSE FOR THE DISTRICT 11 GIFTED PROGRAM

1. To determine whether and to what extent gifted students

- are having their individualized learning needs met.

- are experiencing ongoing challenge through differentiated instruction.

- have the opportunity to work with other gifted students.

- are developing and using critical-thinking skills.

- are benefiting from the staff's being trained to understand and challenge their unique learning needs.

- are having their affective needs met.

2. To identify specific ways the school can better serve gifted students

- in areas where goals are not fully met.

- in additional areas that may emerge through the evaluation process.

Figure 5.4

Rather than look for general impressions or overall views, you will want to focus on specific aspects of your gifted programming. A truly meaningful evaluation will analyze all areas of the program, including the identification system, program design, instruction, and staff development, among others. The evaluation should produce data that will be useful in reinforcing or modifying these elements of the program.

In thinking about the purpose of this evaluation, it is important that you plan to identify and document both successes and problems. Finding what you're doing right is critical. This allows you to show concrete evidence that gifted programming is worthwhile and provides a rationale for present or increased levels of funding. It invites buy-in, too. Yet successes do more than validate and affirm: they also offer models for making changes in different areas that call for improvement. As a colleague of ours is fond of saying, "You don't have to be sick to get better." Choosing not to evaluate an aspect of programming that has been controversial, or that you may feel is not as well conceived or as effectively implemented as it could be, is a sure way to harm your gifted education initiative. In reality, rather than damage the program, constructive criticism will add credibility to the evaluation. For just as no person is perfect, neither is any gifted program.

Who Will Take Part?

You will want your evaluation to address key questions raised by all of the interested parties—parents, teachers, students, administrators, and community members. To do this, these stakeholders must be involved in both planning and contributing to the study of your gifted program's value and impact. This means that the "who?" question is two-pronged,

addressing both those who will guarantee that your evaluation has integrity and those who will provide input. We categorize these two groups as the Conductors (the people who actually plan and carry out the evaluations) and the Information Providers (the people who provide the data).

The Conductors. The task of the Conductors is an ongoing one: to plan and direct a process of both formative and summative evaluations. Many gifted education specialists recommend an evaluation steering committee comprised of key school and district personnel (administrators, a school board member, G/T and regular classroom teachers, and a parent) as well as outside consultants. An external evaluation from an objective assessor can strengthen your program, enhancing both its validity and credibility for a wide variety of audiences. While outside expertise may seem expensive, the cost in most cases is very defensible. It can be extremely challenging for a district or school to manage its own evaluation process, for intentionally or not, people bring their own biases to the table. Also, it's not unusual for individuals from within the school to bring their own personal agendas into the picture. In addition to this, the process of evaluation calls for expertise. Outside consultants offer experience in working with other schools. They are in a position, too, to challenge assumptions or mediate disagreements objectively. Together, outside evaluators and school personnel stand the best chance of carrying out an evaluation process that is comprehensive and has integrity.

"External evaluators offer training and experience and an 'objective eye' rarely found inside a program."
—David M. Fetterman

The Information Sources. Input from stakeholders is essential. You'll want to seek information from:

- identified gifted students who are receiving services

- teachers who work with gifted children—both those in the regular classroom and those who specialize in gifted education

- parents of identified gifted students

- administrators—principals, assistant principals, and school counselors as well as school board members and central administrators

- other members of the school and community who are interested in contributing their perceptions of or experiences with the gifted program

When and How Will You Gather Information?

While you'll need to consider several means of gathering information, one excellent starting point is to take a look back at the needs assessment you had teachers, parents, and administrators complete. (For information on needs assessment, see pages 12–14.) Then, using a very similar format, design your evaluation surveys. You might use or adapt the surveys for teachers, parents, students, and administrators on pages 99–113, and then delineate the results on a graph.

Other means of evaluation should incorporate the following:

- **Test data.** Out-of-level achievement tests (for example, having fourth graders complete standardized tests generally intended for sixth graders) often provide valuable information about the difficulty or complexity of a curriculum. Testing in this way raises the "ceiling" on students' performance so that even academically gifted students can show growth that may not be noticed when using grade-level tests. You cannot be sure that students' high performance on these out-of-level tests is due solely to their participation in the gifted classes or program—there are simply too many other possible factors involved. You can, however, use this type of test data as evidence that at least some of your district's gifted students are performing enough above grade level that they need a more rigorous curriculum than they're currently experiencing.

- **Student portfolios.** Portfolios of student products often provide hard evidence of the impact of the curriculum. Student portfolios can include anything and everything: essays or artwork, photographs of student products and written comments from teachers or other audiences, student self-reflections on the effort it took to complete a particular project, and examples of first and final drafts of the same assignment. Importantly, the teacher or student should add calendar dates to each piece in the portfolio, inserting the items chronologically so that growth over time can be noted.

- **Interviews.** Interviews and observation of students can provide anecdotal documentation. Interviewing teachers, parents, and administrators (as well as students) provides another way to gather information without calling on contributors to labor over written surveys. You might use your survey forms to conduct these interviews and note responses, or hold briefer interviews or focus groups where you record responses on a simpler form.

Bear in mind that by collecting data along the way, rather than just once a year, you will increase respect for and acceptance of your program. Information exists everywhere:

- Track the number of experts who come in to talk with your students; record the number of parent volunteers involved in your program's activities; keep tabs on how often you conduct enrichment lessons in other teachers' classrooms. In other words, document the number of students whose education your programming is enriching and the number of community people and agencies who are benefiting your gifted students (and others).

- When your students go on a field trip or participate in another out-of-school activity, take photos and record students' achievements and reactions to their learning. Send letters home to parents about these events. This may not appear to be related directly to evaluation, but the emails and letters you receive from parents in response to these letters will be useful in showing how a gifted program's offerings affect individual children and families. At times, these personal testimonials carry as much weight as other pieces of evaluation data, as they are unsolicited expressions of support and gratitude.

- When you hold a staff inservice or parent evening, count how many people are in attendance and ask them to complete a *short* evaluation form (for example, one that asks a single question, such as, "What one thing did you learn today that was useful to you?"). Compile these data into a summary statement to distribute to building principals and central office administrators and to the evaluation steering committee.

- Maintain a log of the number of phone calls you receive from parents and others who are interested in the gifted program; document both the concerns and comments raised and how you respond to them. Also, make copies of any written correspondence sent to you by parents, teachers, or students grateful for your efforts on their behalf.

- Establish a gifted advisory group composed of interested educators and parents. This group's purpose will be to meet at least twice a year to discuss specific issues—both positive and negative—regarding the gifted program. At each meeting, have the group document the gifted program's greatest successes and continuing needs, along with recommendations for improvements or changes.

- Conduct exit interviews with gifted students who are switching schools. Also survey gifted program "graduates"—older students and young adults who once took part in the gifted program. Ask them to reflect on any elements of the program that they found beneficial. Further, ask if there were significant gaps in the program that they believe should have been addressed. Compile and use this information as additional evidence about the merits or shortcomings of your gifted program.

- Seek out some form of input from the community at large. Sometimes community leaders are aware of needs that might not otherwise be voiced. A good way to invite community input that can help you evaluate people's impressions of the quality and performance of your gifted programming is through the local media. A blurb in the community paper or a quick public service announcement (PSA) on the TV or radio inviting people to attend a meeting where they can provide input may yield helpful information and suggestions. As with the other data you gather, document the issues people raise. You might write your own PSA or use or adapt the form on page 114. Community interest and support can yield many benefits for the gifted program in terms of program options, funding, innovation, and getting the word out. Reaching out in this way may also give you access to ideas for meeting the needs of traditionally underserved populations, such as kids whose first language isn't English or whose parents aren't as visible or assertive at school.

- Arrange to meet two times each year with the individual building principals in the schools where you are located. During these meetings, share with them the data you've gathered from parents, teachers, students past and present, and others in the community. Ask if any particular concerns are brewing from the administration's vantage point.

Informal methods of collecting information can't replace the more formal data you will document through surveys, test results, interviews, portfolios, and focus groups. Yet they can contribute greatly to the big picture.

How Will You Report the Results?

For evaluation to have real "teeth," all of the people involved must learn the results of it—both the findings and the recommendations for change that have emerged. You'll want to formally present the results to the administration and to other school policymakers as designated in your particular school or district. Someone from or appointed by the steering committee can present an in-person report to teachers at a teacher meeting, to parents at a PTO or PTA event, and to students during pull-out times. It is also wise to report a brief summary of findings through a school newsletter, on the school Web site, and in the local newspaper.

At the same time, a clear and complete written document—one that is readily available and readable for all audiences—is a must. Your report can provide an organized resource that both verifies results and expands on them. Most important, this report can serve as a collective "memory" to all involved.[4] You will have on record a document that can show you where you are and where you need to go, and also provide a baseline for comparisons with later evaluations.

Returning to NAGC's recommendation of both summative and formative evaluation, take care that your report not only presents results, but also encourages follow-through. For example: "We now have this program in place in fifth grade, and for continuity, the services need to be extended into sixth grade."

What Will You Do to Follow Through?

The ultimate purpose of any evaluation is to document what is going well and to address what needs to be done better. Once you have collected sufficient data and reviewed the results with all of the interested parties (staff, parents, students, and the community), the next step is to take action on your recommendations.

One way that has proven effective in our evaluation efforts is to follow the "Olympic Approach" to implementing evaluation results by going for the GOLD, the SILVER, or the BRONZE. In this case you won't be seeking medals, but levels of quality and improvement in your gifted program. Start by considering the optimum (GOLD) plan for program growth, and then determine what level to set as your present goal.

- **Going for the GOLD.** This approach would be to immediately implement virtually every suggestion for improvement, from expanding the grade levels served by a pull-out program to hiring new staff to do so. Money is not the biggest concern here—quality is. Of course, some of the suggestions for improvement might need to be phased in over time, but the GOLD decision would be to buy into them all now and begin acting upon multiple suggestions simultaneously.

- **Going for the SILVER.** To go for the SILVER, you pinpoint the most essential recommendations from the GOLD level, keeping an eye on budget concerns. Perhaps you'll establish a three-, four-, or five-year plan for improvement, including most of the suggestions that emerged from the evaluation but beginning with those changes deemed most important or necessary.

- **Going for the BRONZE.** When resources (people, money, and time) are limited, the BRONZE approach lets you focus on the bare minimum that needs to occur for sustaining and supporting the integrity and usefulness of the gifted program. Often, this involves tweaking what exists rather than introducing entirely new projects or programs. While going for the BRONZE may not be the ideal, if you keep a SILVER and GOLD plan on the back burner, your program will be maintained and you'll know the direction you want to take once your district's economic or philosophical situation becomes more favorable in regard to gifted education.

The bottom line is this: Don't just sit on your evaluation data—act on it! Ultimately, that is the only way that your gifted program will prosper and flourish.

Notes

1. "National Association for Gifted Children Pre-K–Grade 12 Programming Standards" (Washington, DC: NAGC, 1998), Table 4. Gifted Education Programming Criterion: Program Evaluation.

2. Jan B. Hansen, "Selecting an Evaluation Steering Committee: A Critical Step," *MEGT Voice,* Winter 2001, page 1.

3. Jan B. Hansen and Karen B. Rogers, University of St. Thomas, printed in *MEGT Voice* (Winter 2001). Used with permission.

4. *Aiming for Excellence: Annotations to the NAGC Pre-K–Grade 12 Gifted Program Standards* edited by Mary S. Landrum, Carolyn M. Callahan, and Beverly D. Shaklee (Waco, TX: Prufrock Press, 2001), page 86.

Resources

The following resources apply specifically to topics addressed in this strategy's chapter. For a complete list of gifted education resources, see pages 146–154.

"Evaluate Yourself" by David M. Fetterman (Storrs, CT: NRC/GT, 1993); research monograph 9304. This report offers information on conducting self-examinations and external evaluations. See NRC/GT contact and ordering information on page 51.

"How Should We Evaluate Programs for Gifted Learners?" This brochure, part of the "Frequently Asked Questions" packet from NAGC (see page 147), is brief, clear, and easy to read.

"Instruments and Evaluation Designs Used in Gifted Programs" by Carolyn M. Callahan, et al. (Storrs, CT: NRC/GT, 1995);

research monograph 95132. Provides detailed information on instruments and evaluation design, with a focus on documenting current and promising practices in the evaluation process and on the usefulness of evaluation for decision making. See NRC/GT contact and ordering information on page 51.

"National Association for Gifted Children Pre-K–Grade 12 Gifted Program Standards" *(www.nagc.org)*. Find the document at the NAGC Web site and look up the table for program evaluation. The table cites guiding principles along with both minimum and exemplary standards for conducting systematic evaluation of programs and services for gifted children.

Practitioner's Guide to Evaluating Programs for the Gifted by Carolyn M. Callahan and Michael S. Caldwell (Washington, DC: NAGC, 1995). This guide was developed to explain the evaluation process in concrete, sequential, and intelligible steps. The authors present a strategy for evaluating programs; offer help in developing a specific evaluation at the state or local education agency level; and provide a means to review selected assessment strategies and instruments and to construct instruments for evaluating G/T programs.

"Selecting an Evaluation Steering Committee: A Critical Step" by Jan B. Hansen, in *MEGT Voice,* Winter 2001. This article (one in a series *MEGT Voice* is running in order to cover all five steps in evaluating a gifted program) describes detailed rationales, pitfalls, and best practices for building a steering committee composed of both stakeholders and outside leaders and consultants. The same newsletter includes a pull-out page with step-by-step program evaluation guidelines developed by Hansen and Karen B. Rogers. For more information, visit MEGT online *(www.megt.org)*.

★ Teacher Survey: Evaluating Gifted Services ★

Dear Teacher:

Our school/district is evaluating the programming and services provided for identified gifted students, and we need your input. Would you please take a few minutes to complete this anonymous survey, based on your experience during the time period from _____ to _____ , and return it to _____ at _____ on or before _____ .

Thank you for your continued efforts to make our gifted education program a success and for taking the time to help us with this evaluation. We will get back to you with a summary of the results and recommendations.

Sincerely,

_____

---

1. For each statement, write the letter that best expresses your view:

A=Agree   N=Not Sure   D=Disagree

A. _____ I understand how gifted children are identified in our school/district.

B. _____ I understand my role in the identification of gifted children.

C. _____ In general, I feel that the right students have been selected to participate in gifted programming.

D. _____ I have adequate time to serve gifted students in my classroom.

E. _____ I understand the school's goals and objectives for effectively differentiating instruction within the regular classroom.

F. _____ There is adequate communication among parents, teachers, and administrators about the gifted program.

G. _____ I am comfortable communicating with the parents of gifted students.

H. _____ Inservice training and/or support from gifted education staff has helped me understand both the academic and affective needs of gifted children.

I. _____ Inservice training has addressed areas and issues that are important to me.

MORE ➔

J. _____ I have benefited from the services of the gifted teacher and/or coordinator.

K. _____ Gifted education staff have been readily available to me.

L. _____ I believe the school is providing valuable services to gifted students.

For items marked N or D, please note your questions or concerns:

_____

_____

_____

_____

_____

_____

2. Which services has the gifted teacher/coordinator provided to you? Check all that apply.

A. _____ taught one or more lessons in my classroom

B. _____ assisted with differentiation

C. _____ met to discuss students' or individual students' learning needs

D. _____ provided curriculum materials

E. _____ other: _____

F. _____ none of the above

3. Of the items in question 2, what teaching support has been most helpful?

_____

_____

_____

_____

MORE ▶

4. Of the items in question 2, what teaching support has been least helpful?

_____

_____

_____

5. What teaching support presently available would you like to have available more often?

_____

_____

_____

6. What teaching support *not* presently available would be most helpful to you if it were made available?

_____

_____

_____

7. What specific changes or improvements would you like to see in gifted education services?

_____

_____

_____

8. In terms of gifted education, what do you think the school is doing especially well?

_____

_____

_____

9. Additional comments:

_____

_____

★ Parent Survey: Evaluating Gifted Services ★

Dear Parent:

Our school/district is evaluating the programming and services provided for identified gifted students, and we need your input. Would you please take a few minutes to complete this anonymous survey, based on your experience during the time period from _____ to _____ , and return it to _____ at _____ on or before _____ .

Thank you for your continued efforts to make our gifted education program a success and for taking the time to help us with this evaluation. We will get back to you with a summary of the results and recommendations.

Sincerely,

_____

---

1. For each statement, write the letter that best expresses your view:

A=Agree   N=Not Sure   D=Disagree

A. _____ I understand how gifted children are identified in our school/district.

B. _____ I understand my role in the identification of gifted children.

C. _____ In general, I feel that the right students have been selected to participate in gifted programming.

D. _____ My child feels that she/he has had a positive experience participating in the gifted education program.

E. _____ I feel that my child's academic needs are being well met.

F. _____ My child is being appropriately challenged within the regular classroom.

G. _____ My child is being appropriately challenged when participating in out-of-class programs.

H. _____ My child's social and emotional needs related to being gifted are being adequately addressed at school.

I. _____ School staff are readily available to address my questions and concerns about gifted programming and services for my child.

J. _____ I am comfortable communicating with the classroom teacher(s) about my gifted child's needs.

MORE ➤

K. _____ I am comfortable communicating with gifted education staff about my gifted child's needs.

L. _____ The school has provided helpful opportunities for me to learn more about my gifted child's academic and social/emotional needs.

M. _____ I have adequate opportunities to meet and talk with other parents of gifted students.

For items marked N or D, please note your questions or concerns:

_____

_____

_____

_____

_____

_____

2. In which type of gifted education programming does your child participate? Check all that apply.

A. _____ pull-out class(es)

B. _____ differentiated instruction in the regular classroom

C. _____ ability or interest groups with other gifted students

D. _____ ability-based classes

E. _____ enrichment programs

F. _____ other: _____

G. _____ none of the above

3. In which type of gifted education programming would you like to have your child participate? Check all that apply.

A. _____ pull-out class(es)

B. _____ differentiated instruction in the regular classroom

C. _____ ability or interest groups with other gifted students

MORE ➡

D. _____ ability-based classes

E. _____ enrichment programs

F. _____ other: _____

G. _____ none of the above

4. What gifted education service or program currently available do you consider especially important or valuable? Why?

_____

_____

_____

_____

5. What specific changes or improvements would you like to see in gifted education services?

_____

_____

_____

_____

6. Additional comments:

_____

_____

_____

_____

_____

_____

_____

Dear Parent:

Our school/district is evaluating the _____ program in order

to assess its strengths and weaknesses, and we need your input. Would you please take a few minutes to

complete this anonymous survey and return it to _____ at

_____ on or before _____.

Thank you for your continued efforts to make our gifted education program a success and for taking the time

to help us with this evaluation. We will get back to you with a summary of the results and recommendations.

Sincerely,

_____

1. For each statement, write the letter that best expresses your view about the _____ program:

A=Agree   N=Not Sure   D=Disagree

A. _____ My child's participation in the program has been a worthwhile experience.

B. _____ The program contributed much to my child's academic growth.

C. _____ My child showed an increased interest in school as a result of participation in the program.

D. _____ My child benefited from the opportunity to interact in the program with students who have similar abilities.

E. _____ My child's relationships with students in the regular classroom suffered as a result of being in the program.

F. _____ The time spent out of the regular classroom for participation in the program activities was worth it.

G. _____ My child's regular classroom teacher(s) supported my child's participation in this program.

H. _____ My child missed too much of his/her regular schoolwork during the time spent in the program.

I. _____ The extra program work, beyond that in the regular classroom, overburdened my child.

J. _____ Overall, the program activities were more of a challenge to my child than those in the regular classroom.

MORE

K. _____ Without this program, my child's classroom teacher would probably have created activities that would have sufficiently challenged and motivated my child.

L. _____ Students who are not performing well in the program should be removed from it.

M. _____ Classroom teachers should be able to keep a student from attending the program under certain conditions (such as unfinished class assignments or discipline concerns).

N. _____ There has been sufficient communication between the program teacher and myself.

O. _____ The screening process to select students for the program was appropriate and fair.

2. Please circle the response that most closely reflects your opinion:

A. The actual time allotted for this program was:

   too short   just about right   too long

B. My child's feelings about being in the program can best be described as:

   enthusiastic   positive   mixed   indifferent   negative

3. What aspects of the program have been most beneficial to your child?

_____

_____

_____

_____

4. Briefly describe any problems or difficulties your child has had as a result of participating in the program:

_____

_____

_____

_____

MORE ➤

★ Parent Survey: Gifted Program Evaluation (cont'd)

5. What suggestions do you have for improving the program?

_____

_____

_____

_____

_____

6. Additional comments:

_____

_____

_____

_____

_____

_____

_____

_____

_____

_____

_____

_____

_____

Dear Student:

The teachers and school have been working hard to provide you with interesting and challenging learning options. We want your opinion about how we are doing. You don't have to put your name on this form, and we want you to be very honest. After you have answered each of the questions, please take time to add any comments that you believe would make our program better.

Thanks for your help! Please return this form to _____

on or before _____. We'll let you know what we learn

from the survey and what changes may happen as a result.

Sincerely,

_____

What gifted program or activities do you take part in? Please list them here.

_____

_____

_____

For items 1–8, check the choice that BEST expresses your view.

1. Overall, I like my gifted program:

_____ a lot

_____ some

_____ not at all, because _____

[MORE →]

2. The amount of time I spend in the gifted program is:

_____ too long

_____ just about right

_____ not long enough

3. When I think about being with the other gifted students:

_____ I find that I usually enjoy spending time with them.

_____ I don't have an opinion about them that is either good or bad.

_____ I don't enjoy spending time with them most of the time.

4. How would you rate your level of learning in this program?

_____ I'm learning more than in my regular class(es).

_____ I'm not learning anything more than I usually learn in school.

5. The level of expectations set by my gifted program teacher(s) is:

_____ too high

_____ just about right

_____ not high enough

6. Because of my involvement in the gifted program, my classroom teacher(s):

_____ expect too much from me

_____ treat me the same as everyone else in class

_____ cut out some work that I already know how to do

MORE▶

7. Students **not** in the gifted program:

_____ seem jealous of my participation in it

_____ treat me the same as they always have

8. Most or all of the time, this is how I feel about my participation in the gifted program (check all that are true for you):

_____ I enjoy working with students of similar abilities.

_____ I enjoy working on group projects.

_____ I enjoy talking about the ups and downs of being gifted.

_____ Participation in gifted program(s) has added a lot to my homework load.

_____ Participation in gifted program(s) has caused problems with my friends.

_____ Participation in gifted program(s) has caused me to think about new and different ways to learn.

_____ Participation in gifted program(s) has helped me to better understand and accept my abilities.

_____ Participation in gifted program(s) has caused me to think about future careers I might like to pursue.

_____ I would like to continue to be in gifted classes.

Please answer items 9–12 with full and honest statements.

9. What I enjoy the most about the gifted program is:

_____

_____

_____

_____

_____

MORE

10. Something I have learned in the gifted program that I always want to remember is:

_____

_____

_____

_____

_____

11. One of the best ways to improve the gifted program in the future would be to:

_____

_____

_____

_____

_____

12. What else would you like to share about your participation in the gifted program?

_____

_____

_____

_____

_____

Dear Administrator:

Our school/district is evaluating the programming and services provided for identified gifted students, and we need your input. Would you please take a few minutes to complete this anonymous survey, based on your experience during the time period from _____ to _____ , and return it to _____ at _____ on or before _____ .

Thank you for your continued efforts to make our gifted education program a success and for taking the time to help us with this evaluation. We will provide you with a summary of the results and recommendations.

Sincerely,

_____

1. In regard to programming and services for identified gifted students in our school/district, please check items about which you have concerns and provide specific comments that explain your concerns. Space for these comments is provided beneath the list:

A. _____ identification and placement of students

B. _____ program planning

C. _____ program administration

D. _____ particular programs

E. _____ accommodations in the regular classroom

F. _____ accommodations outside the regular classroom

G. _____ staffing for gifted services

H. _____ staff development of gifted education personnel

I. _____ staff development of regular classroom teachers

J. _____ program evaluation

MORE

K. _____ parent involvement

L. _____ community concerns

M. _____ other: _____

_____

_____

_____

2. In terms of gifted education, what do you think the school/district is doing especially well?

_____

_____

_____

_____

3. What specific changes or improvements would you like to see in gifted education services?

_____

_____

_____

_____

4. Additional comments:

_____

_____

_____

_____

Evaluating Gifted Programming
(30 seconds)

_____ is evaluating the programming and services
(Name of school district)

provided for identified gifted students, and is interested in input from members of the community. A public

hearing will be held on _____ , _____ ,
(day) (date)

at _____ at _____.
(location) (time)

Please join us to share your ideas about how we can better serve gifted children in our schools. For more

information, call _____ at _____.
(name of contact person) (phone)

Strengthen Your Program by Communicating and Building Relationships

DO's for the Gifted Teacher*

DO remember, always, whom you're here to support: gifted kids. They need you!

DO keep a personal folder of "kid notes." They will come in handy. Some notes may become old and tattered, but they'll still perform the same magic.

DO know what you want for kids and look for people who see that vision and can work with you to get the job done!

DO seek out teachers who love kids. You can teach them about giftedness, but you can't teach them to like kids.

DO maintain a healthy sense of humor. Laugh frequently—it's cheaper than therapy.

DO guide parents in making choices for their gifted children. Parenting takes on a whole new look with these kids, so move over Dr. Spock!

DO always make sure you communicate your messages to campus administrators. Keep them over-informed! They hold so much power, and you need them as allies.

DO meet the experts in the field and call on them for help. Get to state and national conferences! Just like gifted kids need each other, so do our gifted colleagues.

DO thicken your skin. Most of the controversy about meeting gifted students' needs is not about you. Keep your eyes on the children!

Top Ten Tips for Being a Successful Gifted Coordinator*

10. Know your craft. Be a practitioner.

9. Keep current with general educational trends; they will affect you.

8. Take the money, no matter how or where it comes from.

7. Don't apologize for gifted-child education. Act on the students' behalf.

6. Don't accept mediocrity, in other staff or yourself.

5. Train, train, train.

4. Be as flexible and open-minded as you expect students and other teachers to be.

3. Accept the challenge—any challenge.

2. Don't sign on as a member of a monthly book club!

And the #1 way to be a successful gifted coordinator...

1. Never, never, ever lose your PASSION!

---

* "DO's for the Gifted Teacher" is adapted from "Keeping Your Own Stories" by Dr. Janis Fall, Gifted Coordinator, Killeen (Texas) Independent School District. "Top Ten Tips for Being a Successful Gifted Coordinator" is adapted from "The Hardest Job You'll Ever Love" by Ellen Sloane, GATE Coordinator, Clark County School District, Las Vegas, Nevada. Both are used with permission in *The Survival Guide for Teachers of Gifted Kids* by Jim Delisle, Ph.D., and Barbara A. Lewis (© 2003, Free Spirit Publishing).

The challenges of implementing a gifted education program are many. Some, like goal setting, identification, and evaluation, can be met by seeking information from resources that are readily available and reasonably clear. Other challenges seem more prickly: How do we, as gifted educators, state the case for funding G/T programs? Gain the trust of other teachers? Effectively harness and channel parent support? Guide kids who need help with troubling behavior and difficult feelings? Keep ourselves going in the face of all the "not-enoughs"—not enough money, time, space, people, energy?

These are questions that occur wherever people come together to work in the interests of gifted children's education. We can't hope to offer all the answers—any more than we can point you to resources that will resolve every funding challenge, solve every conflict with a fellow teacher, smooth relations with all parents, or ease every gifted child's social and emotional burdens. What we *can* do is share some time-tested strategies and tricks to help you as you work to sustain your program and the human relationships on which it depends. Survival Strategy 6 offers a mix of ideas, ours and those of other gifted educators, to help you keep communicating and forging effective relationships for the sake of the gifted kids you serve.

In building these alliances, you will continually face the same key challenges:

- **Working with your administrator.** Administrators *do* hold power, and your ability to work effectively with them is critical for your gifted education program. If your principal isn't an enthusiastic supporter of gifted programming, prod her or him into your gifted class to see the kids in action; this experience has converted many a skeptic. As you work to develop a connection between you and your principal or curriculum coordinator, it can be helpful to imagine yourself in this person's shoes. A building principal, for example, must have the whole educational picture in mind. This person has to answer to parents, teachers, the superintendent, the school board, and the entire community. To win your administrator's cooperation and support, start by earning trust. Show your administrator that you can be counted on to provide reliable information efficiently and succinctly, giving this person essential tools for gifted advocacy and, in the process, gaining his or her buy-in.

- **Funding.** Funding issues, large and small, might come up every biennium, every year, or even every week. Wrapping-paper sales and car washes may help you eke out one special activity or buy a

few books for the resource library, but how do you ensure a solidly funded *program*? One of your most important challenges may be that of helping your principal or central administrator recognize and communicate to others why gifted education requires a meaningful and reliable budget.

- **Teacher support.** As a coordinator or pull-out teacher, you are a resource for classroom teachers, and it falls to you to provide information, materials, hands-on help, and training. As a colleague or supervisor of other gifted educators, you are constantly called upon to shore up those whose time, energy, or spirits are flagging and to pitch in and help when needed.

- **Parent involvement.** Parents can be a gifted program's best allies, yet their help will mean the most when you and they are working as a team in the interests of their children and the program itself. It's a mistake to expect the worst from parents—who, after all, are their children's first and staunchest advocates. It's also a mistake to dismiss parents' interest in the gifted education program or to underestimate their ability to play a key role in sustaining it.

- **Gifted kids' affective needs.** The unique emotional and social needs that come with being gifted can take their toll—on students and on you. You are challenged to find ways to help these gifted young people help themselves.

- **And what about *your* needs?** A program can't thrive if the teachers who are implementing it are frazzled, short-tempered, and stretched beyond their means. Because you're human, you may tend to put yourself and your needs last on your list of school priorities. But sustaining yourself and keeping burnout at bay can have a positive impact on your program, your colleagues, and your gifted students.

"Mountains cannot be surmounted except by winding paths."
—Johann Wolfgang Von Goethe

Keeping the Program Visible

One of the hardest things about managing a gifted program is saying enough about what you are doing in it to achieve some level of notice, while not saying so much that others get tired of hearing from you. Added to this is the challenge of presenting gifted education in such a way that others do not view it as elitist. Yes, visibility is tricky territory, but keeping the gifted education program visible is crucial to ensuring its acceptance and establishing it as a source of pride for the entire school and community. There are several key ways to enhance the gifted program's visibility.

Make Connections

Connections with parents, students, teachers, and administrators will help build support for your program. Parents are particularly powerful when they advocate for their own children; they can often be instrumental in convincing administrators that there is a need for gifted services or program modifications. Students, too, are often excellent spokespersons and persuasive campaigners on behalf of gifted education in general and of particular programs and services. Regular classroom teachers who become involved can also spread the word and influence other teachers to be open, interested, and enthusiastic about gifted education. And connections to administrators are critical—not just to administrators who are known to support gifted services, but also to those who seem disinterested or skeptical. Here are a few ideas for developing partnerships and heightening awareness among the key players in gifted ed:

Establish a gifted advocacy council. Be sure the council includes teachers, parents, administrators, students, community members, and anyone who has power to improve policies for the education of gifted students. The charge of every council member will be to lobby informally (and formally—see "Get Political," this page) for gifted education, keeping it visible. Together, those on the council will also strategize ways to address concerns and issues that are raised at school or in the media.

Schedule regular meetings with key school personnel. Arrange regular meetings with administrators and teachers to keep them fully apprised of research on gifted education. (For more on locating research information, see page 118.) Get scheduled on one school board meeting agenda a year, preferably near the end of the year. Use your time to share what the program is doing, highlight successes, and pinpoint one or two key areas for growth and improvement. Even if you only have fifteen minutes, your presentation can make an impact.

Put gifted students forward. Gifted students themselves can be compelling and persuasive in their own cause. Seeing is believing. As a coordinator or teacher of gifted kids, be sure to place your students and their achievements before those who have power to provide for them. If possible, create an opportunity for students to present their program and needs before the school board (or those who hold the purse strings for their program). Gifted students will be your program's best advertisement. If students present their needs, their hopes, and some examples of their amazing work before skeptical or ambivalent school boards, they will create a better shot at winning support.

Make service a key part of gifted programming. Provide opportunities for your gifted students to serve the school, the community, and other students with worthwhile contributions. Obviously, this benefits the gifted students and those they are supporting. It also allows for children in the gifted program to make their presence known and appreciated. If you involve students in problem based service that really makes a difference in the community (such as improving safety in and around the school, creating a directory of services for newcomers, or recording histories from seniors), encourage the students to contact the media in your area so that their contribution will be presented before a larger audience.

At the same time, make a link between administrators, principals, and classroom teachers and the contributions that gifted students make. If those people are given some connection with the projects of gifted kids, you will go a long way toward bringing school boards and community leaders as well as administrators and classroom teachers on board with support. For example, when students receive recognition in the newspaper or on television, be sure that the report names, along with the students involved, the administrators and classroom teachers connected to the project or event. Then these people can not only derive a sense of accomplishment from and identification with the gifted program, but also receive the credit and recognition they rightly deserve for their supportive efforts.

Get political. Be ready and willing to maintain a connection to local, state, and federal government agencies. With the gifted advocacy council, lobby for any funds or bills that might be in progress which could impact gifted students. Federally, gifted education has no mandate, but rather a program that must be funded by Congress each year—which translates into an ongoing need to bring your case to legislators.

Get to know your state funding sources for gifted education as well. Know who is on the school board, which members are supportive of gifted ed and which are not. Let the decision makers hear your voice—and the voices of students and parents.

Develop a list of district, city, county, state, and federal lawmakers along with phone numbers, mailing addresses, and email contacts. Whenever an issue comes up for a hearing or a vote, contact these decision makers and let them know where you want them to stand. Make this list available to parents and teachers of gifted kids as well. When issues arise, you can also write short letters or statements that can serve as templates others can adapt to send to their representatives.

Provide Usable Information and Data

For decisions to be made about gifted programming, policymakers need compelling information and data. You can be a huge help to your administrator—and help ensure funding and programming levels for your gifted students—if you do the necessary research and information gathering. You'll want to provide both outside research and research that addresses the needs and successes of your particular school or district. Put the data in a usable form so you can readily present it or so another person (such as the school principal or curriculum coordinator) can share it with participants at administrative meetings and school board meetings. Charts, graphs, and talking points are especially helpful.

Where can you find the information you need? Here are some places to start:

- **The National Association for Gifted Children (NAGC).** Go to the NAGC Web site *(www.nagc.org)* and print out the programming standards for gifted kids, available there in a series of tables. These research-based standards demonstrate the best practices to aim for in educating gifted children. At the NAGC Web site you'll also find the status of the funding for the Jacob K. Javits Gifted and Talented Students Education Act for the current fiscal year. The Javits Act is the main source of federal support for gifted education in the United States, and Congress determines its funding levels each year.

- **The National Research Center on the Gifted and Talented (NRC/GT).** This nationwide cooperative of researchers, practitioners, and policymakers is funded through the Javits Act. NRC/GT conducts and disseminates research geared to promoting both high-level learning and total school improvement as a way to help educators work with gifted young people. Among the wealth of information NRC/GT can provide practitioners and parents are brochures and study results geared to policymakers. Visit the Web site at *www.gifted.uconn.edu/nrcgt.html.*

- **ERIC Clearinghouse on Disabilities and Gifted Education.** ERIC stands for Educational Resources Information Center and is another invaluable resource, particularly online, for research reports and a broad spectrum of information on gifted education. Start your search at *www.ericec.org.*

- **Information you have gathered from needs assessments and program evaluations.** You'll find a discussion and forms on needs assessment in Survival Strategy 1, and on program evaluation in Survival Strategy 5. Use the data you have gathered to document the value of existing programs, demonstrate areas of need, and make recommendations about program changes and improvements.

- **The students themselves.** Never underestimate the power of allowing students to speak directly to administrators (principals, superintendents, board members). However, the students will be much more believable if they speak in their own voices, as opposed to canned speeches that smack of teacher involvement. Students might talk about what the gifted program, or a particular aspect of it, has meant in their lives. They might report the results of their work on a complex project, in community service, or in problem solving. They might demonstrate or show the products of their work. Choose students for this task who are well spoken and capable of sticking to a time limit.

Develop a Newsletter for Parents

A newsletter provides a wonderful vehicle for keeping parents interested and informed and promoting dialogue. Better yet, you can share a parent newsletter with teachers and administrators; this will keep these professionals in the know, too, and enhance communication. (It also helps ensure that no teacher has to be in a bind if approached by a parent who wants to discuss something that was in the newsletter.)

Plan to publish and distribute three or four newsletters a year, perhaps one each quarter. Here are some ideas for developing content:

- Document individual and group achievements of students, and name the classroom teachers who are involved with these students. If you work in regular classrooms, highlight the work of students done there while downplaying your own role in these accomplishments.

- Take care not to go overboard in mentioning the "fun" field trips you had or speakers you invited in. Make sure these special events are written about within the context of a specific goal or long-term project in which your students were involved. This way, the emphasis stays on what students are learning and accomplishing.

- Use the newsletter as a vehicle to share resources with which you have become familiar—a Web site, perhaps, or a new book that has captured your attention. Also, reprint a short article about giftedness that you may have come across in your readings. (Be sure to obtain permission, which is required when using copyrighted material.) In general, avoid reproducing a contentious article that may incite controversy. Or, if you feel the need to address a controversial issue, do so in a complete and balanced way that objectively cites pros and cons of a topic. Then, if the newsletter editorial board (this may be you or the gifted education committee or council) wants to take a stand, do so in a straightforward and reasonable way, solidly refuting arguments with which you disagree and supporting those you endorse.

- Announce upcoming events or conferences. To save yourself many phone calls, include full information on the date, time, place, registration fees, and deadlines. Stick to local events, for few parents or teachers are likely to venture to the next World Council for Gifted and Talented Children conference in Tokyo.

- Also include current research on gifted issues, classes that will be offered, strategies parents can use to help their gifted children, and other types of useful information.

Design your newsletter with margins and spacing wide enough to leave some eye-relieving blank space. This makes the text more readable. Also, use photos or graphics that are appropriate for the content. If you use the same color paper for each issue, people will come to recognize it as "the gifted newsletter." Avoid fluorescent paper or paper stock that has a background of any kind, because these are almost impossible to copy or to read.

Give the newsletter a name, preferably with your program's or school's name in the title. Establish an issue and volume designation, too, such as Fall 2003

or Volume 1, Issue 2. Use a logo or a masthead (you could make this a contest for your students) and keep this logo throughout the year.

Proofread . . . and proofread again. Make sure more than one person handles this task. Never rely on a computer spellchecker to get you through. You don't want your readers distracted by unintentional errors, like the name Myron appearing as Moron, Shelly as Smelly, or worse. Your newsletter represents the caliber of your gifted program, so let it reflect quality and high standards in both content and appearance.

There are always a few students who seem to be allergic to taking papers home to parents. To circumvent this problem, include an additional stack of newsletters in an appropriate place in or near the school office. Another idea is to enclose the newsletter in gifted students' report card envelopes. If possible, also make the newsletter available on the school or program Web site.

Seek and Create Publicity

Your newsletter is one form of publicity, but it will mainly operate within the school or district. It's equally important to reach out to the community at large. The media can provide your program with wings to carry information to a larger audience. Outlets like newspapers, magazines, Web pages, radio, and TV offer a powerful public relations tool. But you must be sure they receive and report accurate information.

- Check with your district to find any regulations that are in place in regard to working with the media. At the beginning of the year, you will need to get permission from parents to display their children's names, quotes, photos, and work in the media. This written authorization is essential; many—but not all—parents will be eager to support this kind of publicity.

- Create a one-page flyer that you provide to media folks *any time* you (or others in the gifted program) make contact with them or they contact you. This flyer should present the school or district's gifted education philosophy statement and a *brief* outline of your program. (If you make it longer than one page, a reporter might not take time to read it.) The flyer is convenient for you and for media outlets; it also helps assure that reporting about the program will be accurate.

- Whenever students are involved in presentations before school boards or in community groups, competitions, or projects, inform the media before the event. Students who gain public attention for designing robots, attending a space camp, participating in a district debate, or cleaning up wetlands can sometimes do more to drum up support for gifted programs than a stack of written evaluations. Media spots focused on gifted students' contributions create positive images of the schools and districts involved.

- Write editorials and newspaper or magazine articles about what gifted students are doing. If you don't feel you have the expertise to do this, find a freelance writer or a capable volunteer who cares about the needs of gifted students. You can also write for smaller markets or bulletins, like school or district newsletters.

- When your students do something noteworthy (such as sharing picture books they have written with younger children, attending a state or regional competition like Odyssey of the Mind, or surveying their school to discover causes of aggression among students), make sure the local media are informed. Reporters will be more likely to cover your event if a student creates a press release announcing the project or activity. Be sure the press release is designed to catch the attention of a reporter whose desk already has a foot-high stack of announcements. Try adding color or a student's original design. You also might encourage a student to call media offices and read the release, although in some cases phone announcements are not welcomed. It's a good idea to ask the reporter to fax you an article before it is printed so that you can check for errors. Some reporters will do this, while others won't.

- Keep a camera with you so that you can take photographs of student experiences and projects. Sometimes, even though students have informed the press that they are organizing something terrific, journalists will end up covering the bank robbery across town and miss your students' event. If you take photos and provide reporters with the basic details of your event, they will sometimes carry a news item about your students anyway.

- Make sure administrators get copies of all articles and photographs that occur anywhere in print. The same goes for radio and Internet or television coverage—both commercial and public-access TV.

There are other publicity strategies as well. One that bears mentioning, if you have something you are proud of, is to share it with a wider audience: the state or national gifted conference, a regional education conference, or even one of the "big" general conferences for organizations like the Association for Supervision and Curriculum Development (ASCD), the National Association of Elementary School Principals (NAESP), the National Middle School Association (NMSA), the National Council for Teachers of Mathematics (NCTM), or the National Science Teachers Association (NSTA). If at all possible, have at least one other staff member join you as a copresenter. And, of course, include students if it's feasible.

Becoming a Resource for Parents and Teachers

Sustaining your program means sustaining the people who keep it going. A key responsibility here lies in becoming a helpful, reliable resource for parents and teachers alike.

Involve, Inform, and Support Parents

Parents provide a powerful voice for gifted students. They are the people who are usually most interested in what happens with their children's education. Often, too, parents are acutely eager to learn all that they can about gifted ed and how to address their children's unique needs. You will greatly strengthen your program if you reach out to include and support parents. Here's a starter list of tips:

- Hold parent meetings regularly—at least once every quarter, and more often if a parent volunteer can help orchestrate them. The meetings might include only parents of students who have been identified for a gifted program, or they might include all interested parents. Either way, your focus will be on gifted children's education. To encourage wide participation, alternate the meeting times so that some gatherings take place during the school day and others occur in the evening. Among other ideas, you might call on a parent educator to offer guidance on parenting gifted kids, a teacher to share information about how gifted students are being served in the regular classroom, or a resource teacher or volunteer parent to give insight into a particular enrichment program. Advocacy groups often result from parent meetings, so consider inviting a dynamic guest speaker who can present convincing information and anecdotes about the needs of gifted students. Provide handouts and light refreshments.

- Organize a parent committee to advocate for gifted education and to help disseminate information to other parents. Parent volunteers can also assist in administering and teaching support programs. Create a phone tree to get out pertinent information. This can be set up at a parent meeting.

- Be informed at parent-teacher conferences. Know the school, district, and state policies. Know the students and their needs. Be prepared to show that you have a challenging differentiated curriculum, that you are providing specialized challenges for the students involved, and that you're willing and eager to find ways to improve programming to meet individual students' learning needs.

Build a Bridge to Teachers

With a few thoughtful strategic moves, you can become an ally in the eyes of classroom teachers. Following are two "don'ts" and an important "do" for forging ties with teachers:

- **Don't overstate your worth.** We know one gifted coordinator, new to the school district, who introduced herself to the seasoned staff in her middle school by stating, "Hello, my name is Marge, and I'm here to make you look good."

  Ouch! Needless to say, the staff didn't take well to Marge's implication that they needed *her* to make *them* look good. And Marge set up expectations that she could hardly hope to reach. That's not to say that a single errant comment will result in a permanent lack of cooperation, but it can be an uphill climb to get back on neutral turf. That means time and effort spent reclaiming lost ground rather than making progress in the interest of gifted kids.

- **Don't inundate teachers with information or requests.** It's great to be conscientious, but if there is a memo in the teachers' mailboxes every week reminding them of something they owe you, you will be seen more as a pest than as a partner and support person. We have found that the *best* thing to put into teachers' mailboxes is not a request but rather a note that reads, "I saw you were doing a study on pond life with your fifth graders. Here's a book I've come across that I thought might be useful." This kind of action demonstrates that you're (1) paying attention and (2) interested in providing meaningful help; it can go a long way toward showing your colleagues that you are someone who is there for *them* as well as for the students. (A word to the wise: keep a list of what materials you've lent to whom, or you'll quickly lose track of where your resources have gone.)

- **Do respond to teacher requests.** If teachers request particular information, give them specific (not general) resources that are current. The most helpful materials to provide are those that give doable lessons or useful resource information, with the pertinent pages flagged. Of course, you can keep your eye out for journal articles that cover topics more generally, but reserve these for administrators or for teachers who are taking a graduate class in education in order to renew their teaching certificate. Believe us, if you provide materials that call for lots of extra preparation on the teacher's part, your first request from that teacher is likely to be the last.

  Teachers might ask for curricular support for a gifted student in the classroom. They might, for example, request a more advanced math or language arts book, or information about Newton's Laws of Motion. They might ask how to handle a challenging behavioral issue. Should a teacher approach you and ask about meeting a specific student's need, make an appointment to sit and talk with the teacher. This will ensure that you provide the types of resources—material or emotional—that will be truly beneficial.

Start a Resource Library

If you have funds for developing a library, consider yourself fortunate. If funds are low or nonexistent, parents might be willing to fund-raise. (See page 134 for a resource on how to raise money for this and other program needs.) And, if you're like most teachers, you'll probably purchase some materials on your own and make them available for others to use. We both have an extensive collection of curricular resources, categorized by content area, that we've made available for teacher use. You can keep track of materials by inviting teachers to check them out by signing a form and leaving it in a special folder.

Don't wait for a teacher to come asking to borrow this book or that lesson plan. Instead, bring a resource to a teacher whom you believe will use it, with particular pages flagged. Soon, this teacher will be telling others about your stash of helpful stuff, and the materials will be where they belong: off the shelf and in teachers' classrooms.

A good resource library also includes resources on the theory and practice of gifted education as well as materials for parents and students. Keep the library up-to-date and pertinent. You will find many suggestions for resources that address a wide range of topics in the "Resources" section at the end of each Survival

Strategy in this book; also see "Additional Resources" (pages 146–154) for more recommended books, articles, and journals along with a list of organizations and publishers in the area of gifted education.

Provide Opportunities for Staff Development

Staff development is a key component of any gifted program. In its programming criteria, NAGC recommends comprehensive, ongoing professional development so that all people who work with gifted kids are fully qualified to do so. This means that both G/T and regular classroom teachers need to have a variety of inservice opportunities.

Although many district and state philosophies support educating gifted students, the core curriculum is usually aimed at the bull's eye (directly in the middle). Not surprisingly, teachers get comfortable teaching particular material in particular ways. Teachers seldom make major changes in their instruction until they have been taught principles and strategies many times and have had ample opportunity to apply and practice them. A one-time shot at an inservice can do little more than raise awareness; it will not bring about significant improvement in instruction.

One of the secrets to the success of any well-developed gifted program is to provide instruction to those working with gifted students on an ongoing basis. You might feel qualified to lead some instruction yourself; you might also find qualified people within your own local or state organizations or through universities. Contact your state gifted organization or those in surrounding states for expert consultants in gifted education as well. Here are some hints on inservice training:

- Hold regular curricular meetings with small groups of teachers, such as already scheduled grade-level meetings. During this time, help teachers to design differentiated curricular experiences for their students.

- Join forces with other districts to offer special classes on strategies for teaching gifted students. You might also include instruction on special support programs such as Future Problem Solving, Community Problem Solving, debate, writing contests, Math and Science Olympiads, or others.

- If possible, provide opportunities for teachers to obtain state endorsements for teaching gifted students. Some states, but not all, have established guidelines for teaching credentials that are either required or optional for serving gifted students. This can be as simple as a certificate verifying that a teacher has obtained thirty clock hours of staff development on serving gifted children or as complex as obtaining twenty-one

SUGGESTIONS FOR A STAFF DEVELOPMENT PLAN[1]

Participants	Consultant	Focus
Teachers of gifted, school staff, parents, community, administrators, program coordinators, school board members, students	Local, district, or state experts	Informational, motivational, philosophy, overview
Teachers of gifted, administrators, program coordinators, classroom teachers, parents	District or state experts	Awareness, rules, requirements, characteristics of gifted, identification
Teacher of gifted, administrators, program coordinators, classroom teachers	District or state experts, national consultants	Programming, classroom management, differentiation
Teachers of gifted, classroom teachers, administrators, program coordinators	District or state experts, national consultants	Special populations (underperformers, learning disabled, culturally diverse, economically disadvantaged, girls, boys, etc.)
Teachers of gifted, program coordinators	University	University credit courses, advanced coursework

Figure 6.1

graduate course hours in order to receive a license to teach gifted children. Be sure to keep abreast of your state's requirements regarding teaching credentials needed or encouraged when it comes to teaching gifted kids—and then, share these with your colleagues and your administrator. Sometimes teachers can receive financial support from schools, districts, or state or federal funding for obtaining endorsements or higher degrees in gifted education. However it is accomplished, your program will be greatly strengthened if you have endorsed teachers at every school or every grade level.

- Don't limit your training efforts to teachers. As noted in Figure 6.1, many staff development initiatives can also provide essential information for parents, administrators, and even students.

Every school district handles inservice differently. Some have required staff development days several times a year. Others have early-release days for students monthly, with individual schools planning programs for these afternoons. Still others do little more than provide an opening-day convocation speaker, with all other staff development programs optional. A few

---

SECURING A GUEST SPEAKER: 20 STEPS TO SUCCESS[2]

1. Contact the proposed guest speaker and make arrangements to meet with him/her to discuss the details you have in mind. If the speaker is from out of town, make the first contact by phone or email.

2. Discuss the type of presentation you have in mind and come to an agreement that fits both your requirements and the speaker's expertise.

3. Secure a date that fits your schedule.

4. Present a contract to the speaker (or request one from her/him) that outlines the speaker's fee, travel expenses, type and length of presentation, and session date.

5. After signatures have been received, present the speaker with a signed copy of the contract.

6. Contact the speaker again within one month of the presentation to review details.

7. Secure a location for the event; keep in mind potential audience size. Most speakers prefer a small room that looks crowded to a cavernous room that looks empty.

8. Ask the speaker to give you a list of needed audio-visual items and any handouts to be reproduced. Also, ask how the speaker would like to be introduced (most have a standard introduction that they can send to you).

9. Publicize the event at least two months prior to its occurrence. Send flyers and personal invitations to school administrators as well as teachers. Be sure the flyer includes all necessary information: date, time, location, speaker's name and affiliation, presentation title, directions to the site. Send this information to local newspapers, too.

10. Arrange a reservation list for participants and a phone number to call. If a fee is being charged to the audience, make arrangements for collecting the money at the door or by mail.

11. A week prior to the presentation, call or visit the location site to make sure all arrangements are set.

12. Meet the guest speaker at the airport or provide travel directions for local presenters.

13. Arrive at the presentation site at least forty-five minutes prior to its beginning. (If the speaker does not need this much time on site, arrange for someone else to bring the speaker to the site while you check the on-site arrangements.)

14. Unless the speaker has requested a different arrangement, offer handouts to audience members as they arrive.

15. Introduce the guest speaker, taking no more than three minutes to do so. Avoid personal anecdotes or jokes unless you know the speaker well.

16. After the presentation, thank the speaker and audience and (if approved in advance by the speaker) entertain audience questions.

17. Return the guest speaker to the hotel (or provide directions home if the person is driving) and ask if you can help with anything else prior to his/her departure.

18. Within a week, follow up with a phone call, an email, or a letter thanking the speaker and providing any evaluative comments you received. Check on the status of payment and inform the speaker when she/he can expect a check.

19. Thank the establishment that hosted the event. If a rental fee was required, make sure the bill has been paid.

20. Congratulate yourself on a job well done!

Figure 6.2

districts even restrict their staff development to the summer, where teachers are encouraged through extra pay to participate in week-long sessions.

Whatever your district's parameters, learn them quickly and then get presentations and workshops in gifted education scheduled in promptly. This is especially important if your gifted program is new or has undergone recent and extensive revision.

In larger districts, it may be difficult to get the hours or days you need scheduled. Other important topics—school violence, a new grading system, information on blood-borne pathogens—may take precedence over training in how to provide gifted services. Still, if you present a solid rationale and work within the structure provided, you may find the people who schedule these meetings very accommodating. In fact, in some districts your willingness to sponsor an inservice may actually be welcomed, especially if few people want this responsibility.

Once you get the go-ahead, you have several options for topics. You may plan presentations about characteristics and identification of giftedness, differentiating curriculum and instruction, emotional needs of gifted children, working with gifted students who underperform, or other issues you have identified as being of particular importance to the teachers. Whatever your selected topic, make sure that you give teachers at least one practical idea, strategy, lesson, or material that they can use tomorrow. If all you do is talk theory, research, or "shoulds," prepare to see participants snoring and grading papers.

Sometimes when you are preparing a seminar, no one signs up to come. This is not uncommon in a beginning gifted education program. If you're not getting any response from an announcement or from distributing flyers, take the time to call a few people and invite them to attend.

If you are the person conducting the inservice and are doing this for the first time, be prepared for the possibility of awkwardness with some teachers, at least temporarily. Why? Because as soon as you transcend the role of participant and become a presenter, there tends to be an automatic reshuffling of attitudes about who you are. There are those who will think, "Gosh, better he than I." Others may question, "What qualifies him to be training me?" In the eyes of a few, once you've become a presenter, you have made a shift from being one of "us" to one of "them." Try not to be too bothered by this. In most cases, over time, your consistently respectful and professional interactions will overcome people's discomfort.

If you are hiring another presenter to come in, make sure that you have seen or heard this person present firsthand—do *not* rely on someone else's glowing recommendation. Remember, the guest presenter will be at your school for one day, but if the person bombs, *you* will have to live with the fallout for a long time to come. In one district we know, an expensive full-day speaker's presentation was so off the mark that the superintendent had to intervene, which she did by announcing at lunch that due to a districtwide emergency, the afternoon session would have to be cut. This was a half-truth—and a very costly one—but it removed teachers from an excruciatingly awkward setting. Why had this speaker been chosen in the first place? Because someone in the district had seen a portion of a video recording of his presentation and recommended him as a speaker on the strength of it. Unfortunately, the recorded snippet was not representative; the tape was more than ten years old, as was the man's presentation.

With that lesson in mind, do still be prepared to pay for quality. To keep expenses under control, you might be able to swap with another district, enlisting someone there to conduct a session for you while you or someone else from your gifted program presents one for them. When bringing in an outside presenter from any source, look outside your area of expertise and that of your colleagues. Take the opportunity to reap the benefits of reliable new information from a fresh perspective.

A final word to the wise: have food and drink available. Whether it's donuts and fruit in the morning or cheese and a vegetable tray in the afternoon, you will automatically win a degree of buy-in when teachers know you have thought of their bellies as well as their brains. And don't forget that other "b" word: "behinds." If you sit teachers on hard, metal folding chairs and expect them to concentrate, you have more faith in the human spirit (and anatomy) than we do. Keep people comfortable, and half the job is done for you.

Sustain Veteran G/T Teachers

If you supervise other teachers, you know that keeping the "veterans" of gifted education enthused and involved can create a challenge. Workloads, time commitments, funds, and policy decisions can have a cumulative effect of wearing down long-term teachers. Here are some ideas to help boost morale and sustain veteran teachers' mental and physical energy:

- Financially support their attendance at national, state, and local meetings, university seminars, and conventions.

- Hold semiannual or annual retreats where teachers can recharge their enthusiasm. A nonschool setting is best for this purpose, because it allows a welcome change of scenery. Yet, even if you must hold your retreat in a school facility, it is still beneficial to get together for the sole, focused purpose of sharing ideas, resources, frustrations, and solutions.

- Provide articles and up-to-date reading material that will be of interest and will support experienced teachers' current efforts and passions.

- Recognize and award teachers' accomplishments in newsletters and at parent meetings, school or district awards ceremonies, and school board meetings.

- Visit their classroom so they can demonstrate their accomplishments.

- Invite veteran teachers to mentor beginning instructors in gifted education; invite beginners to visit the classes of veterans.

- Encourage veteran teachers to teach small classes and seminars, using their particular strengths.

- Include G/T veterans on gifted committees.

- Hold regular meetings with veterans. Encourage them to actively problem-solve the issues that come up in the gifted education program.

- Give veteran teachers a break and lighten their extraneous workloads whenever possible.

Perhaps most important, don't neglect to sustain yourself. Begin each year with a *manageable-sized* set of specific objectives you hope to achieve—for example, being invited into at least one teacher's class per grade level to work on curriculum differentiation; refining the identification procedure to include teacher nomination; expanding the gifted program to an additional grade level; and meeting with school counselors to review methods for serving gifted students who underperform. Then, at midyear, evaluate which of these objectives you have met and what steps you can take to reach or modify the others. Later in this chapter (pages 132–133) you'll find additional thoughts about injecting balance into your work and keeping yourself refreshed.

Supporting Gifted Students' Social and Emotional Needs

Although all kids experience social and emotional problems at times, gifted children's needs may be different and require special support. This is formally recognized by NAGC, which has included socio-emotional guidance and counseling standards as part of its overall programming principles. Here are a few examples of the types of social and emotional challenges gifted students may face.

Perfectionism. Some gifted children are prone to perfectionism. They know the difference between what's "okay" or "good enough" and what's truly exceptional, and because they are capable of superior performance, come to expect the absolute best of themselves at all times.

*Marcos refuses to hand in his creative writing story. His teacher gives him an F. The story the teacher hasn't seen is actually highly creative. The problem is that Marcos doesn't think he's finished—and might not **ever** think so—because in his mind it isn't perfect yet. As a result, Marcos feels bad about himself and isn't succeeding in language arts.*

Lauren refuses to try out for the dance club for fear she might not make it. Although she's a skilled dancer, she is afraid of making a mistake or failing. Lauren's desire to be perfect is paralyzing her and keeping her from developing her talent and feeling confident about herself.

In their book on the social and emotional needs of gifted kids, Jim and coauthor Judy Galbraith describe the difference between perfectionism—a negative drive—and the positive pursuit of excellence:[3]

*Perfectionism means that you can **never** fail, you **always** need approval, and if you come in second, you're a loser. The pursuit of excellence means taking risks, trying new things, growing, changing—and sometimes failing. Perfectionism is not about doing your best or striving for high goals. Instead, it can block your ability to do well. And it can take a heavy toll on your self-esteem, relationships, creativity, health, and capacity to enjoy life. Because perfection* *isn't possible, deciding that's what you want—and that you won't be satisfied with anything less—is a recipe for disappointment.*

This perspective can help you and other adults as you work with perfectionistic students like Marcos and Lauren. To support these students:

- Guide them to manage a tendency toward perfectionism by finding a different perspective about what constitutes quality. Discuss the difference between perfection and excellence.

- Encourage teachers and parents to relax expectations, if they are too high.

- Emphasize that mistakes are part of the learning process. Help gifted students be less hesitant to tackle difficult tasks for fear of failing. You can reward these children for trying and not just for succeeding.

- Help gifted students to set reasonable goals. For example, it isn't possible or necessary for a student to set a goal to read all the books in the library over the summer. Help a student with this aspiration think about why he or she has set the goal and about what meaningful result the child wants to accomplish.

- Hold weekly conferences with your perfectionistic student to reinforce setting realistic goals.

- Point out what's positive about seeking excellence. It can motivate a student to higher achievement. Great accomplishments in the world have been achieved by people who had tendencies for perfection, such as Olympic champions, research scientists, musicians, and artists. Help students see that pursuing their best spurs them on, while expecting perfection can be defeating.

Ridicule by peers who don't understand their interests. Gifted kids often suffer from a sense of estrangement from kids who don't understand them and who may dismiss or taunt them.

Wade's classmates are discussing video games, while Wade wants to talk about world hunger. His classmates look at Wade with blank stares. Some call him a nerd.

Being gifted is normal for Wade and kids like him. Wade's teacher needs to help Wade understand that his concern for feeding all the children in the world is a noble one and that Wade has a gift that causes him to recognize and focus on this. What else can a teacher do to deflect and discourage the ridicule that gifted kids often face?

- Start a lunchtime get-together for gifted kids. It's important to provide opportunities for gifted and talented kids to meet other children of similar abilities and interests. In this setting, Wade can talk with his new friends about collecting cans of food. Megan can share her latest math tricks. Chan can share her beautiful drawings. There aren't likely to be blank stares and cruel taunts here.

- Create an emotional support group for gifted kids to discuss problems and to express their feelings in a safe atmosphere. You might schedule group meetings before or after school or even during the day.

- Foster an academic atmosphere in classrooms so that achieving is rewarded, expected, and appreciated. When possible, do all you can to see that a gifted child like Wade is placed in classrooms with teachers who like and understand gifted kids.

Worry and a sense of helplessness about world problems. It's not uncommon for a gifted child to feel overly worried and responsible about issues like war, poverty, violence, and the environment. This kind of sensitivity can lead a student to feel deeply guilty, anxious, and even immobilized. The following suggestions offer ways you can help ameliorate these feelings:

- Help gifted children share their gifts in a larger audience of adults or other gifted children who will reinforce the positive value of their concerns and give the children ways to address them. Wade might speak about his concerns before the city council, faculty, school board, or a relief organization.

- Help gifted students make a contribution within their sphere of influence. Wade might collect cans of food to contribute to a food shelf to feed hungry children in his city. This would result in reducing the world hunger problem.

- Relieve children's feelings of guilt by reminding them that there is time for growing up, that they are not responsible for taking on adult problems at this point in their lives.

- The school psychologist or another mental health professional can help a gifted, anxiety-ridden student develop coping and stress management skills. This counselor should be knowledgeable about the characteristics and unique needs of gifted children.

Uneven development. Though intellectually far ahead of other students their age, gifted kids are rarely as advanced socially, emotionally, or physically. At times, certain types of development may even lag.

An eight-year-old boy may have the ability to do calculus, but on the playground he may act like a six-year-old. A fifteen-year-old girl may look and sound like an accomplished adult when contrasting the views of the Greek philosophers, yet feel awkward and childish in a social setting like a party or school football game. A twelve-year-old may be talented athletically, but feel too shy to participate in team sports. A ten-year-old who is a fierce debater might feel embarrassed and inadequate when struggling with the mechanics of spelling or math.

Educators use various terms to describe having intellectual abilities that are out of sync with other areas of development: two you may often hear are *uneven integration* and *asynchronous development*. Gifted kids aren't the only students who develop unevenly; the difference is that their abilities and talents shine so brightly that they cast a stark spotlight on limitations. Some suggestions for helping students cope include the following:

- Help children accept differing abilities. Point out that *all* people develop differently and have varying skills, capabilities, and talents. Reassure gifted kids that no one expects them to have exceptional ability in every area.

- Help children learn needed social skills by role-playing with them.

- Encourage students to feel pride in their gifts and talents rather than despair over uneven development. One way to do this is by assisting gifted students to pursue topics and projects that tap into already developed talents or interests.

- Seek help from a qualified professional in dealing with an area of need. For example, if a gifted child needs to develop study skills, arrange for the student to take a how-to-study class. If a student is highly able in language arts but struggles with geometry, connect the child with a patient and creative math tutor. If you or parents suspect a learning difference or disability, have the student evaluated for special services in the area of need.

Intensity. Gifted children often are strong-willed, intuitive, and independent, with a sense of purpose, destiny, or ethical sensitivity. Perceiving layers of complexity in the world around them, these kids are often obsessed with particular issues or phenomena that are compelling to them. Like the composer who persistently hears musical strains or the mathematician who constantly visualizes formulae, gifted kids are often on their own intense "wave length," deeply focused on a particular problem, concern, or idea. This intensity can alienate other students, and gifted students in turn might be quick to judge others and bristle at any sign of mediocrity or hypocrisy.

To support intense gifted kids, teachers need to be flexible in the scheduling, pacing, and choice of projects. Allow students a breadth of time for working on topics and in areas they care deeply about. To support all kids, it's essential to teach tolerance toward differences. Talk about tolerance; set an example of it. Encourage students to accept, respect, and value the unique individual qualities students have to offer themselves and their classmates.

Stress and burnout. Because of their intensity and drive for perfection, gifted children can experience high levels of stress. To help with stress:

- Encourage gifted kids to take part in classroom games and other leisure activities. Provide opportunities for them to be in charge of some of these activities, too.

- Reduce the homework load by allowing gifted students to prove competency in an area so that they can skip unnecessary assignments. (This accommodation is known as curriculum compacting.)

- Encourage journaling so that the intense gifted student can express feelings and fears and let off steam through the cathartic experience of writing personal thoughts. Visual arts, music, or performing arts can also offer release from stress.

- Allow gifted students to choose some of their challenges, both by providing many choices in curricular extensions and by giving gifted kids opportunities to choose curricular experiences in which they can develop and share their talents.

- Help gifted students learn to laugh and take themselves less seriously. Share humorous cartoons; watch a funny movie in class; make puns and jokes. Tickle students' funny bones and encourage laughter. Laugh at yourself when you do something ridiculous, and point it out: "Yesterday I locked the keys in my car—with the engine running." Make the classroom a safe atmosphere where everyone can relax and be human.

- Teach gifted kids how to say no. "No, I don't have time to do that." "No, I'm too busy." "No, I'm not interested." "No, but thanks for asking." Help them practice by role-playing so that they can get better control of their busy lives.

Beyond perfectionism, teasing, worry about social concerns, uneven development, intensity, and stress, there is a long list of social and emotional issues that can plague gifted students and those who care about them. Some of these include alienation, isolation, boredom, hypersensitivity (both physical and emotional), extreme perceptiveness, high involvement, frustration, expectations from others, and a feeling of being overwhelmed by their own capabilities.

WHAT I'VE LEARNED IN MY ROLE AS A GIFTED EDUCATOR

Over the years, we have heard hundreds of comments from gifted education teachers about the unique social, emotional, and learning needs of gifted students. Here is a sampling of what these teachers have told us:

- "I've learned that gifted kids do not necessarily know what it means to be gifted."

- "I've learned that gifted kids don't always feel smart."

- "I've learned that gifted kids can be very hard on themselves at times."

- "I've learned that gifted kids like discussions that cover mature subjects."

- "I've learned that gifted kids need to have the opportunity to discuss openly their feelings, strengths, and weaknesses in a safe, nonthreatening environment."

- "I've learned that a child who is gifted might not earn the top grades and that a child who earns all A's is not necessarily gifted."

- "I've learned that there is more variety in the learning needs among my small group of gifted children than there ever was in my regular classroom of twenty-five students."

- "I've learned that gifted kids can be lonely."

- "I've learned a new respect for children who think in different ways from the norm."

Figure 6.3

Not surprisingly, along with these social and emotional concerns can come behavior problems. One excellent strategy for working with gifted kids on behavior issues is through growth contracts.[4] Growth contracts are written agreements between individual students and teachers (though parents may find

them useful as well), specifying a plan for personal change or growth within a set period of time. Growth contracts differ from learning contracts in that they are geared toward affective rather than academic concerns. For example, a growth contract might focus on meeting and making new friends, finding something that holds a student's interest (particularly helpful for students who underperform), changing one's attitude about school, or changing a specific behavior. You'll find a growth contract you can use and share with other teachers on page 135. While a contract is being worked on, be sure to meet with the student regularly to discuss how things are going.

In using a growth contract, keep in mind that it's less important for a student to fulfill the contract to the letter than it is for the child to gain skills and information needed to better manage the issue of concern. The contract can help a child learn to set goals, design strategies to meet those goals, work on the strategies, improve, and see what works (and what doesn't). Learning and developing these skills will go a long way toward improving many behavior problems while helping a gifted child develop needed life skills.

"Theories and goals of education don't matter a whit if you do not consider your students to be human beings."
—LOU ANN WALKER

Addressing Parents' and Students' Concerns

Although educators can disagree professionally about specific gifted program components or practices, this dialogue does not typically have the level of personal investment parents are likely to feel when it comes to their son or daughter. For this reason, probably one of the more ubiquitous challenges you face on a day-to-day basis is responding to parents (and at times to students) about their concerns and complaints in regard to the gifted program.

And parents *will* come to you with these concerns and complaints. "Why isn't my daughter in the gifted program?" "I'm worried about my son's performance in school." "My child just isn't being challenged." When you receive the inevitable phone call, email, or letter from a parent, keep this in mind above all else: the parent wants someone to hear the full story. Often, too quickly, we rush in with advice for changing or improving a situation when it could have been more productive to simply *listen*.

When a parent of a gifted child calls you, this person has may have already discussed the issue with the child's classroom teachers, the counselor, the school principal, other parents, and various neighbors and family members. If the parent's concern hasn't been satisfied (and since you're getting a phone call, you can assume that it hasn't), at this point Mom or Dad is probably impatient, anxious, angry, or all three. Listening to the parent's entire story is a sign of both courtesy and wisdom. All the details are going to come out eventually, so it is most efficient if they come out all at once. Too, parents will appreciate that you respect them enough to not interrupt their flowing thoughts.

Take notes during the conversation or, if the communication is written, make a copy of it and write marginal notes to yourself on the copy. Understand that you are getting a biased view of the situation, but also recognize that the principal, counselor, or teacher the parent has spoken to earlier will also present a biased view, albeit from a different perspective. You won't be looking for who's "right" and who's "wrong" (assigning blame sure as heck never solved a problem *we've* ever addressed). Instead, your goal is to arrive at a solution that makes sense in light of the particular circumstance.

Once the parent has fully explained the worry or concern, one of the best responses is not a statement from you, but a question: "How do you think I can be helpful here?" Or, "Is there something specific you'd like me to act on or do?" Or, "What can I do to help resolve this?" In our experience, surprisingly often the parent's response will be, "Well, there's nothing really to do at this point, I just wanted someone to know my feelings about _____." In a case like this, simply by listening, you will have resolved or assuaged a problem.

Of course, the situation won't always be that simple. The parent may be looking for a particular action from you, or for suggestions on how to deal with the issue. Often, too, a solution will need to be provided or a decision made that has the potential of leaving at least one person unhappy. Frequently, concerns revolve around three or four themes.

"I want my child placed in the gifted program." As noted in Survival Strategy 2 (pages 47 and 48), it is best to take time to patiently and thoroughly respond to this concern, referring to the specific identification guidelines your district has established and showing the parent the child's test scores and rank-ings among other students. (*Never,* however, show the tests scores of another child for comparison.) Before saying much of anything, check the child's cumulative folder for available test scores and anecdotal records (such as teachers' report card comments). You may well need to be the bearer of what the parent perceives to be bad news. Although you may do this with a heavy heart, remember this: The criteria established for gifted identification were put together purposefully—the school is able to serve a certain number of students who fit specific characteristics and measures. If you decide to accept every child who comes close to meeting the criteria, you might as well have no criteria at all.

Be sure to talk with the parent about the other opportunities available for the child's growth and enrichment. (Remember the "Inventory of Excellence"—pages 63–64?) Initially the parent may see these as second-rate alternatives. But they're not. It's your job to help the parent recognize the many benefits the school's other options offer, both academically and socially. The last thing you or the school wants is for *any* parent to think that the gifted program is the only thing that could enhance children's education—which is patently untrue.

"My child is not challenged in the regular classroom." Since *unchallenged* and *bored* are vague descriptions, the first thing to ask for here is specifics. A probing question like, "What is your child being asked to do that you feel is inappropriate?" would be a good starting point, followed up by, "If your child could do something different from the work he's now doing, what would it look like?" Unless and until these questions are addressed, there will be little hope for change in the classroom. In addition, make sure that the parent has discussed the issue with the classroom teacher before coming to you. If not, send the parent back to this "first base," and let the teacher(s) know about the phone call that's in the offing.

The teacher in this situation may want advice or help from you. In this case, the more specific your suggestions or action, the better. For example, if a student is skilled in math but is being bogged down by repetitive homework assignments, suggest specific ways to compact the child's curriculum (perhaps by having the child complete the chapter's test early) and provide some enrichment materials for the teacher to use in lieu of the regular assignments. You may find that you need to be more hands-on at first in providing resource help of this sort. Once they've worked through it a time or two, most teachers will be willing and confident about taking on this responsibility.

In some cases it can be helpful to arrange a meeting with the parent, principal, gifted coordinator or resource teacher, and classroom teacher focused on discussing the educational needs of the student. Alert the classroom teacher to the purpose of the meeting ahead of time, so he or she can prepare some strategies. In this situation the teacher is more likely to become engaged; express appreciation for the teacher's willingness to create challenges for the gifted student. Usually, this positive approach will encourage a teacher to be more open to the needs of gifted students now and in the future, and will allow her or him a way to help design and become part of a solution.

If a parent has talked with the teacher and remains unsatisfied, defer further discussion until you have a chance to talk with the teacher involved and discussed ways you can help out. Most of the time showing respect for the classroom teacher and inviting this person's active participation in finding solutions for gifted students' concerns leads to a better experience for students and a stronger working relationship among all of the adults involved as well. Many classroom teachers are eager to seek better educational solutions for gifted students.

In the event (relatively rare) that the teacher admits to not modifying the curriculum or to not actively working to challenge this child at all, and indicates little or no interest in doing so, then the issue is one that no longer involves you directly, but is a matter of administrative concern. Talk to the school principal, relaying the facts as you understand them, and ask for further guidance. This is not "ratting" or going behind a teaching colleague's back. Rather, it is doing your job—going in search of a solution that will best help a gifted child in your care. A strong principal, too, wants to hear about news of this nature before it becomes a major problem, for if a teacher is unwilling or unable to try to appropriately teach one gifted student, the same is likely to be true when it comes to other gifted students.

"I'd like my child removed from the gifted program." When this issue rears its head, it is typically because a gifted student is not performing well outside of the gifted program. That's what happened in the case of a student of Jim's:

A parent contacted Jim regarding her son, Joel, who was in pull-out classes for kids gifted in math and science. Joel loved the G/T program, and performed well in it. Unfortunately, reported his mother, Joel didn't feel the same about some of his everyday schoolwork, *and was on the verge of failing English and social studies. Joel's parents didn't want to pull their son from the gifted classes, but they had concluded that it was necessary so that Joel could experience the consequences of not working up to his potential in important core subjects. "Also," the mother confided to Jim, "we think taking Joel out of the gifted program would make his teachers happier, because some of them have commented that other gifted kids are more responsible than he is."*

After listening to Joel's mother's concerns, Jim scheduled a conference with her and Joel's dad. Before meeting with them, he got input from Joel's teachers about specific ways Joel could improve his performance. The teachers suggested that Joel needed to turn in his daily homework on time and, when projects had to be late, turn them in late for partial credit rather than not at all for no credit. They also recommended that he meet weekly with an aide to help organize his notebook and assignments. The teachers (and Jim) saw an intermediate step focused on these improvements as a better alternative than punishing Joel by banishing him from the challenging science and math classes. Jim and Joel's classroom teachers met with the parents and discussed this course of action. Seeing that the classroom teachers *didn't* want Joel pulled from the G/T program and that school personnel wanted to support Joel's education both in and out of the program, his parents were persuaded to try the recommended approach. For their part, they agreed to monitor his assignments more closely, and Jim agreed to have lunch with Joel one day a week to check in on his progress. Joel didn't become a straight-A student, but both his study habits and his grades gradually improved. As a result, his teachers and parents were comfortable keeping him in the gifted program, and Joel began to take responsibility for his own education.

Having a policy in place to address how homework will be handled when a student misses work because of a gifted pull-out program will set the stage for cooperation among teachers, students, parents, and the administration. Figure 6.4 shows an example of a policy that is simple and straightforward.

Sometimes, of course, a parent will be determined to remove a child from programming, or a gifted student will decide not to cooperate. At times, too, the gifted program itself may not be the right fit, for one reason or another. The exit policy action plan described in Survival Strategy 2 (pages 49–50) will be helpful in these circumstances.

DISTRICT 11 HOMEWORK POLICY

Students participating in the gifted program will spend some time outside of the regular classroom. The work completed by the student in the gifted class should replace the regular class work, and the student should not be expected to make up missed assignments, with the following exceptions:

- The student will be responsible for learning new material that was presented to the class during his or her absence. This can be accomplished through teacher explanations, student explanations, or short study assignments given by the teacher. The student should not be required to complete all written assignments connected with the new work that has been missed, but should be given an opportunity to demonstrate her or his understanding of the concepts involved through oral discussion or partial written assignments.

- The student will be responsible for completing long-term assignments such as research projects and written reports that may be due on the day a student is in the gifted program. It will be the student's responsibility to arrange for a time to present his or her work to the teacher, either the day before or the day after the assignment is due.

- The student will be required to make up all tests which are given in her or his absence unless excused by the classroom teacher.

- It is essential that students not be penalized for work they missed as a result of gifted program participation. Report card grades should reflect the level of student progress during the time he or she is in the regular classroom. An additional progress report from the gifted education teacher(s) will be sent home with quarterly report cards for all gifted students.

Figure 6.4

"What can I do to get into the gifted program?"

While parents often initiate dialogue about gifted program concerns, occasionally you will face student questions as well. Sooner or later, anyone charged with teaching or coordinating in a gifted program will face a request like this one that Barbara was met with at the beginning of one school year:

Hi, Ms. Lewis:

I hope you have had a nice summer. You probably don't know me, but you taught my sister, Chantel, in your gifted program last year. I used to be in gifted, but they took me out in sixth grade. I'm doing better in school, now, and I would like to be in your gifted program again because Chantel says it's great. What can I do to get back into gifted?

Sincerely,
Ross Sherman

This is tough, especially when a child *did* not, and may well *still* not, meet the qualifications for entrance into the gifted program. Barbara's first response to this note was to check Ross's history in and out of the gifted program. He was a sensitive and talented boy with a creative mind, whose gifts had not fit well within the cooperative problem-solving and critical-thinking program he had been placed in during fifth grade. Barbara saw that the best options for Ross lay outside the gifted program in other opportunities at school.

After speaking with his dad on the phone, Barbara met with Ross and talked with him about how things were going so far in school. Ross described several classes and teachers he was especially enjoying. Then Barbara mentioned his note and explained that the school district had to follow certain guidelines for the gifted program. This meant that even a lot of bright and creative students like Ross had talents that fit better in other places than the gifted program. She asked Ross if he knew about two other programs, Destination ImagiNation and the Middle School Writers' Guild (both open to all students and well suited to Ross's introspective approach to writing and thinking). They discussed these activities, and Barbara encouraged Ross to take part in one or both of them. The meeting ended on an upbeat and helpful note, with Ross visibly happier about the situation and clearly eager to explore some of the ideas he and Barbara had talked about.

Of course, not every situation as touchy as this ends up with such a rosy solution. For those that do not, try to keep tabs on the student, directly and indirectly. Ask the student to stay in touch with you in the weeks ahead—and then, follow up, even with a brief hallway conversation. In addition, contact one or two of this child's more receptive teachers, asking for a status report on the child's progress and what additional resource materials you could provide that might be helpful with this student. A call to the parent might even be in order, especially if you know that some good changes have, in fact, occurred in this child's education.

These are four of the more common issues that you are likely to face in your communication with parents and students. Of course, there will be others. Whatever the concerns, as long as you are aware that you don't need to have an immediate solution for everything, and as long as you remember to follow through on phone calls and other contacts that you have promised to make, your communication about even sticky issues need not be awkward, tense, or combative. In fact, communicating and working effectively with parents and students can lead to a strengthened home-school bond and a more positive experience for the student over time.

A Few Final Thoughts

Every state (and province) has its own parameters and guidelines in regard to gifted education. Unique circumstances come in to play in each district and school as well. Yet, regardless of these differences, there are some constants about the job of being a gifted education teacher:

- It is a job that requires intelligence, on-your-feet thinking, and at times, the ability to hold your tongue.

- It is a job that requires you to stand up for what you believe is right for the gifted children in your charge.

- It is a job that requires as much energy as you can muster.

Where can you find that energy? Like the gifted educators quoted at the beginning of this chapter, you may come up with your own "Top Ten" list or set of "do's." Or, perhaps you'll find inspiration in a combination of factors both large and small, as this gifted coordinator has done:

WHERE EAGLES SOAR[5]

By Jane F.G. McDonald

What keeps me going from day to day?

- Gifted kids with whom I've made a difference. (Jen, an "underground" gifted girl, came back into the fold today. "I missed you and the G/T program, Mrs. McD. What are we going to do this year?" Also, today I heard that fifth-grade Sarah will be allowed to take sixth-grade math. A small victory!)

- G/T parents who need us to be advocates. (The phone call of a parent from seven years and two states ago asking for parenting information.)

- Our incredible G/T teaching team. (They are my best "forever friends." Shoulders to cry on, blessings to share.)

- Designing and implementing quality programs. (Gifted kids are gifted 100 percent of the time; programming should reflect this.)

- Having incredible administrative support. (The best superintendent I've ever known.)

- Networking with G/T professionals nationally.

- A laptop computer that works; a swivel chair.

- A roof that no longer leaks.

Yep, some days it's a stretch. As I leave my elementary school in Helena, Montana, and drive the incredible journey home through Lewis and Clark territory, passing antelope and elk and watching eagles soar over the Missouri River banks, I ponder the worthiness of this position with personal binoculars. I realize that it comes down to one strong belief: that what I do makes a real difference to children, parents, teachers, and the community. Today I pass the test. Tomorrow?

In hopes of continuing to make a difference, I keep a toolbox, including:

- G/T professional development tools. (I arm myself with a staff that knows how to deal constructively with difficult people and situations. I also schedule "Power Days" with the staff—to get them out of their typical day's schedule and build our team relationship.)

- The valuable involvement of parents. (I tap into parents' talents by having them create a Speaker's Series, develop Web sites and newsletters, and hold parent discussion groups—we call them "G/Teas.")

- Cost-conscious staff development. (I give teachers time to meet with their G/T students, in and out of the classroom. Also, we developed a Parent Cadre, a group of community members and parents who come into the classroom as substitutes so that classroom teachers can attend professional development opportunities about gifted kids—at no cost to the district!)

- Direct services that matter to gifted students. (I make sure that what is done in the G/T resource room is strategically different from what is being done in the regular classroom. This means mapping out the G/T curriculum for multiple grade levels.)

- Living beyond the classroom. (I recognize stress and address it actively—through friends, diet, and exercise. Also, I find a beautiful place and become a part of it, taking time to laugh and watch the eagles soar.)

With our district's budget cuts and downsizing, we've had the opportunity (note the optimism) to evaluate and redesign our gifted services. Transitioning to a "leaner, meaner" place is not easy, but with a strong and flexible staff, and a ride home every day through nature's beauty, it's all worthwhile.

Figure 6.5

Another gifted education professional offers this perspective on the rewards of working with gifted children:

KEEPING YOUR OWN STORIES[6]
By Jan Fall

I have worked in gifted-child education for twenty-two of my twenty-nine educator years. When I raised my hand in 1977 to work with the new gifted program, I had no idea it would lead me to where I am today. Gifted kids have changed my life; they have given my own need for challenge and curiosity a run for its money.

My training is solid, with leaders in the field, but nothing prepared me for the day-to-day pursuit of doing what is best for kids. People everywhere still believe in the myths surrounding the education of gifted children. It is part of this job to dispel those myths.

What keeps me going year after year is simple: I've met gifted kids. They give me energy and hope. They give a vision into tomorrow. Their excitement for learning is contagious. Just this week, in great frustration with adults, I headed back into the schools to reclaim the reason for what I do. It didn't take long: a third grader describing his abstract Expressionist painting; fourth graders talking about a "crime scene" in a forensics class; high school students preparing vignettes to present the Victorian Era to the community. I returned to my office with a much lighter step.

Don't think that I haven't thought at times that a career change looked inviting! But then I would meet a gifted child or get an email from one I had taught. A note that I received in 1997, from a student I last taught in third grade in 1988, says this:

"Ms. Fall: Thank you so much for being the first person to show me the power of knowledge, optimism, and confidence. Sorry our paths split so soon. Tim."

I can always put my hand on this note when I need it. Tim knows how important he and his note have been to my career. I had the chance to tell him when he graduated from college, in three years, with a double engineering degree. I still get phone calls from a mom at my previous district every time she makes headway for her profoundly gifted son, whose educational path we began to propel forward when he was just four years old and taught himself German from the Internet.

Keep your own stories; rely on them and the good people around you. Make your own difference. The kids need us.

Figure 6.6

Knowledge, optimism, confidence. Tim put it right in his letter to Jan, his former teacher. With these talents and attitudes, the field of gifted-child education will survive—indeed, it will grow—despite the shifting sands that come with the conflux of politics and educational reform and seem to threaten our field's very existence. For those days when you need a lift, a reminder of all that you know and all that it means for you and your students, you can turn to these testimonials about the gifted education profession.

As long as children exist, there will always be that group of able kids whom we choose to call *gifted*. All of them—each of them—require advocates who respect and understand their needs. And that, of course, is your biggest, most complex, and most fulfilling job.

Enjoy the ride!

"There will come a time when you believe everything is finished. That will be the beginning."
—LOUIS L'AMOUR

Notes

1. Adapted from material by Sally Yahnke Walker in *Gifted Education Resource Guide,* Illinois State Board of Education (Springfield, Illinois: 1999). Used with permission.

2. Steps for securing a guest speaker come from Michelle L. Watson, Coordinator of Gifted Services, Tuscarawas-Carroll-Harrison Educational Service Center, New Philadelphia, Ohio, and are adapted with permission.

3. Jim Delisle and Judy Galbraith, *When Gifted Kids Don't Have All the Answers: How to Meet Their Social and Emotional Needs* (Minneapolis: Free Spirit Publishing, 2002), page 64. Used with permission.

4. Ibid., page 119. Used with permission.

5. Adapted from "Where Eagles Soar" by Jane F.G. McDonald, Gifted Coordinator, Helena, Montana, Public Schools. Used with permission.

6. Adapted from "Keeping Your Own Stories" by Dr. Janis Fall, Gifted Coordinator, Killeen (Texas) Independent School District. Used with permission.

Resources

The following resources apply specifically to topics addressed in this strategy's chapter. For a complete list of gifted education resources, see pages 146–154.

Counseling the Gifted and Talented edited by Linda K. Silverman (Denver: Love Publishing Company, 2000). A highly comprehensive work, this book is a must for counselors, teachers, and coordinators of programs for the gifted. Presents sound advice for orchestrating a program of prevention in counseling the gifted. Also check the Web site of the Gifted Development Center, which offers many excellent publications and other useful information *(www.gifteddevelopment.com).*

"How to Make Parent-Teacher Conferences Worthwhile and Productive" by Arlene R. DeVries, Home and School Report (Washington, DC: NAGC, 1996). This helpful article is available from NAGC (page 7). You can also find an excerpt online *(www.nagc.org).*

"National Association for Gifted Children Pre-K–Grade 12 Gifted Program Standards" *(www.nagc.org).* This Web page is the online source for a document that delineates both requisite and exemplary standards for gifted education programming in seven areas, including Professional Development and Socio-Emotional Guidance and Counseling.

Perfectionism: What's Bad About Being Too Good?, rev. ed., by Miriam Adderholdt and Jan Goldberg (Minneapolis: Free Spirit Publishing, 1999). This fun text for students is a must-read for teachers, too. It offers research and statistics on the causes and consequences of perfectionism, plus tips on how perfectionistic kids can learn to relax.

"Recent Research on Guidance, Counseling and Therapy for the Gifted" produced by the NAGC Counseling and Guidance Division. This document presents conclusions about research studies on the affective needs of gifted students and cites implications for school counselors, teachers, policymakers, parents, and mental health professionals. Also provides an extensive reading list. Find the document at *www.nagc.org.*

Staff Development: The Key to Effective Gifted Education Programs edited by Peggy A. Dettmer and Mary S. Landrum (Waco, TX: Prufrock Press, 1998). Presents guidance through the staff development process—from organizing, planning, and conducting to following up.

Ultimate Guide to Getting Money for Your Classroom and School by Frances A. Karnes with Kristin R. Stephens (Waco, TX: Prufrock Press, 2002). This book offers practical, hands-on ways to find the resources you need. The authors present a step-by-step guide to grant writing; proven fund-raising ideas; and a practical how-to for long-term fund development.

"What Are the Social and Emotional Needs of Gifted Students?" by H.L. Nevitt. This brochure, part of the "Frequently Asked Questions" packet from NAGC (see page 7), provides a useful handout for meetings with parents and teachers.

When Gifted Kids Don't Have All the Answers: How to Meet Their Social and Emotional Needs by Jim Delisle and Judy Galbraith (Minneapolis: Free Spirit Publishing, 2002). Here you'll find in-depth background information along with real-life strategies and solutions for meeting the social and emotional needs of gifted kids. Includes information on identification, sensitivity, self-esteem, underachievement, and the "Great Gripes" of gifted kids.

★ Student Growth Contract ★

Growth Goal

What is it that you want to change about yourself or your life?

1. I'd like to be _____

_____

_____

_____

Working on the Goal

How will you make this change?

2. Steps I'll take to reach my goal:

_____

_____

_____

_____

3. Resources that will help me (including people I can turn to for support):

_____

_____

_____

_____

4. Possible roadblocks I'll need to get around:

_____

_____

_____

_____

Adapted from *When Gifted Kids Don't Have All the Answers* by Jim Delisle, Ph.D., and Judy Galbraith, M.A. (2002), pages 123–124. Used with permission of Free Spirit Publishing. From *The Survival Guide for Teachers of Gifted Kids* by Jim Delisle, Ph.D., and Barbara A. Lewis, copyright © 2003. Free Spirit Publishing Inc., Minneapolis, MN; 800-735-7323; www.freespirit.com. This page may be reproduced for individual, classroom, or small group work only. For other uses, contact www.freespirit.com/company/permissions.cfm.

★ **Student Growth Contract** (cont'd)

Checking Progress

How will you know when things are better?

5. I'll know when _____

_____

_____

_____

6. How close to my goal did I come? Explain:

_____

_____

_____

_____

7. Did I achieve as much as I hoped or expected? Explain:

_____

_____

_____

_____

_____

8. Did I achieve less than I hoped or expected? Explain:

_____

_____

_____

_____

Adapted from *When Gifted Kids Don't Have All the Answers* by Jim Delisle, Ph.D., and Judy Galbraith, M.A. (2002), pages 123–124. Used with permission of Free Spirit Publishing. From *The Survival Guide for Teachers of Gifted Kids* by Jim Delisle, Ph.D., and Barbara A. Lewis, copyright © 2003. Free Spirit Publishing Inc., Minneapolis, MN; 800-735-7323; www.freespirit.com. This page may be reproduced for individual, classroom, or small group work only. For other uses, contact www.freespirit.com/company/permissions.cfm.

Who's Who in Gifted Education?

A Short List of Key Players, Past and Present

G ifted education began in ancient Greece. High ability was valued and nurtured during China's Tang Dynasty, and in Renaissance Europe, governments and moneyed private citizens supported talented artists, musicians, writers, and architects. In the United States, public-school provisions for gifted children came about slowly and somewhat erratically. Most of the research and support for today's bright and talented kids can trace its roots to the twentieth century. This "Who's Who?" is intended to provide a very brief reference concerning many of the pioneers of gifted education in North America (and, occasionally, Europe), past and present. Our list, arranged alphabetically, is by no means comprehensive; indeed, without doubt many individuals *not* mentioned here have made and continue to make significant contributions to the field. With that caveat, use this list as a quick introduction to some of the teachers, psychologists, researchers, and gifted advocates who influence gifted-child education and to the strides and innovations these folks have made for gifted and talented kids.

GEORGE BETTS

In his early role as a high school counselor, Betts saw the need to develop a child's passions, many of which had little to do with school. Using this as his theme, Betts developed the Autonomous Learner Model, a multiyear program model that includes academics, counseling, and "passion learning." The program is designed to reach children who might otherwise be ignored by gifted programming as well as to attend to students' affective development.

ALFRED BINET

A French psychologist, Binet developed a scale for measuring ability in Parisian schools at the turn of the twentieth century. The scale, intended to measure students' "judgment" or "mental age," was later used as the basis for Lewis Terman's *Stanford-Binet Intelli-gence Scale*. Binet believed that intelligence could be learned, expanded, and improved with time.

BENJAMIN BLOOM

In his effort to expand teachers' views on all children's learning, educational psychologist and researcher Benjamin Bloom introduced his *Taxonomy of Educational Objectives* in 1956, which outlined six levels of thinking that build upon one another in terms of complexity. The taxonomy led to substantial improvement in designing curriculum that emphasized higher levels of thinking and remains an important component of gifted education theory.

BARBARA CLARK

From her early work as a teacher of gifted children to her current emphasis on the importance of brain research toward understanding gifted development, Clark's efforts have spanned a generation. Her book *Growing Up Gifted* is a staple on every gifted specialist's bookshelf. Clark's other professional interests include underachievement and identifying and serving gifted children internationally.

NICHOLAS COLANGELO

Interested in the social and emotional needs of gifted children, Colangelo is a leading researcher and writer on counseling the gifted. He is the director of the Connie Belin National Center for Gifted Education at the University of Iowa and the coauthor of several textbooks that are widely respected in the field of gifted education.

JOHN FELDHUSEN

A strong proponent for enrichment programs that could potentially bring out the talents of many children, Feldhusen has developed gifted programming at both the elementary and secondary levels. His work at Purdue University has helped to broaden our conception of gifted programming. His Super Saturday

Programs (enrichment classes for children led by community professionals) have been emulated in countless cities and towns nationally.

DONNA FORD

Donna Ford has spent her career advocating for underrepresented populations of gifted students, especially among the African American population. Focusing on cultural, academic, and family issues related to underachievement among black students, Ford's work emphasizes both the socio-emotional and intellectual factors that need to be considered when trying to increase the achievement of this population of students.

MARY FRASIER

A staunch advocate for addressing the needs of gifted children from minority cultures, Mary Frasier has developed extensive identification procedures for locating gifts and talents masked by cultural differences. In addition, her work in bibliotherapy—using fictional characters to help children better understand themselves—has been instrumental in the counseling of gifted children.

JAMES GALLAGHER

Gallagher's *Teaching the Gifted Child* is one of the best-recognized texts in gifted education and has appeared in five separate editions over a thirty-year span. Gallagher's work in political advocacy, curriculum development, and other areas places him among the most influential and broadly based individuals in gifted education. If it happened in gifted, Gallagher was probably involved to some degree.

SIR FRANCIS GALTON

Working in the mid-eighteenth century, Galton was one of the first researchers to explore concepts of fixed intelligence and intelligence testing. The English statistician and psychologist, influenced by his cousin Charles Darwin, maintained that intelligence is primarily genetic, a line of thought that continues today, although to a lesser degree.

HOWARD GARDNER

Believing the conventional understanding of intelligence to be too limited, Harvard psychologist Howard Gardner formulated a theory of multiple intelligences (MI). MI theory acknowledges that there are many different ways in which people learn and think and that individuals have relative strengths and weaknesses related to each. Gardner calls these different ways of taking in and processing information intelli-gences; the eight he identifies are linguistic, logical-mathematical, musical, visual-spatial, bodily-kines-thetic, interpersonal, intrapersonal, and naturalist.

ARNOLD GESELL

Believing that maturation led development, Gesell developed a scale that tracked the ages at which children typically are able to perform mental and motor functions. As a student of G. Stanley Hall, Gesell believed that behavior and learning are strongly influenced by heredity.

J.P. GUILFORD

A former president of the American Psychological Association, Guilford used his keynote address at the organization's 1950 conference to challenge his colleagues to research the yet-unexplored field of creativity. Over the next twenty years, a great deal of work was done on creativity. Guilford also developed the theoretical Structure of the Intellect (SOI), which demonstrated in detail at least 120 elements that comprise human knowledge and ability.

G. STANLEY HALL

A pioneering figure in American psychology, Hall centered his interests on child development and evolutionary theory. He believed that maturation led learning and that behavior and intellectual development were strongly influenced by genetics.

LETA HOLLINGWORTH

A founding figure in gifted education, Hollingworth studied high-ability children in the New York City Public Schools while working as a professor and researcher at Teachers College, Columbia University. She also taught at the first public school for the gifted, Speyer School, where she concentrated her work on a small number of highly intelligent kids. Her insight into their intellectual and emotional development, though from the 1930s, remains a fundamental reference point for understanding the special needs of high-ability children.

JEAN ITARD

In the late eighteenth century, Itard discovered "Victor," a feral child approximately twelve years old, in the woods of France. Today, Victor might be considered autistic. Itard kept a journal of his attempts to "train" the boy to be more intelligent. Itard's book, *The Wild Boy of Aveyron,* remains a classic, as it details one of the first efforts to increase intelligence by direct intervention.

SANDRA KAPLAN

A former teacher and coordinator of gifted programs, Kaplan is noted for her work in the area of curricular differentiation, advocating for programs that emphasize depth, complexity, and interdisciplinary themes. She is a former president of the National Association for Gifted Children and has authored many books and articles on gifted education.

BARBARA KERR

Barbara Kerr is most noted for her work on gifted females, having written the extremely popular book *Smart Girls: A New Psychology of Girls, Women, and Giftedness* (revised several times from the original edition known as *Smart Girls, Gifted Women*). Examining cultural, educational, and personal factors that keep some gifted girls from reaching the fullest extent of their abilities and interests, Kerr's practical work has influenced many school personnel in their conceptualization of programs that serve gifted children. More recently, Kerr has also examined the unique dynamics in raising and educating gifted boys.

C. JUNE MAKER

Maker's work on the development of curriculum for meeting the needs of children from underrepresented populations—children who are disabled or economically disadvantaged and those from minority groups—is extensive. She was among the first to advocate for thematic instruction for gifted students, integrating her ideas with program models developed by other leaders in gifted education.

MARY MEEKER

A student of J.P. Guilford, Meeker took his theoretical construct of intelligence as composed of at least 120 separate elements and designed curriculum and instructional materials to address these widely varying abilities. Her SOI Institute continues to actively support all gifted individuals, but especially those with abilities that may be suppressed by learning disabilities or whose learning styles may be visual-spatial in orientation.

A. HARRY PASSOW

A researcher at Columbia University, Passow worked toward differentiating curriculum long before the current focus on its importance. A staunch advocate for teachers, he believed gifted education strategies to be valuable for all classrooms. Passow also studied underachievement, coauthoring *Bright Underachievers* in 1966, the first book on the topic.

JEAN PIAGET

Piaget theorized the growth and development of intelligence and maintained that students needed active participation in learning opportunities during stages of development. He is a founding figure in child development whose influence is apparent even today.

MICHAEL PIECHOWSKI

Educator and psychologist Michael Piechowski has long championed giftedness as an internal trait rather than one visible in achievements. His research on overexcitability in intellectual, emotional, and other realms is influential and is derived from the studies of psychiatrist Kazimierz Dabrowski.

SALLY REIS

At the center of many recent developments in gifted education, Reis has worked with Joseph Renzulli to promote excellence in schools, offering unique learning opportunities. Their Schoolwide Enrichment Model focuses on student portfolios, performance assessment, theme-based studies, and hands-on learning that encourages the application of knowledge toward solving complex problems.

JOSEPH RENZULLI

Director of the National Research Center on the Gifted and Talented at the University of Connecticut since its inception, Renzulli is a vocal critic of identification practices based strictly on high IQ scores, believing instead that giftedness is observable only in actions and accomplishments. Renzulli's special programming (extended enrichment opportunities for up to twenty-five percent of the school population) attempts to prompt "gifted behavior" from students and has received both praise and criticism from colleagues.

ANNEMARIE ROEPER

With the guidance of A. Harry Passow, Annemarie Roeper and her husband transformed their school in Michigan to a school for the gifted in 1956. It is today considered one of the world's preeminent pre-K–12 schools exclusively serving gifted children. Roeper's model for education, the Self-Actualized Interdependence Model (SAI), focuses on gifted children as global citizens with intellectual *and* affective needs. Her research on gifted adults is also acclaimed in the field.

KAREN ROGERS

Among the most renowned researchers in gifted education today, Rogers has done work encompassing many important areas, including the benefits of ability grouping and acceleration for academically gifted students. Her continuing follow-up work on the people who were the subjects of Lewis Terman's research (and their children) also holds much promise in the years ahead.

LINDA SILVERMAN

A clinical psychologist who focuses on the needs of highly gifted children, Silverman has championed the continued use of the individual IQ test as an accurate barometer of intellectual ability—a view not as politically popular as it once was. Her diverse body of research includes studies on gifted-child counseling, gifted females, and visual-spatial learners, among other topics.

DOROTHY SISK

Sisk works in the fields of creativity and leadership at Lamar University, where she also coordinates teacher training in gifted education. Beyond her extensive involvement with national and international gifted organizations, she is the author of many books and articles about creativity and gifted education. Sisk was the first director of the federal Office of Gifted and Talented (OGT) and was instrumental in securing federal funds for gifted students in the 1970s and '80s.

JULIAN STANLEY

Stanley is a strong proponent for the "radical acceleration" of children with extreme mathematical abilities. His work at Johns Hopkins University resulted in the establishment of the Study of Mathematically Precocious Youth (SMPY). This program was the genesis of nationwide talent searches that allow gifted children in middle school to take college-level classes for which they are already intellectually prepared.

ROBERT STERNBERG

Researcher and psychologist Robert Sternberg formulated a theory in which three dimensions of intelligence (the proficiency to analyze, synthesize, and apply thinking to problems) determine overall ability, incorporating the element of practical knowledge into intelligence.

RUTH STRANG

Following Leta Hollingworth's premature death, Strang took over much of her work at Columbia University, with a particular emphasis on parenting gifted children—the first substantial work in this area. She emphasized the social and emotional needs of gifted children and reminded parents that students should not become martyrs to their own unfulfilled ambitions.

ABRAHAM TANNENBAUM

A prolific historian of gifted education, Tannenbaum also published in 1983 *Gifted Children: Psychological and Educational Perspectives,* a comprehensive text on giftedness that remains influential today. His long career branched out to include sub-specialties that had seldom been considered by others: underachievement, social aspects of giftedness, benefits of grade skipping, and the role of fate in being selected as a gifted child.

LEWIS TERMAN

A founding figure of giftedness, Terman began testing children in the early twentieth century using the *Stanford-Binet Intelligence Scale,* a test he developed after Alfred Binet's scale for measuring ability. He followed up this mass testing by studying 1,500 kids with IQs above 140 and documenting their physical, intellectual, and emotional development in *Genetic Studies of Genius,* in which he dispelled many myths about gifted individuals.

CAROL ANN TOMLINSON

A classroom teacher for most of her career, Tomlinson has emerged as a leader in differentiating curriculum for all learners. The author of widely read books on the topic, she takes care to point out that gifted children's academic needs will be met if differentiation is seen as essential for every student, but that gifted children will continue to have nonacademic needs as well.

E. PAUL TORRANCE

Torrance developed a view of creativity that included four facets—fluency, flexibility, originality, and elaboration—which became the criteria by which children's creativity was judged on the *Torrance Tests of Creative Thinking,* introduced in 1966. He later established the Future Problem Solving Program, which now is an international enrichment program serving thousands of children annually.

JOYCE VAN TASSEL-BASKA

Coupling the academic needs of gifted children with the reform efforts currently underway to make school curriculum more rigorous and hands-on, Van Tassel-Baska has produced volumes of books and articles related to these areas. As much programming guides as textbooks, Van Tassel-Baska's practical works have special importance for a seldom-reached audience of gifted students: those in high school.

VIRGIL WARD

Though a philosopher by trade, Ward was a strong advocate for gifted students receiving a differentiated curriculum. His classic 1961 book, *Educating the Gifted: An Axiomatic Approach,* remains among the best sources for designing educational options that respect the intellects of gifted young people.

JOANNE WHITMORE

Whitmore has been a tireless advocate for underachieving children. Her book *Giftedness, Conflict and Underachievement* (published in 1980) showed that children with severe emotional or learning disorders could also be gifted. Whitmore's later work emphasized the presence of intellectual giftedness among populations of people with disabilities.

PAUL WITTY

A researcher and professor, Witty is best known for expanding the view of giftedness beyond IQ. He believed that individuals were gifted if they exhibited consistently outstanding ability in any potentially valuable human activity, including art, writing, and social leadership. Today, this view is the baseline for many expanded views of intelligence.

What's What in Gifted Education?

A Glossary of Terms

ability grouping
Grouping students of like ability to work together on a short- or long-term basis.

acceleration
Allowing students to move to a higher level of schoolwork than their age would ordinarily dictate, be it in the form of early entry to school, placement in a self-contained gifted classroom, earning credit by examination, skipping grades, completing two grades in a single year, or concurrent enrollment in both high school and college.

achievement test
A test that measures what students have learned or have been taught in a specific content area relative to the expected achievement of average students; does not gauge potential.

ADHD (Attention Deficit Hyperactivity Disorder)
A medically diagnosed condition with symptoms that include being overly physically active and having difficulty sitting still or paying attention.

Advanced Placement (AP)
A formalized system that allows students to enroll in intense, high-level courses in high school and possibly gain college credit simultaneously.

Asperger Syndrome
A condition characterized by severely impaired social skills and the occurrence of repetitive or restrictive behaviors that keep highly able children from learning some skills and developing socially.

assessment
Traditionally, the process of evaluating student learning with standardized testing and a clearly defined portfolio of individual work samples. In gifted education, teachers attempt to evaluate student products or performance to tailor education to student needs and interests.

asynchronous development
Also referred to as uneven integration, this is development in which intellectual growth is ahead of physical and social and/or emotional development.

autism
A condition characterized by self-absorption, inability to interact socially, repetitive behavior, and language dysfunction.

Bloom's Taxonomy
Classification of thinking into six levels of increasing complexity: knowledge, comprehension, application, analysis, synthesis, and evaluation.

categorical funds
Supplemental funding for programs that targets specific groups of students (for example, gifted ESL) or specialized programs (for example, Title I reading).

ceiling of difficulty
The highest level of performance that a test can assess.

cluster grouping
Assigning students of the same grade level who have been identified as gifted to a small instructional group within a class of otherwise heterogeneously grouped students.

concurrent enrollment
Also referred to as dual enrollment, this is the instance where students take a course for both college and high school credit. College credit is granted by the post-secondary institution offering the course while high school credit is dependent upon state education guidelines.

content acceleration
The faster presentation of curriculum to more closely match the speed at which a gifted student learns.

creativity/creative thinking
Artistic or intellectual intuitiveness that allows students to conceive and create innovative concepts or products.

critical thinking
Cultivated analytical skills allowing students to logically comprehend and solve complex concepts or problems.

curriculum compacting
Sometimes called telescoping, this adaptation eliminates (or shortens) work that students have already mastered at a pace faster than their classmates. Compacting allows students time and opportunity for enrichment or acceleration options during the school day.

differentiation
Adapting the pace, level, or kind of instructional curriculum to meet each student's individual learning needs, styles, or interests.

early entrance
The enrollment of children in educational programs before the common starting date or age; early entrance is most commonly associated with kindergarten.

EBD (emotional and/or behavioral disorders)
Students in this group often experience academic difficulties due to an inability to maintain social relationships and a tendency toward chronic behavior problems.

emotional giftedness
A type of giftedness where students perceive thoughts and events intensely and think about them more deeply than age peers.

emotional intelligence
A form of intelligence characterized by profound self-awareness, self-motivation, empathy, persistence, and social ability.

enrichment programs
General term for a wide range of challenging student learning opportunities outside of the regular curriculum.

ESL (English as a Second Language)
Students in this group are not native English speakers but are developing English-language proficiency. Communication problems often mask these students'
gifts and talents, causing them to be underrepresented in gifted programming.

flexible grouping
Grouping students based on interests and abilities on an assignment-by-assignment basis.

formative evaluation
Evaluation geared toward improving programming and services.

grade acceleration
Placing a student in an advanced grade or course on a full- or part-time basis.

growth contract
Student agreement geared toward affective rather than academic concerns.

heterogeneous grouping
Grouping students with differing abilities, achievements, interests, perspectives, and backgrounds. Also referred to as mixed-ability grouping.

homework policy
Policy established for gifted students participating in pull-out programs outlining the regular classroom work that students must make up and the guidelines for its completion.

homogeneous grouping
Grouping students of similar ability, regardless of their age. Also referred to as like-ability grouping.

honors classes
Advanced courses with an accelerated and challenging curriculum provided by the middle or high school.

hypersensitivity
Acute physical and/or emotional perception of the surrounding world.

**IDEA
(Individuals with Disabilities Education Act)**
Federal legislation providing for an appropriate education to students with special needs; does not include provisions for intellectually or academically gifted children.

identification
Methods used to determine which students are best suited for gifted services.

IEP (Individualized Educational Plan)
A carefully documented plan, geared to a child's unique characteristics and needs, that outlines educational goals and how they will be pursued. A legal document, an IEP is jointly developed by educators (in special and regular education), parents, and sometimes students.

inclusion
Practice where students of differing abilities and conditions are grouped together in the regular classroom.

intelligence test
A test that measures children's potential for achievement in intellectual pursuits.

IQ (intelligence quotient)
Measure of child's cognitive ability that compares a child's mental age and actual age.

Jacob K. Javits Gifted and Talented Students Education Act (Javits Act)
The Jacob K. Javits Gifted and Talented Students Education Act of 1994 is federal legislation that allocates grant money for gifted education and research each year.

LD (learning difference or learning disability)
A neurological condition that interferes with the brain's ability to process information.

learning centers/interest centers
Classroom stations or collections of materials students can use to explore new areas or to reinforce earlier lessons. For gifted students, interest centers should offer greater depth, breadth, and sophistication of materials.

learning style
A student's preferred mode of learning, such as visual, auditory, or kinesthetic.

LEP (Limited English Proficiency)
Students in this group are not native English speakers and have very little, or minimally developing, English-language proficiency. Communication problems often mask these students' gifts and talents, causing them to be underrepresented in gifted programming.

looping
Practice where teachers from one grade level advance to the next along with their class. Teachers return to the original grade level with a new group of students after a cycle of two or more years.

magnet schools
Special public schools that offer a concentrated curriculum in designated areas of study (for example, fine and performing arts, science and technology, and so forth). Some charter schools and most Governor's Schools are types of magnet schools.

mastery learning
An instructional method where students advance through the curriculum according to ability rather than grade level, allowing them to progress at their own pace.

mentorship
The one-on-one learning relationship between a student and an expert in a specific topic or discipline. The mentor supports and guides the student to develop in that area of interest.

mission statement
A concise statement of purpose that clearly describes the reasons for programming. A mission statement for a gifted education program should reflect or align with the general educational mission of the school or district and with the gifted education philosophy statement. Mission and philosophy statements are often combined. Together, they provide a compass for setting program goals.

multiple intelligences
Different ways of learning and processing information, as identified by psychologist Howard Gardner in his theory of multiple intelligences. Gardner's eight intelligences are linguistic, musical, logical-mathematical, visual-spatial, bodily-kinesthetic, interpersonal, intrapersonal, and naturalistic. Each student has relative strengths and weaknesses within these domains.

multipotentiality
Concept that gifted children have the ability to succeed in several areas of work or study, making career selection difficult.

needs assessment
Process of examining educational programs and curriculum to locate specific student needs that are going unmet with the intention of establishing the focus for additional programming.

off-track programs
Learning opportunities available to students during periods when they are not attending school.

overexcitability (OE)
Intense and deep response often found in gifted students that allows for greater feeling, imagination, energy, sensuality, and cognitive ability.

perfectionism
Having exceedingly high (often impossible) expectations about how one can or should perform academically or in other areas.

philosophy statement
A concise focus statement helpful in identifying and describing a programming approach based on specific needs the program seeks to address. A philosophy statement for a gifted education program should reflect or align with the general educational philosophy of the school or district and with the gifted mission statement. Philosophy and mission statements are often combined. Together, they provide a compass for setting program goals.

portfolio assessment
A collection of student products used to demonstrate and measure achievement, abilities, and talents, often toward the purpose of placing the student in a gifted program or evaluating work done in a gifted program.

problem-based learning
An instructional method that compels students to think critically, analytically, and cooperatively, individually or in groups, toward finding solutions to real-world problems or imaginary scenarios (based in truth) using appropriate learning resources.

program evaluation
A systematic appraisal of the impact and value of the services a program provides.

pull-out program
Also referred to as a send-out class or resource-room program, this is a part-time program where gifted children leave the regular classroom for a limited time to attend specialized classes with a resource teacher.

resource center/resource room
A designated location in the school or district where special program services are provided for gifted students. Sometimes called the pull-out classroom.

school-within-a-school
A program with concentrated offerings in designated curricular areas that, rather than occupying a different building, operates within the walls of a general education facility.

self-contained program
An arrangement where students are grouped on a full-time basis with intellectual peers, often for consecutive years, to promote high achievement and reduce the social and emotional problems that can come with giftedness.

standardized testing
Testing of students under identical conditions that allows for results to be statistically compared to a standard.

summative evaluation
Assessing the quality of programming and measuring success in light of program goals.

tiered assignments
Varied levels of activities to ensure that students explore ideas at a level that builds on prior knowledge and prompts continued intellectual growth.

tracking
Permanently grouping students by ability, such as in the "low," "middle," or "high" math or reading group.

twice exceptional
Quality of being both gifted and having a physical, an emotional, or a learning disability.

underachievement/underperformance
School performance that falls far short of a student's ability.

underrepresented populations
Groups traditionally excluded from many gifted education programs, including gifted girls, ethnic and cultural minorities, economically disadvantaged students, kids who misbehave, and those with learning differences. Also referred to as underserved populations.

weighted grades
Offering equal credit for a lower grade in a more difficult class. For example, a grade of B in Honors English is equivalent to a grade of A in Basic English.

Additional Resources

This is a list of some of the many resources for supporting educators and families as gifted education is planned and implemented. See also the "Resources" sections at the end of each Survival Strategy for additional recommendations.

Educators

Publications

Aiming for Excellence: Annotations to the NAGC Pre-K–Grade 12 Gifted Program Standards edited by Mary S. Landrum, Carolyn M. Callahan, and Beverly D. Shaklee (Waco, TX: Prufrock Press, 2001). This is an excellent resource for implementing and evaluating gifted programming. Based on research, the book expands upon and offers practical information on NAGC standards in seven program areas of gifted education.

Assessment of Exceptional Students: Educational and Psychological Procedures, 6th ed., by Ronald L. Taylor (Needham Heights, MA: Allyn and Bacon, 2003). This book provides up-to-date information on assessment instruments, techniques, and procedures for identifying students with different learning needs. Also find information on different methods for evaluating student products and performance.

Autonomous Learner Model: Optimizing Ability by George T. Betts and Jolene K. Kercher (Greeley, CO: ALPS Publishing, 1999). This revised edition of a classic resource shows teachers and gifted coordinators how to plan gifted programs for grades 6–12. For use in the regular classroom, in a pull-out program, as an individual elective course, or in specific curricular areas, the model focuses on the cognitive and emotional aspects of learning to promote students' growth into complete individuals.

Barefoot Irreverence: A Guide to Critical Issues in Gifted Child Education by James R. Delisle (Waco, TX: Prufrock Press, 2002). Reviews all aspects of the emotional development of gifted students as well as other topics such as standardized testing, parenting gifted children, and continuing controversies in the field.

Being Gifted in School: An Introduction to Development, Guidance, and Teaching by Laurence J. Coleman and Tracy L. Cross (Waco, TX: Prufrock Press, 2001). Offers a survey on the field of gifted and talented education. A great resource for those interested in the development of giftedness.

Celebrating Gifts and Talents (Washington, DC: NAGC, 1999). A nine-minute video featuring gifted and talented youth, this resource offers an overview of G/T educational needs. Excellent for staff development or for parent meetings, the video is available from NAGC (see page 152).

Choosing and Charting: Helping Students Select, Map Out, and Embark on Independent Projects by Lindy T. Redmond (Mansfield Center, CT: Creative Learning Press, 2002). Written for students, this book offers step-by-step instructions for choosing a topic, finding information, taking notes, conducting interviews, and developing an appropriate product. Also offers topic ideas and product suggestions.

Crossover Children: A Sourcebook for Helping Children Who Are Gifted and Learning Disabled, 2d ed., by Marlene Bireley (Reston, VA: Council for Exceptional Children, 1995). A great resource for meeting the educational needs of twice-exceptional students, this book includes strategies for educational planning and programming, advice for meeting behavioral, social, and academic concerns, and suggestions for enrichment options.

Curriculum Development and Teaching Strategies for Gifted Learners, 2d ed., by C. June Maker and Aleene B. Nielson (Austin, TX: Pro-Ed, 1996). For use in elementary classrooms, this book offers ideas for differentiating curriculum to meet the unique needs of gifted students. It examines the learning environment, content, process, and product, and details teaching strategies like interdisciplinary units and task-card activities.

Curriculum Planning and Instructional Design by Joyce Van Tassel-Baska (Denver: Love Publishing, 2002). This resource for K–12 curriculum development includes planning, developing, implementing, and evaluating the curriculum. Teaching strategies and curriculum examples are offered, as well as discussion of the most important issues in gifted education today.

Developing the Gifts and Talents of All Students in the Regular Classroom: An Innovative Curricular Design Based on the Schoolwide Enrichment Model by Margaret Beecher (Mansfield Center, CT: Creative Learning Press, 1995). This resource explains interest-based teaching, curriculum mapping, interdisciplinary curriculum, self-directed learning, learning centers, and other approaches to meeting the needs of individual students. Also find planning and management techniques for implementing outlined programming options.

Education of the Gifted and Talented, 4th ed., by Gary A. Davis and Sylvia B. Rimm (Needham Heights, MA: Allyn and Bacon, 1997). Outlining the most prominent ideas from gifted education's past, this resource discusses program planning, identification, social and emotional needs, and much more. Find tips for not only teaching gifted youth, but also for developing and evaluating programming.

Emotional Intelligence: Why It Can Matter More Than IQ by Daniel Goleman (New York: Bantam Books, 1995). A well-researched volume that looks at the link between intellectual and emotional intelligence and examines the inner characteristics of people who excel in life.

Enriching the Curriculum for All Students by Joseph S. Renzulli (Mansfield Center, CT: Creative Learning Press, 1995). This practical, research-based book is full of strategies to help raise achievement in all students. Offering helpful advice to administrators and teachers for integrating higher-order thinking skills and a broad range of learning experiences into the classroom, the book presents strategies for schoolwide improvement and tips for staff development and parent involvement.

Excellence in Educating Gifted and Talented Learners, 3d ed., edited by Joyce Van Tassel-Baska (Denver: Love Publishing Company, 1998). Read about personality types, learning styles, stages of giftedness, and much more in this unique book. Intended as a practical resource, the book translates the latest research into working strategies for grouping, acceleration, and many other instructional methods.

Fostering Creativity in Children K–8: Theory and Practice edited by Mervin D. Lynch and Carole Ruth Harris (Needham Heights, MA: Allyn and Bacon, 2001). This book presents leading strategies for encouraging students to be creative while producing appropriate products that can be evaluated. Also find information for reaching special populations including children with learning disabilities and those from minority groups.

"Frequently Asked Questions" (Washington, DC: NAGC). A set of twelve brochures from NAGC, this packet covers many topics in gifted education today. Including everything from instructional strategies for educators to information on social and emotional development, this packet is helpful for both parents and educators. For a full listing of brochures and ordering information, visit *www.nagc.org/Publications/majorpubs.htm*.

Gifted and Talented International. Published twice a year, Gifted and Talented International shares current theory, research, and practices in gifted education with its audience of international educators and parents. The journal is available from the World Council for Gifted and Talented Children (see page 152).

Gifted Child Quarterly. Published by NAGC in January, April, July, and October of each year, this journal documents the latest in gifted education research and methods. A subscription is available with membership in NAGC (see page 152).

Gifted Child Today. This quarterly magazine features ideas from gifted education teachers around the country. Find current research and practical methods for bringing the latest gifted ideas into the classroom. Features also address the social and emotional needs of the gifted. Subscriptions are available from Prufrock Press (see page 154).

Gifted Education Communicator. Published four times a year by the California Association for the Gifted (CAG), this practitioner's journal is for parents and educators of gifted children. Focus is on providing practical strategies for applying theory and research. A benefit of membership in CAG (see page 151), the journal is available on a yearly basis to others who are interested.

Growing Up Gifted: Developing the Potential of Children at Home and at School, 5th ed., by Barbara Clark (Upper Saddle River, NJ: Prentice Hall, 1997). Widely acknowledged as a definitive textbook on gifted education, this resource offers solid advice for educators of high-ability children. Discover what makes gifted children unique, learn how to address their social and emotional needs, and find ways to nurture learning.

Guiding the Social and Emotional Development of Gifted Youth: A Practical Guide for Educators and Counselors by James R. Delisle (New York: Longman Publishing Group, 1992). Find here advice for meeting the social and emotional needs of gifted children in the school environment. Background information explores gifted development and practical strategies offer suggestions for addressing students' unique needs. Though out of print, the book should be available through libraries.

Handbook of Gifted Education, 3d ed., edited by Nicholas Colangelo and Gary A. Davis (Needham Heights, MA: Allyn and Bacon, 2002). Experts in the field address a wide variety of topics, including identification, classroom practices, creativity, and counseling. A balance of theory and practical suggestions, this is a respected resource in gifted education.

Handbook of Intelligence edited by Robert J. Sternberg (New York: Cambridge University Press, 2000). Offering a broad review of current research into the nature of intelligence, this book includes discussions of emotional intelligence, measuring and testing intelligence, information processing, and many other aspects of intelligence.

How to Differentiate Instruction in Mixed-Ability Classrooms by Carol Ann Tomlinson (Alexandria, VA: Association for Supervision and Curriculum Development, 1998). A helpful resource for educators with only slight experience differentiating instruction, this book describes what differentiation is and isn't, offers a look inside some differentiated classrooms, and details how to plan differentiated lessons.

Intelligence Reframed: Multiple Intelligences for the 21st Century by Howard Gardner (New York: Basic Books, 1999). This revision of a classic book examines multiple intelligences in detail. Gardner broadens his theory of multiple intelligences to include a naturalist intelligence. The other types of intelligences include linguistic, logical-mathematical, musical, visual-spatial, bodily kinesthetic, interpersonal, and intrapersonal.

Learning Styles Inventory—Version III: Technical and Administration Manual by Joseph S. Renzulli, Mary G. Rizza, and Linda H. Smith (Mansfield Center, CT: Creative Learning Press, 2002). The latest version of this popular assessment tool is designed to measure students' preferences among instructional strategies common in elementary and middle school classrooms. Find samples of instruments, explanations of student talent portfolios, and insight on how to use these and other tools in making selections for programming.

Mentorship: The Essential Guide for Schools and Businesses by Jill Reilly (Scottsdale, AZ: Great Potential Press, 1992). Mentoring can enrich the education of students through motivating experiences not otherwise available. This practical resource discusses all of the aspects of and steps toward installing mentorship programs in schools.

Multicultural Education: Issues and Perspectives, 4th ed., edited by James A. Banks and Cherry A. McGee Banks (New York: Wiley, 2002). Find current and emerging research on the education of students from different cultural, racial, ethnic, and language groups and explanations and exercises for ensuring that classrooms are open to and address the needs of all students.

Multicultural Gifted Education by Donna Y. Ford and J. John Harris III (New York: Teachers College Press, 1999). A comprehensive and practical resource for raising the level of instruction for gifted minority students, this book offers case studies of multicultural gifted education in practice, suggests methods for classroom teachers, and provides guidelines for evaluating multicultural education programs.

Multicultural Mentoring of the Gifted and Talented by E. Paul Torrance, Kathy Goff, and Neil B. Satterfield (Waco, TX: Prufrock Press, 1998). Written for mentors working with culturally diverse groups, this resource explains characteristics of minority students, offers helpful advice for overcoming racial and cultural stereotypes, and provides tips for becoming a lasting positive influence in students' lives.

Multiple Intelligences in the Classroom, 2d ed., by Thomas Armstrong (Alexandria, VA: ASCD, 2000). A practical guide to incorporating multiple intelligences curriculum in the classroom, this book includes information on assessment, teaching strategies, cognitive development, and more. Included are reading lists and lesson plans.

"National Association for Gifted Children Pre-K–Grade 12 Gifted Program Standards" *(www.nagc.org/webprek12.htm)*. This Web page is the online source for a document that delineates both requisite and exemplary standards for gifted education programming in seven areas: Curriculum and Instruction, Program Administration and Management, Program Design, Program Evaluation, Socio-Emotional Guidance and Counseling, Professional Development, and Student Identification.

Nurturing the Gifts and Talents of Primary Grade Students edited by Susan M. Baum, Sally M. Reis, and Lori D. Maxfield (Mansfield Center, CT: Creative Learning Press, 1998). Compiled from the experience of leading figures in gifted education, this resource offers practical advice for teaching young children with advanced abilities, intense interests, and unique talents. Find tips on identification, programming, curriculum strategies, and classroom management.

Once Upon a Mind: The Stories and Scholars of Gifted Child Education by James R. Delisle (Belmont, CA: Wadsworth Publishing Company, 2000). This book explores the history of gifted-child education through a series of personal reflections of practitioners in the field. Special focus is maintained on the emotional lives of gifted children and those who have promoted this aspect of giftedness in their work.

The Parallel Curriculum: A Design to Develop High Potential and Challenge High-Ability Learners by Carol Ann Tomlinson, et al. (Thousand Oaks, CA: Corwin Press, 2001). This resource for developing curriculum and instruction takes a different approach to the task. The resulting parallel curriculum model, intended for use in both heterogeneous and homogeneous classroom settings, offers four parallel options for developing curriculum, ensuring interesting and enjoyable learning opportunities for all students.

Planning for Productive Thinking and Learning: A Book for Teachers by Donald J. Treffinger with John F. Feldhusen (Waco, TX: Prufrock Press, 2000). A guide for instilling thinking skills into curriculum, discovering how to identify objectives, building learning activities, and evaluating programming.

Reaching New Horizons: Gifted and Talented Education for Culturally and Linguistically Diverse Students edited by Jaime A. Castellano and Eva Díaz (Needham Heights, MA: Allyn and Bacon, 2002). A comprehensive overview of gifted education for culturally diverse and ESL students, this book features discussions of bilingual education, gifted programming models for ESL and minority students, advice for identification and assessment, and other topics. A discussion of the problems most encountered in these special populations is included, as well as the inclusionary strategies that have proven most effective in bringing out the gifts and talents of linguistically and culturally diverse students.

Reversing Underachievement Among Gifted Black Students: Promising Practices and Programs by Donna Y. Ford (New York: Teachers College Press, 1996). This book on underachievement among African American youth includes strategies and programs to encourage gifted minority students to achieve. Offering an analysis of the psychological, social, emotional, and academic factors that shape student development, Ford describes programs

designed to better serve this underrepresented population in gifted education and urges teachers, administrators, and families to form a partnership toward finding and keeping more students in gifted programs.

Schoolwide Enrichment Model: A How-To Guide for Educational Excellence, 2d ed., by Sally M. Reis and Joseph S. Renzulli (Mansfield Center, CT: Creative Learning Press, 1997). This revised edition detailing the renowned Schoolwide Enrichment Model offers practical, step-by-step advice for implementing successful instructional strategies that meet the needs of all students. Included are instruments, charts, assessment tools, and planning guides for organizing, administering, and evaluating different aspects of the model.

Smart Boys: Talent, Manhood, and the Search for Meaning by Barbara A. Kerr, Sanford J. Cohn, et al. (Scottsdale, AZ: Great Potential Press, 2001). Believing that boys with high ability often diminish the importance of their own intellect and curiosity to fit within accepted masculine roles, the authors of this book document the challenges that gifted boys face, which can include underachievement, social isolation, and "dumbing down" to fit in. Educators and parents will find ideas for nurturing the talents of gifted boys while helping them to overcome ambivalence about their gifts and concerns over expected masculine behaviors.

Smart Girls: A New Psychology of Girls, Women, and Giftedness, rev. ed., by Barbara A. Kerr (Scottsdale, AZ: Great Potential Press, 1997). This book explores why gifted girls so often fail to realize their potential as they reach adolescence and adulthood and offers practical advice to teachers, parents, and policymakers about ways to help gifted girls continue to grow and succeed. Kerr also presents current research on gifted girls, summarizes biographies about eminent women, their lives, and achievements, and examines the current educational and family environment.

So You Want to Start a School for the Gifted? A Practical Guide to Help You Help the Highly Able and Talented edited by Eileen S. Kelble (Washington, DC: NAGC, 1999). This publication from NAGC outlines the practical steps toward establishing a school for the gifted, including staffing, admissions, and curriculum issues.

The Social and Emotional Development of Gifted Children edited by Maureen Neihart, et al. (Waco, TX: Prufrock Press, 2002). Examining the social and emotional lives of gifted children, this resource hones in on the major afflictions that often complicate giftedness. Discussions of underachievement, depression, oversensitivity, and other conditions are posed, with the authors suggesting that appropriate educational strategies, counseling, and research need to be available to prevent such conditions.

Some of My Best Friends Are Books: Guiding Gifted Readers from Preschool to High School, 2d ed., by Judy Halsted (Scottsdale, AZ: Great Potential Press 2001). This resource describes how books have the power to affect the lives of bright children, not only by sparking their imaginations, but also by providing a means of bibliotherapy in light of their unique social and emotional needs. Included in this edition are summaries of approximately 300 books, information on issues like creativity, intensity, and sensitivity, and questions for follow-up discussion.

Special Populations in Gifted Education: Working with Diverse Gifted Learners by Jaime A. Castellano (Needham Heights, MA: Allyn and Bacon, 2003). Illuminates the realty that gifted students are from all backgrounds and that their talents transcend handicapping conditions, poverty, geography, and cultural, ethnic, and linguistic ties.

Successful Intelligence: How Practical and Creative Intelligence Determine Success in Life by Robert J. Sternberg (New York: Plume,

1997). A thought-provoking look at the nature of intelligence and how creativity and practicality can often trump IQ, this book documents why raw intelligence does not necessarily determine success.

Talented Children and Adults: Their Development and Education, 2d ed., by Jane Piirto (Upper Saddle River, NJ: Prentice Hall, 1999). A comprehensive resource on both the characteristics of gifted students and appropriate instructional methods, this book contains the latest research and offers suggestions for inclusion, definitions of giftedness, information on gifted adults, and much more.

Teaching Kids with Learning Difficulties in the Regular Classroom: Strategies and Techniques Every Teacher Can Use to Challenge and Motivate Struggling Students by Susan Winebrenner (Minneapolis: Free Spirit Publishing, 1997). This handbook for helping students labeled "learning disabled" in the classroom is full of practical ideas for improving performance in language literacy, social studies, science, and math without simplifying curriculum to the point where other students are no longer challenged.

Teaching the Gifted Child, 4th ed., by James J. Gallagher and Shelagh A. Gallagher (Needham Heights, MA: Allyn and Bacon, 1994). This resource helps educators examine characteristics of gifted students and presents curriculum models for meeting their needs. Also find current discussions on intelligence, problem-based curriculum, student evaluation, and underrepresented populations.

Tempo. A quarterly journal from the Texas Association for Gifted and Talented (TAGT), this publication for educators and parents includes the latest research and instructional strategies and features articles on the most current issues in gifted education. To subscribe, contact TAGT (see page 152).

Understanding Our Gifted. For educators, counselors, and parents of gifted kids, this quarterly journal features up-to-date information on giftedness from national leaders in the field. Contact Open Space Communications (see page 153) for subscription information.

Uniquely Gifted: Identifying and Meeting the Needs of the Twice-Exceptional Student edited by Kiesa Kay (Gilsum, NH: Avocus Publishing, 2000). A large collection of insightful essays from experts on twice-exceptional students, this resource covers topics that include family perspectives, teaching strategies, and administrative issues. A thorough bibliography and Internet resources offer direction for expanding classroom options.

Work Left Undone: Choices and Compromises of Talented Females by Sally M. Reis (Mansfield Center, CT: Creative Learning Press, 1999). Here you'll find an exploration of the internal and external barriers talented females face in a society where girls and women often downplay accomplishments in order to maintain relationships and blend in with the crowd. Read about external barriers like stereotyping and conflicting messages from parents which can also cause some girls and women to settle for the ordinary.

World Gifted. This newsletter of the World Council for Gifted and Talented Children (WCGTC) is published three times a year. It provides current information on gifted education and acts as a forum for an international dialogue between educators reporting from different countries. Contact WCGTC (see page 152) for more information.

Web Sites

Gifted Canada

www3.telus.net/giftedcanada
A forum for Canadian researchers, educators, and families to share information on giftedness, this site sponsors newsletters and provides links to provincial organizations. Also available is information on teaching strategies, current research, a listing of summer programs, and resource lists.

Project Based Learning

pblchecklist.4teachers.org
Find information about project-based learning methods and strategies for including multiple intelligences in the curriculum. The site offers checklists for starting out and ideas for interdisciplinary activities in math, language arts, geography, science, and technology.

Strategies for Differentiating Instruction

www.ascd.org/ed_topics/cu2000win_willis.html
This site offers explanations of differentiation strategies, including ideas specific to gifted programming. Find information on tiered assignments, extension activities, compacting, acceleration, and additional strategies.

Teaching Tolerance

www.tolerance.org
This Web site supports K–12 educators promoting respect for differences and appreciation of diversity in schools. Information is available on programs and activities designed to eliminate bias. A magazine, *Teaching Tolerance,* is also available and is full of ideas to make classrooms safe and supportive environments for all students.

Parents and Gifted Kids

Publications

Becoming a Master Student by David B. Ellis (Boston: Houghton Mifflin, 1994). While bright kids often have the correct answers, those answers are often lost in a sea of papers and folders. This book helps kids get organized, manage their time, and do all of the little things that are required for success in the classroom environment.

The Best 345 Colleges edited by Robert Franek (New York: Princeton Review, 2002). Providing profiles on the major colleges in the nation, this publication, updated annually, offers a listing of the main criteria students look for in colleges and universities and allows them to match those criteria with their individual interests. Check the library or bookstore for the latest edition.

"Considerations and Strategies for Parenting the Gifted Child" by James Alvino (Storrs, CT: NRC/GT, 1995); research monograph 95218. Helpful advice for parents looking to nurture children's gifts and provide excellent learning opportunities.

Duke Gifted Letter. Published four times a year by Duke University for parents of the gifted, the *Duke Gifted Letter* addresses the tough issues that can accompany raising a gifted child. Featuring analysis of exemplary gifted programs, reviews of gifted literature, and parent stories, this periodical offers advice for best providing for children. To subscribe, contact the Duke University Talent Identification Program (page 151).

Freeing Our Families from Perfectionism by Thomas Greenspon (Minneapolis: Free Spirit Publishing, 2002). This resource offers an explanation of perfectionism, its causes and consequences, and a healing process for transforming it into healthy living practices and self-acceptance.

The Gifted Kids' Survival Guide for Ages 10 and Under by Judy Galbraith (Minneapolis: Free Spirit Publishing, 1999). This friendly, straightforward guide for younger gifted kids explains what giftedness is all about, how to make the most of school, how to socialize successfully, and more.

The Gifted Kids' Survival Guide: A Teen Handbook by Judy Galbraith and Jim Delisle (Minneapolis: Free Spirit Publishing, 1996). A guide for older gifted kids, this book provides strategies, practical how-tos, surprising facts, and teen essays and quotes for surviving and thriving as a gifted teen.

"Helping Your Child Find Success at School: A Guide for Hispanic Parents" by Candis Y. Hine (Storrs, CT: NRC/GT, 1994); research monograph 94202. This document for Hispanic parents details ways to ensure school success for children including eight keys to achievement.

High IQ Kids edited by Kiesa Kay, Deborah Robson, and Judy Fort Brenneman (Minneapolis: Free Spirit Publishing, 2007). For parents and teachers who feel out of their depth with highly gifted kids, this book blends personal stories, strategies, scholarly articles, and essays from parents, educators, researchers, and other experts to address the joys and challenges of raising and teaching highly and profoundly gifted children of all ages.

Imagine. Published five times a year by the Center for Talented Youth (CTY) at Johns Hopkins University, this magazine is for middle and high school students who want to take control of their learning and get the most out of their precollege years. Motivated youth will find information on summer programs, college planning advice, career exploration features, book reviews, puzzles, and more. Contact CTY (see page 151) for more information.

Keeping Your Kids Out Front Without Kicking Them from Behind: How to Nurture High-Achieving Athletes, Scholars, and Performing Artists by Ian Tofler and Theresa Foy DiGeronimo (San Francisco: Jossey-Bass, 2000). The authors help parents to draw the line between encouraging children and pushing them too hard, offering practical advice for nurturing talents and social needs without overworking or putting too much pressure on kids.

Parenting for High Potential. Published by NAGC, this quarterly magazine is designed for parents looking to develop children's gifts and talents at home. Special features include expert advice columns, book reviews, parenting tips, and a pullout children's section. Contact NAGC (see page 152) for subscription information.

Parents' Guide to Raising a Gifted Child by James Alvino and the editors of *Gifted Children Monthly* (New York: Random House, 1996). A practical primer for raising and educating gifted children from preschool to adolescence, this book helps parents to identify giftedness in children, make decisions on the care and education of children, nurture gifts, and address a range of other issues.

See Jane Win for Girls: A Smart Girl's Guide to Success by Sylvia B. Rimm (Minneapolis: Free Spirit Publishing, 2003). In this encouraging resource for girls and young women, Rimm offers advice for staying confident, capable, and ready to lead. The book incorporates the experiences of successful women from virtually all fields of employment along with practical advice to help girls make positive changes and choices.

The Survival Guide for Parents of Gifted Kids: How to Understand, Live With, and Stick Up for Your Gifted Child, rev. ed., by Sally Yahnke Walker (Minneapolis: Free Spirit Publishing, 2002). Explains and explores what giftedness is, how kids are identified as gifted, and how to advocate for gifted education. Parents will find answers to many of their questions about having a bright child.

They Say My Kid's Gifted: Now What? by F. Richard Olenchak (Waco, TX: Prufrock Press, 1998). This easy-to-use guide, developed by NAGC, instructs parents how to effectively work with schools to ensure the best educational experience for their children. Find information on identification procedures, gifted education in the regular classroom, and ways to ensure a child's success within a gifted program.

Web Sites

Gifted Child Society
www.gifted.org
Established by parents of gifted kids, this Web site offers support and information for parents of gifted youth. Advocacy and professional training efforts are supplemented with newsletters, seminars, and a forum where parents can share their ideas and concerns about life with bright children.

Gifted Children
www.gifted-children.com
An online parents' newsletter, this site offers information for identifying and encouraging gifted children as well as for developing talents when they are discovered. With articles discussing contemporary events and issues, this is a sound resource for staying abreast of legal and educational developments in gifted ed.

GT World!
www.gtworld.org
An online support community for families with gifted children, this Web site offers ideas for advocacy and information on a wide range of other issues in gifted education. Parents will find a listing of definitions related to giftedness, research articles, reading lists, helpful links, and other pertinent information.

Haven
www.havensrefuge.lunarpages.net
A Web site and chat forum created by and for gifted kids, this site offers a safe and comfortable environment for kids to discuss their interests and concerns. A variety of message boards allow members to address academic, philosophical, social, and other topics. This is a great resource for reminding gifted youth that they are not alone.

Hoagies' Gifted Education Page
www.hoagiesgifted.org
For parents, educators, and children, this site provides information on programs for gifted youth, their special needs, and other topics in gifted ed. Children will find entertaining activities, reading lists, contests, and links to other resources. A well-rounded site with a lot of very useful information.

TAG Project
www.tagfam.org
This online community works to strengthen relationships between individuals, families, and organizations advocating on behalf of gifted and talented youth. Resources address meeting the unique academic, social, and emotional needs of gifted kids.

Organizations

American Association for Gifted Children (AAGC)
Duke University
Box 90539
Durham, NC 27708-0539
(919) 783-6152
www.aagc.org
The oldest advocacy group for gifted students in the United States, this organization continues to work for expanded educational opportunities for the gifted and talented. Visit AAGC online for access to cutting-edge research, newsletters with gifted happenings, and many other resources for parents and educators.

Association for Supervision and Curriculum Development (ASCD)
1703 North Beauregard Street
Alexandria, VA 22311-1714
1-800-933-2723
www.ascd.org
Dedicated to meeting the needs of all students in classrooms throughout the world, this organization performs and shares research, distributing a variety of journals, newsletters, books, and other materials. Also offering worldwide conferences and professional training opportunities for educators, ASCD is an important forum for issues in education today.

California Association for the Gifted (CAG)
11130 Sun Center Drive, Suite 100
Rancho Cordova, CA 95670
(916) 441-3999
www.cagifted.org
CAG is made up of parents, educators, and community members interested in gifted education. It holds conferences throughout California, offers grants to educators, and provides opportunities for professional development. *Gifted Education Communicator* and *Intercom* are benefits to members; both are quarterly journals with reports on meetings, special events, and legislative developments.

Center for Gifted Education
College of William and Mary
P.O. Box 8795
Williamsburg, VA 23187-8795
(757) 221-2362
www.cfge.wm.edu
Working toward an understanding of the needs of gifted and talented individuals of all ages, this center, under the direction of Joyce Van Tassell-Baska, provides graduate programs in gifted education, performs research, develops curriculum, and offers programs to gifted youth and their families.

Center for Talented Youth (CTY)
Johns Hopkins University
McAuley Hall
5801 Smith Avenue, Suite 400
Baltimore, MD 21209
(410) 516-0337
www.cty.jhu.edu
This center, operated by Johns Hopkins University, offers gifted and talented youth advanced educational opportunities in the form of summer programs, distance education, academic conferences, and ceremonies that celebrate the accomplishments of high-ability students. The center is also a leading research and advocacy organization for gifted and talented youth.

Council for Exceptional Children (CEC)
1110 North Glebe Road, Suite 300
Arlington, VA 22201-5704
1-888-232-7733
www.cec.sped.org
This organization offers information on new research findings, federal legislation, classroom methods, and more. It sponsors conferences on topics in gifted education and manages information networks that include the ERIC Clearinghouse, National Clearinghouse on Careers Serving Children with Disabilities, and IDEA Partnerships.

Davidson Institute for Talent Development (DITD)
9665 Gateway Drive, Suite B
Reno, NV 89521
(775) 852-3483
www.ditd.org
This foundation offers advanced learning opportunities and scholarships for profoundly gifted youth and professional development opportunities including presentations and inservice training on giftedness. Also available online are articles from leading researchers and other resources for the profoundly gifted and their families and teachers.

Duke University Talent Identification Program
1121 West Main Street
Durham, NC 27701-2028
(919) 668-9100
www.tip.duke.edu
This program identifies gifted and talented children and provides them with innovative programming designed to help them reach their full potential. Providing services and programs beyond those offered in the classroom while attending to the unique gifted social and emotional needs, this organization offers a range of activities and programs available to parents, teachers, and gifted youth.

ERIC Clearinghouse on Disabilities and Gifted Education
c/o Computer Sciences Corporation
655 15th Street NW, Suite 500
Washington, DC 20005
1-800-538-3742
www.eric.ed.gov
This one-stop site for education information offers parents and educators of disabled and/or gifted children dozens of articles and fact sheets, information on available special programs, and other resources helpful toward giving all children of all ages the best education available.

Gifted Development Center
Institute for the Study of Advanced Development
1452 Marion Street
Denver, CO 80228
(303) 837-8378
www.gifteddevelopment.com
Directed by renowned gifted advocate Linda Kreger Silverman, the Gifted Development Center offers assessment, counseling, tutoring, and telephone consultations for the profoundly gifted. Books, articles, and other learning materials are available online.

National Association for Gifted Children (NAGC)
1707 L Street NW, Suite 550
Washington, DC 20036
(202) 785-4268
www.nagc.org
Of the most important gifted organizations in the nation, NAGC's membership of researchers, parents, and educators work to meet the unique educational and other needs of gifted and talented children. Publications, career opportunities for educators in the field, summer and enrichment programs for gifted youth, and legislative updates are only some of this organization's efforts to support gifted youth.

National Association for the Education of Young Children (NAEYC)
1313 L Street NW, Suite 500
Washington, DC 20005
1-800-424-2460
www.naeyc.org
The nation's largest organization of early-childhood educators and others involved in the education of children from birth through grade three, this organization holds conferences, produces childhood development materials, and offers opportunities for professional development. A catalog of NAEYC's products and resources for parents, including a listing of accredited early-childhood programs, is available online.

National Research Center on the Gifted and Talented (NRC/GT)
University of Connecticut
2131 Hillside Road, Unit 3007
Storrs, CT 06269
(860) 486-4676
www.gifted.uconn.edu/nrcgt.html
This nationwide cooperative of researchers, educators, and others working in gifted education offers cutting-edge information on all aspects of giftedness. Resources provide not only the most current academic research, but also practical ideas for helping children to thrive at home and in the classroom.

Supporting Emotional Needs of the Gifted (SENG)
P.O. Box 488
Poughquag, NY 12570
(845) 797-5054
www.sengifted.org
Focusing on the unique social and emotional needs of gifted children, SENG has advocated for over twenty years on behalf of bright kids and their families. The organization provides education, staff development, and research to promote classrooms where a child's gifts are allowed to shine.

Texas Association for the Gifted and Talented (TAGT)
1524 South IH 35, Suite 205
Austin, TX 78704
(512) 499-8248
www.txgifted.org
One of the largest state gifted organizations in the country, TAGT advocates on behalf of gifted students, produces and distributes current research to its members and to the general public, and offers quality professional development in the field. The Web site includes an overview of materials TAGT has developed and links to further resources.

World Council for Gifted and Talented Children (WCGTC)
c/o The University of Winnipeg
515 Portage Avenue
Winnipeg, Manitoba, Canada R3B2E9
(204) 789-1421
world-gifted.org
Focusing world attention on gifted and talented children, this organization supports gifted research, training, and advocacy internationally. Contact WCGTC for more information on membership, conferences, and publications, which include *Gifted and Talented International,* a professional journal, and *World Gifted,* the organization's member newsletter.

Publishers of Gifted Education Materials

ALPS Publishing
P.O. Box 336052
Greeley, CO 80633
1-800-345-2577
www.alpspublishing.com
ALPS Publishing specializes in producing materials for teachers, parents, and students that encourage independent, lifelong learning. The publishing home of George Betts' Autonomous Learner Model, this company is a resource for student materials promoting research and independent projects.

A.W. Peller and Associates
116 Washington Avenue
Hawthorne, NJ 07507
1-800-451-7450
www.awpeller.com
This company's catalog is a comprehensive source of educational materials for the gifted. Find resources for teaching gifted kids in the regular classroom and in pull-out programs. Available are books, kits, videos, posters, games, and software.

Center for Creative Learning
4921 Ringwood Meadow
Sarasota, FL 34235
(941) 342-9928
www.creativelearning.com
The Center for Creative Learning produces materials on creativity, creative problem solving, talent development, and learning styles. Research-based publications are intended to foster students' critical-thinking, problem-solving, and decision-making skills and help them discover and take advantage of their individual learning styles.

Classroom Connect
6277 Sea Harbor Drive
Orlando, FL 32887
1-800-638-1639
www.classroomconnect.com
This company offers original Web-based curricula for teachers of K–12 students with an emphasis on research and critical-thinking skills. Also available are professional development services featuring a wide network of educators from around the country.

Corwin Press
2455 Teller Road
Thousand Oaks, CA 91320
1-800-233-9936
www.corwinpress.com
Corwin Press provides solutions for those serving the field of K–12 education. Their practice-oriented publications range from very practical, experiential-based manuals to more reflective or research-based books that target school principals, administrators, specialists, teachers, teacher educators, advanced–level students, and other educational practitioners.

Creative Learning Press
P.O. Box 320
Mansfield Center, CT 06250
1-888-518-8004
www.creativelearningpress.com
Publishing home of the Schoolwide Enrichment Model, Creative Learning Press offers a wide range of practical books for installing gifted programming throughout an entire school or district. Materials for assessment, identification, enrichment options, and a range of other educational and instructional needs are available.

Critical Thinking Books and Software
P.O. Box 1610
Seaside, CA 93955
1-800-458-4849
www.criticalthinking.com
This company carries books, software, and other products that are designed to improve content learning while promoting critical-thinking skills in reading, writing, math, science, and social studies. While addressing the learning needs of all students, this publisher also produces materials created specifically for gifted students.

Enslow Publishers
P.O. Box 398
Berkeley Heights, NJ 07922
1-800-398-2504
www.enslow.com
Publishing nonfiction books for grades K–12, Enslow puts out titles on a variety of topics that include biography, history, sports and recreation, math, science, and technology. Additionally, materials for science projects and experiments are available for students.

Free Spirit Publishing
217 Fifth Avenue North, Suite 200
Minneapolis, MN 55401-1299
1-800-735-7323
www.freespirit.com
A publisher of nonfiction resources for children and teens, parents, educators, and counselors, Free Spirit provides research-based and user-friendly materials covering gifted education, learning differences, self-esteem, stress management, creativity, and school success.

Gifted Education Press
P.O. Box 1586
Manassas, VA 20109
(703) 369-5017
www.giftededpress.com
A publisher of books and periodicals on educating gifted children, this publisher produces materials in all subject areas for all grade levels. Teachers and parents of gifted children, and children themselves, will find innovative offerings on a wide range of topics.

Great Potential Press
P.O. Box 5057
Scottsdale, AZ 85261
(602) 954-4200
www.greatpotentialpress.com
Great Potential Press produces books for parents, teachers, counselors, and educators of gifted and talented children on a wide range of topics that include the social and emotional needs of the gifted, creativity, college planning, legal issues, and many more.

Greenhaven Press
P.O. Box 95501
Chicago, IL 60694-5501
1-800-877-4253
www.gale.cengage.com/greenhaven
Greenhaven Press produces titles that offer divergent points of view on controversial social, political, and economic issues. Excellent resources for debate students, these books on history, literary criticism, biography, and other topics aid in research and enhance critical-thinking skills.

Learning Quest
P.O. Box 1698
Carmichael, CA 95609
(916) 332-9544
www.learningquestinfo.com

Learning Quest makes available curriculum and materials that integrate technology and classroom learning. Offering a variety of challenging programs in a number of subject areas, these engaging materials help to motivate all students to learn not only in content areas but also through computers and other technology.

Magination Press
P.O. Box 92984
Washington, DC 20090-2984
1-800-374-2721
www.maginationpress.com
Find books for children on a variety of topics including learning disabilities, self-esteem, school issues, and others, treated in an engaging way that helps kids to understand and cope with circumstances in their lives.

Open Space Communications
P.O. Box 18268
Boulder, CO 80308
1-800-494-6178
www.openspacecomm.com
In addition to publishing books and tapes for gifted education, Open Space Communications also produces *Understanding Our Gifted,* a journal for teachers and parents.

Peytral Publications
P.O. Box 1162
Minnetonka, MN 55345
1-877-739-8725
www.peytral.com
Find practical books and other products for the gifted and talented, twice exceptional, and other special learning populations.

Pieces of Learning
1990 Market Road
Marion, IL 62959
1-800-729-5137
www.piecesoflearning.com
Publisher of games, writing resources, and critical-thinking exercises, this is a resource for motivating and challenging students in a wide variety of content areas including social studies, language arts, math, and science.

Pro-Ed
8700 Shoal Creek Boulevard
Austin, TX 78757
1-800-897-3202
www.proedinc.com
Pro-Ed is publisher of materials for classrooms and professional development, with a focus on special education. Produces both practical, hands-on books and theoretical materials on topics that include reading, writing, math, and social skills.

Prufrock Press
P.O. Box 8813
Waco, TX 76714
1-800-998-2208
www.prufrock.com
Find innovative books, magazines, and software in a virtually all content areas as well as a host of professional development resources.

Zephyr Press
814 North Franklin
Chicago, IL 60610
1-800-232-2187
www.zephyrpress.com
Zephyr Press produces instructional materials that integrate higher-level thinking, problem-based learning, and multiple intelligences theory in the classroom environment. Practical and easy-to-use, these materials allow educators to teach to students' individual needs.

Test Materials

CTB McGraw-Hill
20 Ryan Ranch Road
Monterey, CA 93940
1-800-538-9547
www.ctb.com
This company offers achievement and aptitude testing for all grades. Testing materials are available for evaluating general skills, mathematical ability, and other areas. Special materials are available for testing students and gauging high ability in children from lower grades.

Educational Assessment Service
W6050 Apple Road
Watertown, WI 53098
1-800-795-7466
www.sylviarimm.com
This company offers assessment tools for identifying creatively gifted kids and underachievers in all grade levels. Assessment tools also gauge students' interests and point the way toward appropriate programming options.

Educational Testing Service
Rosedale Road
Princeton, NJ 08541
(609) 921-9000
www.ets.org
This organization offers a broad array of assessments for evaluating student performance and determining placement in special programs. Available products include individualized, portfolio-based, and online assessments.

Pearson AGS Globe
1 Lake Street
Upper Saddle River, NJ 07458
1-800-627-0365
www.pearsonschool.com
Publisher of assessment tools, textbooks, and instructional materials for students with a wide range of special needs, Pearson AGS Globe specializes in publishing individually administered tests that measure cognitive ability, achievement, and behavior. Group tests are also available.

PLATO Learning
10801 Nesbitt Avenue South
Bloomington, MN 55437
1-800-447-5286
www.plato.com
An online assessment program for educators, here you will find tools for evaluating student strengths and needs in relation to state and national standards. Focusing on the entire school community, these tests help educators decide on the best curriculum and instructional strategies for meeting the needs of all students.

Professional Associates
P.O. Box 28056
Austin, TX 78755
1-866-335-1460
www.professionalassociatespublishing.com
This publisher of learning inventories and assessment materials offers practical products designed for easy and effective use. Find many assessment tools and resources including rubrics and tests for measuring students' authentic learning.

Riverside Publishing
3800 Golf Road, Suite 100
Rolling Meadows, IL 60008
1-800-323-9540
www.riverpub.com
Offers a range of achievement and ability assessment tools for measuring student interests and cognitive abilities.

Scholastic Testing Service
480 Meyer Road
Bensenville, IL 60106
1-800-642-6787
www.ststesting.com
This test publisher offers evaluation aids for determining creativity and learning styles, as well as a number of products specifically designed for use with gifted and talented students.

Index

About the Authors

Jim Delisle, Ph.D., is a retired professor of education at Kent State University in Ohio, where he directed the undergraduate and graduate programs in gifted education. He is a former classroom teacher, special education teacher, and teacher of gifted children. He has received several teaching honors, including Kent  State University's most prestigious distinction, the Distinguished Teaching Award, in 2004. However, the most important award came recently when one of his former fourth-grade students selected him, upon high school graduation, as his "Most Inspirational Teacher." Jim also has served as a counselor for gifted adolescents and their families. He is the author or coauthor of more than 200 articles and 14 books, including the best-selling *Gifted Kids' Survival Guide: A Teen Handbook* and *When Gifted Kids Don't Have All the Answers: How to Meet Their Social and Emotional Needs* (both with Judy Galbraith).

Jim and his wife, Deb, have homes in Kent, Ohio and North Myrtle Beach, South Carolina.

Barbara A. Lewis has taught gifted children for more than fifteen years. She was the Coordinator for Gifted and Talented Students in the Park City, Utah, School District where she designed the district's gifted education program. She is the author of *The Kid's Guide to Social Action, Kids with Courage, The Kid's*  *Guide to Service Projects, What Do You Stand For? For Teens, What Do You Stand For? For Kids,* and *The Teen Guide to Global Action.*

Barbara has received many awards for excellence in writing, teaching, and leading youth in service projects and social action. She and her students have been honored for community contributions by President George H. W. Bush and featured in many national magazines and newspapers, in *The Congressional Record,* and on national television.

Barbara lives in Park City, Utah, with her husband, Lawrence, and is a sought-after speaker on topics including gifted education, character development, service, and social action.

Other Great Books from Free Spirit

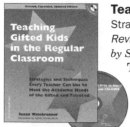

Teaching Gifted Kids in the Regular Classroom (Book with CD-ROM)
Strategies and Techniques Every Teacher Can Use to Meet the Academic Needs of the Gifted and Talented
Revised, Expanded, Updated Edition
by Susan Winebrenner

Teachers call it "the orange bible." *Teaching Gifted Kids* is the definitive guide to meeting the learning needs of gifted students in the mixed-abilities classroom—without losing control, causing resentment, or spending hours preparing extra materials. It's full of proven, practical, classroom-tested strategies teachers love, plus many useful reproducibles. Included CD-ROM has all of the forms from the book, plus many additional extensions menus, ready to customize and print for classroom use.
All grades. *256 pp.; softcover; 8½" x 11"; with CD-ROM*

Differentiating Instruction in the Regular Classroom (Book with CD-ROM)
How to Reach and Teach All Learners, Grades 3–12
by Diane Heacox, Ed.D.

Differentiation—one of the hottest topics in education today—means changing the pace, level, or kind of instruction to fit the learner. This guide is a menu of strategies, examples, templates, and tools teachers can use to differentiate instruction in any curriculum, even a standard or mandated curriculum. The CD-ROM includes all of the forms from the book, plus additional materials. Timely and practical.
For grades 3–12. *176 pp.; softcover; 8½" x 11"; with CD-ROM*

Making Differentiation a Habit (Book with CD-ROM)
How to Ensure Success in Academically Diverse Classrooms
by Diane Heacox, Ed.D.

Following on the heels of Diane Heacox's best-selling teacher resource *Differentiating Instruction in the Regular Classroom,* this book offers new ideas, fresh perspectives, and additional research-based strategies designed to help teachers not only differentiate instruction, but to seamlessly integrate differentiation practices into their daily routines.
For teachers and administrators. *192 pp.; softcover; 8½" x 11"; reproducible handouts on CD-ROM*

The Kid's Guide to Service Projects
Over 500 Service Ideas for Young People Who Want to Make a Difference (Updated 2nd Edition)
by Barbara A. Lewis

This guide has something for everyone who wants to make a difference, from simple projects to large-scale commitments. Kids can choose from a variety of topics including animals, the environment, friendship, hunger, politics and government, and much more.
For ages 10 & up. *160 pp.; softcover; illust.; 6" x 9"*

When Gifted Kids Don't Have All the Answers
How to Meet Their Social and Emotional Needs
by Jim Delisle, Ph.D., and Judy Galbraith, M.A.

Gifted kids are much more than test scores and grades. Topics include self-image and self-esteem, perfectionism, multipotential, depression, feelings of "differentness," and stress. Includes first-person stories, easy-to-use strategies, survey results, activities, reproducibles, and up-to-date research and resources.
For teachers, gifted coordinators, guidance counselors, and other adults working with gifted kids (including parents). *288 pp.; softcover; illust.; 7¼" x 9¼"*

Freeing Our Families from Perfectionism
by Thomas S. Greenspon, Ph.D.

Perfectionism is not about doing our best. It's about feeling that we're never good enough—a burden that takes a heavy toll on our bodies, emotions, relationships, creativity, and every other aspect of our lives. In this groundbreaking book, psychologist and therapist Tom Greenspon describes a healing process for transforming perfectionism into healthy living practices and self-acceptance.
For parents. *128 pp.; softcover; illust.; 6" x 9"*

Teaching Beyond the Test (Book with CD-ROM)
Differentiated Project-Based Learning in a Standards-Based Age, Grades 6 & Up
by Phil Schlemmer, M.Ed., and Dori Schlemmer
This practical classroom resource presents dozens of strategies for differentiation among learners (flexible grouping, choice boards, tiered assignments, and more) and a range of fully developed content-focused projects, each modeling one or more differentiation strategies. All projects are aligned with rigorous, comprehensive content standards in the areas of English/language arts, math, social studies, and science. Designed for use by any teacher, in any classroom, in any school. Includes reproducibles.
For grades 6 & up. *256 pp.; softcover; 8½" x 11"; with CD-ROM*

The Cluster Grouping Handbook: A Schoolwide Model (Book with CD-ROM)
How to Challenge Gifted Students and Improve Achievement for All
by Susan Winebrenner, M.S., and Dina Brulles, Ph.D.
Practitioners will find a wealth of teacher-tested classroom strategies along with detailed information on identifying students for clusters, gaining support from parents, and providing ongoing professional development. Special attention is directed toward empowering gifted English language learners. The included CD-ROM (for Windows and Macintosh) features all of the reproducible forms from the book plus a PowerPoint presentation.
For teachers and administrators, grades K–8. *224 pp.; softcover; 8½" x 11"; with CD-ROM*

The Gifted Kids' Survival Guide
For Ages 10 & Under
Revised & Updated 3rd Edition
by Judy Galbraith, M.A.
First published in 1984, newly revised and updated, this classic book has helped countless young gifted children realize they're not alone, they're not "weird," and being smart, talented, and creative is a bonus, not a burden. The new edition includes fresh illustrations, quizzes, tips, and quotes, plus information on brain development, technology, and self-esteem. Includes advice from hundreds of gifted kids.
For ages 10 & under. *128 pp.; softcover, illust.; 6" x 9"*

The Gifted Kids' Survival Guide
A Teen Handbook
Revised, Expanded, and Updated Edition
by Judy Galbraith, M.A., and Jim Delisle, Ph.D.
Vital information on giftedness, IQ, school success, college planning, stress, perfectionism, and much more.
For ages 11–18. *304 pp.; softcover; illust.; 7¼" x 9¼"*

The Survival Guide for Parents of Gifted Kids
How to Understand, Live With, and Stick Up for Your Gifted Child
Revised & Updated Edition
by Sally Yahnke Walker, Ph.D.
How can parents cope with the unique challenges gifted kids present? Parents learn what giftedness is (and isn't), how kids are identified, how to prevent perfectionism, when to get help, how to advocate for their children's education, and more.
For parents of children ages 5 & up. *176 pp.; softcover; illust.; 6" x 9"*

The Essential Guide to Talking with Gifted Teens (Book with CD-ROM)
Ready-to-Use Discussions About Identity, Stress, Relationships, and More
by Jean Sunde Peterson, Ph.D.
The 70 guided discussions in this book are an affective curriculum for gifted teens. By "just talking" with caring peers and an attentive adult, kids gain self-awareness and self-esteem, learn to manage stress, and build social skills and life skills. Each session is self-contained and step-by-step; many include reproducible handouts. Introductory materials help even less-experienced group leaders feel prepared and secure in their role.
For teachers, counselors, and youth workers in all kinds of school and group settings working with gifted kids in grades 6–12. *288 pp.; softcover; 8½" x 11"; with CD-ROM*